HISTORICAL DICTIONARIES OF AFRICA
Edited by Jon Woronoff

1. *Cameroon,* by Victor T. Le Vine and Roger P. Nye. 1974. *Out of print. See No. 48.*
2. *The Congo,* 2nd ed., by Virginia Thompson and Richard Adloff. 1984. *Out of print. See No. 69.*
3. *Swaziland,* by John J. Grotpeter. 1975.
4. *The Gambia,* 2nd ed., by Harry A. Gailey. 1987. *Out of print. See No. 79.*
5. *Botswana,* by Richard P. Stevens. 1975. *Out of print. See No. 70.*
6. *Somalia,* by Margaret F. Castagno. 1975. *Out of print. See No. 87.*
7. *Benin (Dahomey),* 2nd ed., by Samuel Decalo. 1987. *Out of print. See No. 61.*
8. *Burundi,* by Warren Weinstein. 1976. *Out of print. See No. 73.*
9. *Togo,* 3rd ed., by Samuel Decalo. 1996.
10. *Lesotho,* by Gordon Haliburton. 1977. *Out of print. See No. 90.*
11. *Mali,* 3rd ed., by Pascal James Imperato. 1996.
12. *Sierra Leone,* by Cyril Patrick Foray. 1977.
13. *Chad,* 3rd ed., by Samuel Decalo. 1997.
14. *Upper Volta,* by Daniel Miles McFarland. 1978.
15. *Tanzania,* by Laura S. Kurtz. 1978.
16. *Guinea,* 3rd ed., by Thomas O'Toole with Ibrahima Bah-Lalya. 1995.
17. *Sudan,* by John Voll. 1978. *Out of print. See No. 53.*
18. *Rhodesia/Zimbabwe,* by R. Kent Rasmussen. 1979. *Out of print. See No. 46.*
19. *Zambia,* 2nd ed., by John J. Grotpeter, Brian V. Siegel, and James R. Pletcher. 1998.
20. *Niger,* 3rd ed., by Samuel Decalo. 1997.
21. *Equatorial Guinea,* 3rd ed., by Max Liniger-Goumaz. 2000.
22. *Guinea-Bissau,* 3rd ed., by Richard Lobban and Peter Mendy. 1997.
23. *Senegal,* by Lucie G. Colvin. 1981. *Out of print. See No. 65.*
24. *Morocco,* by William Spencer. 1980. *Out of print. See No. 71.*
25. *Malawi,* by Cynthia A. Crosby. 1980. *Out of print. See No. 84.*
26. *Angola,* by Phyllis Martin. 1980. *Out of print. See No. 92.*
27. *The Central African Republic,* by Pierre Kalck. 1980. *Out of print. See No. 51.*
28. *Algeria,* by Alf Andrew Heggoy. 1981. *Out of print. See No. 66.*

29. *Kenya,* by Bethwell A. Ogot. 1981. *Out of print. See No. 77.*

30. *Gabon,* by David E. Gardinier. 1981. *Out of print. See No. 58.*

31. *Mauritania,* by Alfred G. Gerteiny. 1981. *Out of print. See No. 68.*

32. *Ethiopia,* by Chris Prouty and Eugene Rosenfeld. 1981. *Out of print. See No. 91.*

33. *Libya,* 3rd ed., by Ronald Bruce St John. 1998.

34. *Mauritius,* by Lindsay Riviere. 1982. *Out of print. See No. 49.*

35. *Western Sahara,* by Tony Hodges. 1982. *Out of print. See No. 55.*

36. *Egypt,* by Joan Wucher King. 1984. *Out of print. See No. 89.*

37. *South Africa,* by Christopher Saunders. 1983. *Out of print. See No. 78.*

38. *Liberia,* by D. Elwood Dunn and Svend E. Holsoe. 1985. *Out of print. See No. 83.*

39. *Ghana,* by Daniel Miles McFarland. 1985. *Out of print. See No. 63.*

40. *Nigeria,* 2nd ed., by Anthony Oyewole and John Lucas. 2000.

41. *Côte d'Ivoire (The Ivory Coast),* 2nd ed., by Robert J. Mundt. 1995.

42. *Cape Verde,* 2nd ed., by Richard Lobban and Marilyn Halter. 1988. *Out of print. See No. 62.*

43. *Zaire,* by F. Scott Bobb. 1988. *Out of print. See No. 76.*

44. *Botswana,* 2nd ed., by Fred Morton, Andrew Murray, and Jeff Ramsay. 1989. *Out of print. See No. 70.*

45. *Tunisia,* 2nd ed., by Kenneth J. Perkins. 1997.

46. *Zimbabwe,* 2nd ed., by Steven C. Rubert and R. Kent Rasmussen. 1990. *Out of print. See No. 86.*

47. *Mozambique,* by Mario Azevedo. 1991. *Out of print. See No. 88.*

48. *Cameroon,* 2nd ed., by Mark W. DeLancey and H. Mbella Mokeba. 1990.

49. *Mauritius,* 2nd ed., by Sydney Selvon. 1991.

50. *Madagascar,* by Maureen Covell. 1995.

51. *The Central African Republic,* 2nd ed., by Pierre Kalck; translated by Thomas O'Toole. 1992.

52. *Angola,* 2nd ed., by Susan H. Broadhead. 1992. *Out of Print. See No. 92.*

53. *Sudan,* 2nd ed., by Carolyn Fluehr-Lobban, Richard A. Lobban Jr., and John Obert Voll. 1992. *Out of print. See No. 85.*

54. *Malawi,* 2nd ed., by Cynthia A. Crosby. 1993. *Out of print. See No. 84.*

55. *Western Sahara,* 2nd ed., by Anthony Pazzanita and Tony Hodges. 1994.

56. *Ethiopia and Eritrea,* 2nd ed., by Chris Prouty and Eugene Rosenfeld. 1994. *Out of Print. See No. 91.*

57. *Namibia,* by John J. Grotpeter. 1994.
58. *Gabon,* 2nd ed., by David E. Gardinier. 1994.
59. *Comoro Islands,* by Martin Ottenheimer and Harriet Ottenheimer. 1994.
60. *Rwanda,* by Learthen Dorsey. 1994.
61. *Benin,* 3rd ed., by Samuel Decalo. 1995.
62. *Republic of Cape Verde,* 3rd ed., by Richard Lobban and Marlene Lopes. 1995.
63. *Ghana,* 2nd ed., by David Owusu-Ansah and Daniel Miles McFarland. 1995.
64. *Uganda,* by M. Louise Pirouet. 1995.
65. *Senegal,* 2nd ed., by Andrew F. Clark and Lucie Colvin Phillips. 1994.
66. *Algeria,* 2nd ed., by Phillip Chiviges Naylor and Alf Andrew Heggoy. 1994.
67. *Egypt,* 2nd ed., by Arthur Goldschmidt Jr. 1994. *Out of print. See No. 89.*
68. *Mauritania,* 2nd ed., by Anthony G. Pazzanita. 1996.
69. *Congo,* 3rd ed., by Samuel Decalo, Virginia Thompson, and Richard Adloff. 1996.
70. *Botswana,* 3rd ed., by Jeff Ramsay, Barry Morton, and Fred Morton. 1996.
71. *Morocco,* 2nd ed., by Thomas K. Park. 1996.
72. *Tanzania,* 2nd ed., by Thomas P. Ofcansky and Rodger Yeager. 1997.
73. *Burundi,* 2nd ed., by Ellen K. Eggers. 1997.
74. *Burkina Faso,* 2nd ed., by Daniel Miles McFarland and Lawrence Rupley. 1998.
75. *Eritrea,* by Tom Killion. 1998.
76. *Democratic Republic of the Congo (Zaire),* by F. Scott Bobb. 1999. (Revised edition of *Historical Dictionary of Zaire,* No. 43)
77. *Kenya,* 2nd ed., by Robert M. Maxon and Thomas P. Ofcansky. 2000.
78. *South Africa,* 2nd ed., by Christopher Saunders and Nicholas Southey. 2000.
79. *The Gambia,* 3rd ed., by Arnold Hughes and Harry A. Gailey. 2000.
80. *Swaziland*, 2nd ed., by Alan R. Booth. 2000.
81. *Republic of Cameroon,* 3rd ed., by Mark W. DeLancey and Mark Dike DeLancey. 2000.
82. *Djibouti,* by Daoud A. Alwan and Yohanis Mibrathu. 2000.

83. *Liberia,* 2nd ed., by D. Elwood Dunn, Amos J. Beyan, and Carl Patrick Burrowes. 2001.
84. *Malawi,* 3rd ed., by Owen J. Kalinga and Cynthia A. Crosby. 2001.
85. *Sudan,* 3rd ed., by Richard A. Lobban Jr., Robert S. Kramer, and Carolyn Fluehr-Lobban. 2002.
86. *Zimbabwe,* 3rd ed., by Steven C. Rubert and R. Kent Rasmussen. 2001.
87. *Somalia,* 2nd ed., by Mohamed Haji Mukhtar. 2002.
88. *Mozambique,* 2nd ed., by Mario Azevedo, Emmanuel Nnadozie, and Tomé Mbuia João. 2003.
89. *Egypt,* 3rd ed., by Arthur Goldschmidt Jr. and Robert Johnston. 2003.
90. *Lesotho,* by Scott Rosenberg, Richard Weisfelder, and Michelle Frisbie-Fulton. 2004.
91. *Ethiopia, New Edition,* by David H. Shinn and Thomas P. Ofcansky. 2004.
92. *Angola, New Edition,* by W. Martin James. 2004.

Historical Dictionary of Angola
New Edition

W. Martin James

Historical Dictionaries of Africa, No. 92

The Scarecrow Press, Inc.
Lanham, Maryland • Toronto • Oxford
2004

SCARECROW PRESS, INC.

Published in the United States of America
by Scarecrow Press, Inc.
A wholly owned subsidiary of
The Rowman & Littlefield Publishing Group, Inc.
4501 Forbes Boulevard, Suite 200, Lanham, Maryland 20706
www.scarecrowpress.com

PO Box 317
Oxford
OX2 9RU, UK

British Library Cataloguing in Publication Information Available

Library of Congress Cataloging-in-Publication Data

James, W. Martin.
  Historical dictionary of Angola / W. Martin James. — New ed.
    p. cm. — (Historical dictionaries of Africa ; no. 92)
  New ed. of: Historical dictionary of Angola / Susan H. Broadhead. 2nd ed.
1992.
  Includes bibliographical references.
  ISBN 0-8108-4940-2 (alk. paper)
  1. Angola—History—Dictionaries. I. Broadhead, Susan H. (Susan Herlin),
1939–, Historical dictionary of Angola. II. Title. III. African historical
dictionaries ; no. 92.
  DT1264.J36 2004
  967.3'003—dc22   2004000080

♾™ The paper used in this publication meets the minimum requirements of
American National Standard for Information Sciences—Permanence of Paper
for Printed Library Materials, ANSI/NISO Z39.48-1992.
Manufactured in the United States of America.

To Christopher William Martin James
and Gregory Bennett James—
long may you run.

Contents

Editor's Foreword   xi

Acknowledgments   xiii

Acronyms and Abbreviations   xv

Maps   xxii

Chronology   xxv

Introduction   xxxvii

THE DICTIONARY   1

Appendix 1: Selected Place-Name Changes   183

Appendix 2: Government of Unity and National Reconciliation,
       September 2003   185

Appendix 3: Angola's Oil Production   187

Bibliography   189

About the Author   229

Editor's Foreword

Angola is one of Africa's larger and more populous countries. It is endowed with natural resources and has the potential of great wealth. Unlike other African countries, however, Angola did not achieve independence under a single leader and party but with leadership divided and parties confronting one another even more bitterly than they had faced the Portuguese colonialists before them. The country was torn apart, left devastated, and impoverished by the time the long and destructive civil war was finally resolved. It is only now, more than a quarter century after independence, that Angola can finally begin the long struggle for political, economic, and social advancement with the hope—but not the certainty—of achieving its true potential.

The introduction to this *Historical Dictionary of Angola* describes the country's land and people, as well as their history. Then the dictionary provides several hundred entries on significant people, places, and events and reviews the dearth of political institutions and economic and social achievements. To make sense of the jungle of acronyms that appear in everything written on Angola, a very long list of acronyms and abbreviations is provided. For further information, which is often difficult to find, the comprehensive and well-structured bibliography completes this instructive and well-rounded guide.

This entirely new edition of the *Historical Dictionary of Angola* was written by W. Martin James, a professor of political science at Henderson State University who has been studying Angolan affairs for many years. He has visited Angola several times, most notably as an electoral observer for the 1992 elections. Given the significance of the civil war, it is notable that his doctoral dissertation was on the UNITA insurgency, which he followed with a book on the civil war itself. Aside from that, Dr. James has lectured widely on Angolan history and economics, has written numerous articles on current affairs in the region, and is fluent in Portuguese (one of the languages spoken in Angola).

Jon Woronoff
Series Editor

Acknowledgments

As a graduate student in 1974, I had no idea as to the subject for my master's thesis. The professor for whom I performed research was beginning to explore the situation in southern Africa. Knowing I had no thesis topic yet, he asked me to assist him in research and writing. Our first subject was Angola, a topic I have never left. Retired now, Professor J. Peter Vanneman played an important role in my development as a student, scholar, teacher, professor, and individual.

I would like to thank my colleagues at Henderson State University, especially President Charles Dunn. It is comforting to be able to teach and conduct research where diverse personalities and ideologies play such an important role in keeping the creative juices stirred.

To Jon Woronoff, the series editor, and Kim Tabor, at Scarecrow Press, I owe a special debt of gratitude. Their involvement, persistence, and dedication to this project have expanded the horizon of my scholarship.

My thanks to the U.S. Geological Survey for permission to use the minerals map, the World Food Programme for the southern Africa rail network map, to the United Nations ReliefWeb for the provincial map dated February 2002, and to the Economist Intelligence Unit, 2003, for the political map.

Finally, a special thank you to my parents, William M. and Dorothy James. They have always been there, every time.

Acknowledgments

Acronyms and Abbreviations

AIDS/HIV	acquired immune deficiency syndrome/human immunodeficiency virus
AMANGOLA	Amigos do Manifesto Angolano (Manifesto of Angolan Friends)
ANC	African National Congress
ANGOP	Agência de Notícia de Angola (Angolan News Agency)
ANNA	Agência de Notícia Nacional de Angola (Angola National News Agency)
ARA	Amigos para a Resistência de Angola (Friends of the Angolan Resistance)
ASCORP	Angola Selling Corporation
AU	African Union
BAI	Banco Africano de Investimento (African Investment Bank)
BCA	Banco Comercial Angolano (Commercial Bank of Angola)
BCI	Banco de Comércio e Indústria (Bank of Commerce and Industry)
BESA	Banco Espírito Santo de Angola (Holy Spirit Bank of Angola)
BFA	Banco Fomento de Angola (Promotion Bank of Angola)
BNA	Banco Nacional de Angola (National Bank of Angola)
BPC	Banco de Poupanca e Credito (Angola Credit and Savings Bank)
CCAP	Caixa de Credito Agro-Pecuario e Pescas Bank (Agro-Livestock and Fisheries Credit Bank)

CCP	Congresso da Paz (Congress for Peace)
CDDA	Centro de Desenvolvimento e Democracia para Angola (Center for Democracy and Development in Angola)
CEAST	Conferência Episcopal de Angola e São Tomé (Bishops Conference of Angola and São Tomé)
CEEAC	La Communauté Economique des Etats Africains (Economic Community of Central African States)
CIA	Central Intelligence Agency
CJPRA	Comissão de Justica, Paz e Reconcilição em Angola (Commission for Justice, Peace and Reconciliation in Angola
CNIDAH	Comissão Intersectorial de Desminagem e Assistência Humanitária às Vitimas (Intersectorial Commission for Demining and Humanitarian Assistance)
COIEPA	Comité Inter-Eclesial para a Paz em Angola (Interdenominational Committee for Peace in Angola)
CPAD	Comitê Preparatória de Accão Directa (Committee to Prepare for Direct Action)
CPLP	Communidade dos Países de Língua Portuguesa (Community of Portuguese-Speaking Countries)
CVA	Cruz Vermelha de Angola (Angolan Red Cross)
DIAMANG	Companhia de Diamantes de Angola (Angolan Diamond Company)
DNIC	Direção Nacional de Investigação Criminal (National Criminal Investigation Directorate)
DPRA	Democratic People's Republic of Angola (Repùblica de Pessoa Democrática de Angola)
DRC	Democratic Republic of the Congo
ELNA	Exército Popular de Libertação Nacional de Angola (Army for the National Liberation of Angola) (FNLA)
ENDIAMA	Emprêsa Nacional de Diamantes de Angola (Angolan National Diamond Company)
EO	Executive Outomes (South Africa)
ESINA	Exército Angolan Nacional da Intervenção e do Salvation (National Angolan Army of Intervention and Salvation)

FAA	Forças Armadas de Angolanas (Angolan Armed Forces)
FALA	Forças Armadas de Libertação de Angola (Armed Forces for the Liberation of Angola) (UNITA)
FAPLA	Forças Armadas Populares de Libertação de Angola (Popular Armed Forces for the Liberation of Angola) (MPLA)
FESA	Fundação Eduardo dos Santos (Eduardo dos Santos Foundation)
FGM	female genital mutilation
FILDA	Feira Internacional de Luanda (Luanda International Trade Fair)
FLEC	Frente de Libertação do Enclave de Cabinda (Front for the Liberation of the Enclave of Cabinda)
FLEC–FAC	Frente de Libertação do Enclave de Cabinda–Forças Armadas de Cabinda (Front for the Liberation of the Enclave of Cabinda, Armed Forces of Cabinda)
FLEC–R	Frente de Libertação do Enclave de Cabinda–Renovada (Front for the Liberation of the Enclave of Cabinda, Renewed)
FMU	Forças Militares da UNITA (UNITA Military Force)
FNLA	Frente Nacional de Libertação de Angola (National Front for the Liberation of Angola)
FONGA	Foro de ONGs Angolanas (Forum of Angolan NGOs)
FPRN	Fundo para a Paz e Reconciliação Nacional (National Peace and Reconciliation Fund)
FUA	Frente de Unidade Angolana (United Front for Angola)
GARP	Grupo Angolano de Reflexao para Paz (Angolan Party for the Reflection of Peace)
GRAE	Govêrno Revolucionário de Angola no Exílio (Angola's Revolutionary Government-in-Exile) (FNLA)
GURN	Govêrno da Unidade e da Reconciliação Nacional (Government of National Unity and Reconciliation)
IBA	International Bar Association
ICRC	International Committee of the Red Cross
IDPs	Internally Displaced People

IMF	International Monetary Fund
INAD	Instituto Nacional de Angola Demining (National Demining Institute)
JMPLA	Juventude do MPLA (MPLA Youth)
JURA	Juventude Revolucionaria de Angola (Revolutionary Youth of Angola) (UNITA)
JVMC	Commissão Mista de Verificação e Fiscalização (Joint Verification and Monitoring Commission)
LIMA	Liga da Mulher Angolana (League of Angolan Women) (UNITA)
MFA	Movimento das Forças Armadas (Armed Forces Movement) (Portugal)
MINARS	Ministério da Assistência Reinserção Social (Ministry of Social Affairs and Reintegration)
MONUA	Misión de Observadores de las Naciones Unidas en Angola (United Nations Observer Mission in Angola)
MOU	Memorando de Entendimento Complementar ao Protocolo de Lusaka para a Cessaçáo das Hostilidades e Demais Questões Militares Pendentes (Memorandum of Understanding as an Addendum to the Lusaka Protocol on the Cessation of Hostilities and the Resolution of Outstanding Military Issues in Accordance with the Lusaka Protocol)
MPIA	Movimento Para a Independencia de Angola (Movement for the Independence of Angola)
MPLA	Movimento Popular de Libertação de Angola (Popular Movement for the Liberation of Angola)
MPLA–PT	Movimento Popular de Libertação de Angola, Partido do Trabalho (Popular Movement for the Liberation of Angola, Workers Party)
MSF	Médecins sans Frontières (Doctors without Borders)
NATO	North Atlantic Treaty Organization
NEPAD	New Partnership for African Development (Nova Parceria de Desenvolvimento do Continte Africano)
NGO	nongovernmental organization
NNARP	O Nucléo Nacional de Recolha e Pesquisa da Literatura Oral (National Nucleus of Oral Literature Gathering and Research)

NSHR	National Society for Human Rights
OAU	Organization of African Unity
OMA	Organização das Mulheres de Angola (Organization of Angolan Women) (MPLA)
PADPA	Partido de Apoio Democrático e Progreso de Angola (Angolan Party for Democratic Support and Progress)
PAJOCA	Partido da Aliança da Juventude, Operários e Campesinos de Angola (Alliance Party of Angolan Youth, Workers and Peasants)
PALOP	Países Africanos de Língua Oficial Portuguesa (African Portuguese-Speaking Peoples)
PAPARR	Provincial de Acção para o Retorno e Reassentamento (Provincial Emergency Plan of Action for Resettlement and Return)
PDA	Partido Democrático Angola (Democratic Party of Angola)
PDCA	Partido Democrático Christian de Angola (Christian Democratic Party of Angola)
PDS	Partido do Desenvolvimento Social (Social Development Party)
PEE	Programa de Estabilização da Economia (Program to Stabilize the Economy)
PEG	Programa de Emergência do Governo (Emergency Government Program)
PES	Programa Economica e Social para 1994 (Economic and Social Program of 1994)
PIDE	Polícia International de Defesa de Estado (International Police for the Defense of the State) (Portugal)
PLD	Partido Liberal Democrático (Liberal Democratic Party)
PLUA	Partido da Luta Unida dos Africanos de Angola (Party for the United Struggle of Angola's Africans)
PNLS	Programa Nacional de Luta Contra o Sida (National Program to Fight AIDS)
POC	Partidos Oposição Civil (Civil Opposition Parties)
PREA	Partido Republicano de Angolan (Republican Party of Angola)

PRS	Partido Renovação da Social (Social Renewal Party)
RACN	Rapid Assessment of Critical Needs
RNA	Radio Nacional de Angola (National Radio of Angola)
RPDA	República de Pessoa Democrática de Angola (Democratic People's Republic of Angola) (UNITA/FNLA, 1975–1976)
RUA	Resistência Unido de Angola (United Resistance of Angola)
SA–ACC	South Africa–Angola Chamber of Commerce
SADC	Southern African Development Community
SADCC	Southern Africa Development Coordination Conference
SADF	South African Defense Forces
SEF	Saneamento Económico e Financiero (Economic and Financial Rehabilitation)
Sonangol	Sociedade Nacional de Combustíveis de Angola (National Fuel Company of Angola)
SWAPO	South West Africa People's Organization
SWATF	South West Africa Territorial Forces
TAAG	Transportes Aéreos de Angola (Angolan Airlines Company)
TPA	Televisão Pública de Angola (Angolan National Television)
UCAN	Universidade Catholica de Angola (Catholic University of Angola)
UEA	União dos Escritores Angolano (Angola Writer's Union)
UJA	União dos Jornalistas (Angolan Union of Journalists)
UNACA	União Nacional dos Camponeses de Angola (Angolan Peasants Association)
UNAVEM I	United Nations Angola Verification Mission I
UNAVEM II	United Nations Angola Verification Mission II
UNAVEM III	United Nations Angola Verification Mission III
UNCTAD	United Nations Conference on Trade and Development
UNDP	United Nations Development Program
UNEA	União Nacional dos Estudantes Angolanos (National Union for Angolan Students) (Ovimbundu)

UNESCO	United Nations Education, Scientific and Cultural Organization
UNHCR	United Nations High Commissioner for Refugees
UNIANG	Universidade Independente de Angola (Independent University of Angola)
UNICEF	United Nations Children's Fund
UNITA	União Nacional para a Independência Total de Angola (National Union for the Total Independence of Angola)
UNITA-R	União Nacional para a Independência Total de Angola, Renovada (National Union for the Total Independence of Angola, Renovated)
UNMA	United Nations Mission to Angola
UNOA	United Nations Office in Angola
UNTA–CS	União Nacional dos Trabalhadores de Angola, Confederão Sindical (National Workers Union of Angola, Trade Union Confederation)
UPA	União das Populações de Angola (Union of People of Angola) (pre-FNLA)
UPNA	União das Populações do Norte de Angola (Union of People of North Angola)
USAID	United States Agency for International Development
USSR	Union of Soviet Socialist Republics
Vorgan	A Voz da Resistência do Galo Negro (Voice of the Resistance of the Black Cockerel)
WHO	World Health Organization

Political map of Angola.

Provincial map of Angola.

AREA 1,246,700 km²

POPULATION 9.5 million

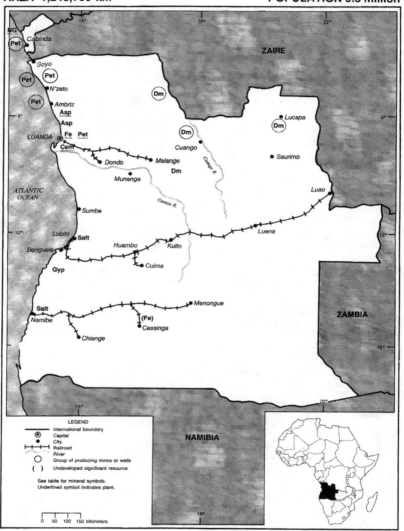

Map of minerals and mines in Angola.

Courtesy U.S. Geological Survey

Chronology

1300–1600   The Bantu settle present-day Angola.

1483   Portuguese explorer Diogo Cão reaches the kingdom of the Bakongo. Later in the same year he encounters the kingdom of Ndongo of the Mbundu people, whose ruler is called Ngola a Kilu-anje. From this title, the Portuguese begin to term the entire region as *Angola*.

1483–1965   The Portuguese, almost from their arrival, begin the buying and selling of slaves. As many as 4 million Angolans may have been sold into slavery.

1491   The first Catholic Church is built in Mbanza; it is later called São Salvador.

1576   The Portuguese found the town of Luanda.

1617   The city of Benguela is established.

1620–1660   Queen Nzinga Mbande attempts to reconquer the territory of Ngola. She will later be revered as the first Angolan revolutionary.

1641–1648   The conflict in Europe allows Holland to capture Luanda and Benguela. The Dutch end slavery, angering Brazilians, who help Portugal evict Holland by May 1648.

1665   Portuguese forces defeat Bakongo at Battle of Mbwila, ending the unified Bakongo kingdom.

1671   **29 November:** A Portuguese force captures the Mbundu fortress at Pungu-a-Ndongo, ending the integrity of the Mbundu kingdom.

1769   Francisco de Sousa Coutinho establishes Caconda in the central highlands.

1774–1776 The Portuguese bring the Ovimbundu kingdoms under control. The kings of Bailundo and Andulo are captured.

1777 The white population of Angola is less than 1,600.

1836 Portugal outlaws the slave trade. The law is ignored until Great Britain enforces it.

1840 Mocâmedes is founded.

1858 Slavery is outlawed in Angola.

1859 Portuguese forces reoccupy São Salvador for the first time since the return of the colonialists sparked the Bakongo nationalist movement in the 17th century.

1880 Three hundred Boers fleeing British rule in South Africa arrive in Huíla.

1885 Portugal signs the Treaty of Simulambuco with Cabindan chiefs. Cabindans view the treaty as proof that Cabinda is not part of Angola.

1901 The Caminho de Ferro de Luanda railroad begins operation. It ultimately links Luanda to Malange, 378 miles away.

1904 Portuguese forces lose 120 troops in a single battle against the Ambo.

1912 Diamonds are found in Lunda province.

1913 Mestico intellectuals found Liga Angolana in Luanda.

1915 **September:** Ambo King Mandume is defeated by the Portuguese.

1919 After 15 military campaigns dating from 1631, the Dembo ethnolinguistic group is conquered by Portugal.

1922 **22 September:** Agostinho Neto is born near Luanda.

1923 **12 January:** Holden Roberto is born at São Salvador.

1926 **May:** A right-wing military coup leads to the establishment of a one-party state in Portugal.

1931 The Caminho de Ferro de Benguela railroad is completed.

1932   Antonio Salazar becomes Portuguese prime minister, until a stroke fells him in 1968. As prime minister, Salazar attempts to incorporate Angola as a province of Portugal.

1934   **3 August:** Jonas Malheiro Savimbi is born at Munhango.

1951   Salazar annexes Angola to Portugal as an "overseas province."

1953   The anticolonial group Partido da Luta Unida dos Africanos de Angola (PLUA) (Party for the United Struggle of Africans of Angola) is founded. It will later merge with others to form the Movimento Popular de Libertação de Angola (MPLA) (Popular Movement for the Liberation of Angola).

1954   The União das Populações do Norte de Angola (UPNA) (Union of People of Northern Angola) is founded.

1956   **10 December:** The MPLA is founded as an offshoot of the Angolan Communist Party, which had strong links to the Portuguese Communist Party.

1957   The Soviet Union starts supporting the MPLA with weapons aid. Ghana receives independence from Great Britain.

1958   Holden Roberto changes the name of the UPNA to União das Populações de Angola (UPA) (Union of People of Angola) in order to attract a broader following in Angola. **September:** Savimbi leaves Angola bound for Europe to further his education.

1959   The Ovamboland People's Organization, later to become the South West Africa People's Organization (SWAPO), is formed.

1960   **3 June:** Belgium grants independence to Zaire. British prime minister Harold Macmillan delivers a speech in Cape Town, South Africa, in which he states "The wind of change is blowing throughout this continent." Seventeen nations with a combined population of 190 million people receive independence from colonial powers.

1961   **4 February:** Members of the MPLA attempt to storm prisons in Luanda. UPA's Holden Roberto receives a $10,000 retainer from the Central Intelligence Agency (CIA). **15 March:** The UPA begins a massive uprising in northern Angola. Savimbi joins the UPA and later becomes foreign minister of Govêrno Revolucionário de Angola no Exílio

(GRAE) (Revolutionary Government of Angola in Exile). **1 July:** Portuguese troop strength in Angola reaches 17,000.

1961–1965 The number of Portuguese troops in Angola rises from 9,000 to over 50,000.

1962 28 March: Roberto merges the UPA with the Partido Democrático de Angola (PDA) (Democratic Party of Angola) to found the Frente Nacional de Libertação de Angola (FNLA) (National Front for the Liberation of Angola). One month later, the GRAE is formed.

1963 Agostinho Neto visits the United States seeking support and presenting the MPLA's policies and positions. Three Cabindan groups merge to form Frente de Libertação do Enclave de Cabinda (FLEC) (Front for the Liberation of the Enclave of Cabinda).

1964 July: Savimbi abruptly quits his post in the GRAE.

1965 Savimbi travels to the People's Republic of China, where he and several colleagues receive military training.

1966 Gulf Oil makes its first significant discovery in Cabinda. **13 March:** União Nacional para a Independência Total de Angola (UNITA) (National Union for the Total Independence of Angola) is founded in Moxico province at Muangai. **25 December:** UNITA launches its first major attack against Teixeira de Sousa.

1967 Savimbi is expelled from Zambia. He reenters Angola the following year.

1973 Roberto visits Beijing, China, in search of weapons and training. The Chinese agree to send 119 instructors to FNLA camps in Zaire. **21 August:** Portuguese officers form the Movimento das Forças Armadas (MFA) (Armed Forces Movement).

1974 25 April: The dictatorship of Prime Minister Marcello Caetano is bloodlessly overthrown by members of the MFA. The MFA immediately signals that independence will be granted to Mozambique, Angola, Cape Verde, Guinea–Bissau, and São Tomé e Principe. **May:** Portugal has 50,000 soldiers in Angola. **August:** Three factions of the MPLA hold a party congress to elect a new leadership. After Neto loyalists walk out, Daniel Chipenda is elected president of the MPLA. **September:** At a second party congress, the MPLA cadre reelects Neto to the presidency. Chipenda rejects the results and flees with his supporters to Zaire. **October:** The Soviet Union increases military aid to the MPLA. **November:** The three liberation movements arrive in Luanda in anticipation of elections and the transitional government.

1975 2–5 January: At Mombasa, Kenya, the three independence movements agree to mutual recognition with equal rights and responsibilities. **15 January:** Portugal, UNITA, the MPLA, and FNLA sign the Alvor Accords, whereby Portugal agrees to free Angola. **Spring:** The administration of U.S. president Gerald Ford (Republican) donates $300,000 to UNITA. **March:** Forces loyal to former MPLA commander Daniel Chipenda are incorporated into the FNLA. **May:** 230 Cuban military advisers arrive in Luanda and establish four training centers for the MPLA soldiers. **Early summer:** The MPLA drives UNITA and FNLA from the capital city of Luanda. **June:** President Jomo Kenyatta of Kenya uses his influence to persuade the MPLA, UNITA, and FNLA to sign a cease-fire known as the Nakuru Agreement. **25 June:** Mozambique is granted independence by Portugal. **Late July/August:** Sizable numbers of Cuban troops arrive in Luanda. From neighboring South West Africa, South African units cross the border to occupy the Cunene Dam complex. Mercenaries from Great Britain, France, Portugal, and other nations enter Angola, most in support of the FNLA. **Fall:** The FNLA forces, supported by Zairian troops, drive from northern Angola toward Luanda with the intention of capturing the city before the scheduled date of independence. UNITA and South African forces undertake a similar drive from the south. **10 November:** The FNLA gathers forces in Quifangondo for a final push against the MPLA. An ambush by MPLA and Cuban troops armed with Soviet-made 122-mm rocket launchers route the FNLA column in what becomes known as Sheila way Luau (Battle of Death Road). **11 November:** Portugal grants independence to Angola. The MPLA declares the People's Republic of Angola (PRA), which is immediately recognized by the Soviet Union, Cuba, Warsaw Pact nations, and Brazil. The FNLA and UNITA declare the República de Pessoa Democrática de Angola (RPDA) (Democratic People's Republic of Angola) with Huambo as its capital. **19 December:** By a vote of 54–22, the U.S. Senate adopts the Clark amendment to deny further funds for covert military aid in Angola. The $8.2 million still "in the pipeline" is delivered.

1976   Sociedade Nacional de Combustiveis de Angola (Sonangol), the state petroleum company, is formed. **January:** Forces loyal to Daniel Chipenda cross into South West Africa, where they are recruited by South Africa. Formed into the 32nd Battalion, they are then rated as "the finest light infantry in the world today." The 32nd will be deployed extensively throughout the 1980s in support of UNITA. The unit will be disbanded after the 1994 elections in South Africa. **8 January:** The Organization of African Unity (OAU) convenes in Addis Ababa, Ethiopia, to debate Angola. After three days, the conference ends with no resolution. Applications for membership from the MPLA, UNITA, and FNLA are rejected. Nations involved in Angola include Belgium, China, Cuba, East Germany, France, Great Britain, North Korea, South Africa, the Soviet Union, the United States, West Germany, Zaire, and Zambia. **Late January:** South African forces announce withdrawal from Angola to be completed by 27 March. **11 February:** The OAU recognizes the MPLA as the legitimate government of Angola and the 47th member of the organization. **February:** UNITA announces a return to guerrilla warfare against the MPLA/Cuba/Soviet Union. **October:** President Neto travels to Moscow to sign the Twenty-Year Treaty of Friendship and Cooperation. **1 December:** Angola is admitted as the UN's 146th member.

1978   **May:** In the first major incursion (Operation Reindeer) since 1975–76, South African forces attack a SWAPO base at Kissing. Estimates are as high as over 1,000 killed and 420 wounded.

1978–1988   South African forces attack African National Congress (ANC) and SWAPO bases in Angola. Later, in support of UNITA, attacks are launched against the Forças Armadas Populares de Libertação de Angola (FAPLA) (Popular Armed Forces for the Liberation of Angola).

1979   **20 September:** Neto, ill with cancer, visits Moscow for medical treatment. While in emergency surgery, he dies. He is succeeded by José Eduardo dos Santos. **November:** Traveling to the United States for the first time, Savimbi visits New York City and Washington, D.C.

1980   Nine southern African states form the Southern Africa Development Coordinating Council. **May:** In an interview with the *Wall Street Journal,* candidate Ronald Reagan states his administration will "provide them [UNITA] with weapons."

1981   Savimbi again travels to Washington, D.C. Unlike during his first visit, Savimbi meets with (Reagan) administration officials. Jamba becomes the provisional capital of UNITA's Free Land of Angola. **August:** South Africa launches Operation Protea, which kills or captures over 1,000 SWAPO members. They also engage the Angolan army for the first time.

1982   UNITA launches the Christmas Offensive throughout Angola.

1983   South African forces launch Operation Asker against government forces. For the first time since 1975–1976, South African troops directly engage Cuban forces. UNITA begins to capture foreign nationals working in Angola, marching them for hundreds of miles then releasing them before the international media.

1984   **16 February:** A first Lusaka Accord between Angola and South Africa provides for the withdrawal of South African forces from Angola by 1988. The agreement quickly falls apart.

1985   **May:** South African commandos, disguised as UNITA rebels, attack the Gulf Oil refinery in Luanda. The U.S. Congress passes legislation that kills the Clark Amendment. In 1986, the United States begins to supply weapons and money to UNITA for the first time since 1976. **October:** The MPLA forces, backed by Soviet weaponry and Cuban troops, fail to capture Mavinga/Jamba, a key staging area for UNITA. Intervention by South African forces saves the day for the rebels. Mikhail Gorbachev becomes general secretary of the Soviet Union. Soon, under prodding from the United States, Gorbachev announces Moscow's "new thinking" about Third World conflicts.

1986   Savimbi visits the United States again. He meets with President Reagan and the secretaries of defense and state. **1–14 May:** President dos Santos, in Moscow, receives Soviet commitment to the integrity of MPLA power.

1987   **July–September:** Again, the MPLA forces, supplied by the Soviet Union and Cuban soldiers, fail to capture Mavinga/Jamba. South Africa intervenes once more with troops and air power. As the MPLA/Cuban column retreats toward Cuito Cuanavale, UNITA and South African forces follow, laying siege to the city.

1988   **January:** The MPLA government introduces the first of many economic reorganization plans. The Saneamento Económico e Financiero

(SEF) will attempt to raise salaries, increase productivity, and spur domestic consumption. **March:** The siege of Cuito Cuanavale ends, with South Africa on the one hand and Cuba and the Soviet Union on the other both claiming victory for their clients. The ambiguous ending of the siege lays the groundwork for the Brazzaville Protocol (a.k.a., the New York Accords). **June:** Savimbi visits the United States for the fourth time, primarily to make contact with Vice President George Bush, who is campaigning against Michael Dukakis for the presidency. After winning the presidency, Bush reiterates U.S. support for UNITA. **July–September:** Cuban troop strength in Angola numbers between 52,000 and 60,000. **22 December:** Angola, South Africa, and Cuba sign the New York Accords. Cuba agrees to a phased withdrawal from Angola. South Africa agrees to halt aid to UNITA and allow elections toward an independent South West Africa, soon to be renamed Namibia. The United Nations Angola Verification Mission (UNAVEM) is deployed to monitor the South African and Cuban withdrawal and oversee Namibian elections.

1989   22 June: At Gbadolite, Zaire president Mobutu Sese Seko hosts Savimbi, dos Santos, and 18 African heads of state. In confusing circumstances, Savimbi and the Angolan president shake hands, indicating a peace accord is near. Both parties later renege on the vague, imprecisely worded document. **July:** Fighting resumes between the MPLA and UNITA despite a 22 June cease-fire. **September:** Angola is admitted as the 152nd member of the International Monetary Fund (IMF) and as a member of the World Bank. **1 November:** Elections are held in South West Africa/Namibia. SWAPO wins. **December:** The Angolan government launches Operation Final Assault against Mavinga/Jamba. Government failure to take the objective leads to direct MPLA–UNITA negotiations. Cuba claims to have lost 2,289 men while on "internationalist missions." More than 2,000 were killed in Angola.

1990   August: In a visit to Luanda, Soviet foreign minister Eduard Shevardnadze says "obviously there cannot be a military solution." **September:** The Soviet Union suggests and all parties accept the "Triple Zero" proposal, which calls for the USSR to halt arms deliveries to the MPLA, the United States to stop supplying UNITA, and both Angolan groups not to seek weapons from other nations. **October:** Jonas Savimbi again visits Washington, D.C., where he meets with

President Bush, Secretary of State James Baker, and key members of Congress. **December:** At the Third Party Congress, the MPLA–PT drops the "PT" from its moniker and adopts policies of "a multiparty political system, a mixed economic system based on market forces and the transformation of the party's nature and orientation."

1991   March: New laws are introduced to permit multiparty politics and guarantee civil liberties. **31 May:** UNITA and the MPLA sign the Bicesse Accords, which call for an immediate cease-fire, creation of a national army, the cantonment of existing armies, and elections. **1 July:** The last Cuban soldiers leave Luanda, as called for by the New York Peace Accords. UNAVEM II is created to oversee implementation of the Bicesse Accords. The force is underbudgeted at $118 million and deploys a total of 476 monitors to a nation twice the size of France.

1992   10 August: The MPLA unilaterally ends voter registration with an estimated 700,000 rural Angolans unregistered. **September:** The first free and fair elections in Angola are held. Parliament is won by the MPLA, but the presidency is not decided due to the frontrunner's failure to win a majority. However, 10 political parties, not including UNITA, charge the elections are fraudulent. **7 October:** Savimbi leaves Luanda for Huambo. **31 October:** The MPLA soldiers and civilians launch a pogrom against Ovimbundu and Bakongo living in Luanda. According to church sources, 20,000 people are killed. The UNITA vice president and chief negotiator are among the dead. **November–December:** The civil war resumes.

1993   28 February: Peace talks between the MPLA and UNITA scheduled in Addis Ababa, Ethiopia, are cancelled when UNITA fails to show. **6 March:** After a 55-day siege, UNITA captures Huambo from the MPLA forces. **12 April:** Peace discussions between the two warring parties begin in Abidjan, Côte d'Ivoire. As negotiations stall, the United States moves toward recognizing the MPLA as the legitimate government of Angola. **19 May:** The United States extends diplomatic recognition to Angola. **July:** UN Secretary-General Boutros Boutros-Ghali appoints former Malian foreign minister Alioune Blondin Beye as UN Special Representative to Angola. He replaces Margaret Anstee. **15 September:** The UN Security Council passes the first of several sanction resolutions against UNITA. Sanctions forbid member states from supplying or selling arms or petroleum products.

1994   10 November: Government forces recapture Huambo. **20 November:** A peace agreement between UNITA and the MPLA is signed in Lusaka, Zambia, calling for a cease-fire, disarming of UNITA soldiers, and UNITA's participation in the government. However, neither Jonas Savimbi nor President dos Santos sign the pact.

1995   8 February: The United Nations Security Council creates UNAVEM III. The estimated cost is $383 million, and the force includes 7,000 UN troops, 350 military observers, and 260 civilian police. **6 May:** The first summit between President dos Santos and Savimbi is held in Libreville, Gabon. **8 December:** President dos Santos meets with U.S. president Bill Clinton in the United States in the first official encounter between the presidents of the two nations.

1996   13 March: UNITA celebrates the 30th anniversary of its founding at Bailundo, Angola.

1997   9 April: UNITA representatives elected in 1992 officially take their posts. Some 15,000 Angolan troops are rushed to the Republic of the Congo to assist former president Denis Sassou Nguessou in a power struggle against then president Pascal Lissouba. **30 June:** The Misión de Observadores de las Naciones Unidas en Angola (MONUA) (UN Observer Mission in Angola) is created to replace UNAVEM III. **30 October:** The United Nations implements more sanctions against UNITA.

1998   11 March: UNITA is recognized as a legal political party. **12 June:** The UN implements further sanctions against UNITA. **August:** Angola sends troops to support President Laurent Kabila of the Democratic Republic of the Congo, who is embattled in a civil war. **24 August:** UNITA ceases collaboration with the troika of nations overseeing the peace process: Portugal, Russia, and the United States. **2 September:** The UNITA splinter group UNITA–Renovada is formed. The government immediately recognizes the new group as a official negotiator. The SADC condemns Savimbi, stating his behavior "is that of a war criminal." **November:** The government army launches an offensive against UNITA. **December:** A UN cargo plane is shot down near Huambo.

1999   January: A second UN plane is shot down near Bailundo. Both incidents are blamed on UNITA. President dos Santos installs a "war cabinet" to pursue total victory against UNITA. **22 February:** Côte d'Ivoire revokes passports of UNITA officials, including Lukamba Gato and Isaías Samakuva. **March:** Under orders from the government, the UN suspends operations in Angola. **24 July:** The government issues an arrest warrant for Savimbi on charges of "armed rebellion, sabotage, and slaughter." **October:** Government troops capture the UNITA strongholds of Bailundo and Andulo. Angola agrees to allow the UN to reopen its office in Luanda. **December:** Jamba is captured.

2000 **11 November:** Angola celebrates 25 years of independence.

2001 **March:** Savimbi tells Voice of America radio in Luanda, in his first interview in over a year, he is ready to discuss peace. **1 May:** Angolan troops capture Mavinga from UNITA forces. **3 June:** Admitting defeat of its army in conventional warfare, UNITA switches to guerrilla warfare. **August:** President dos Santos announces his decision to step down at the next elections, but gives no date for the elections. **21 August:** The government demands Savimbi be arrested and tried as a war criminal.

2002 **22 February:** Savimbi is killed by government forces in Moxico province. **12 March:** The government confirms the death of UNITA's vice president, António Dembo. **25 March:** The London-based NGO Global Witness issues a report accusing the Angolan government of siphoning billions of dollars from the oil industry. **2 April:** Parliament approves a blanket amnesty program for UNITA soldiers and Forças Armadas de Angolanas (Armed Forces of Angola) deserters. **4 April:** The government and UNITA sign a cease-fire agreement. **April–June:** Over 80,000 UNITA soldiers and 300,000 relatives enter demobilization camps. **28 June:** Angola ratifies the Ottawa Convention on the Prohibition of the Use, Stockpiling, Production and Transfer of Anti-Personnel Mines and on Their Destruction. **30 July:** Head of UNITA Renovada Eugenio Manuvakola steps down as party leader, clearing the way for negotiations to transform the rebel group into a political party. **2 August:** The UNITA army is formally disbanded, and 5,000 are to enter the government army, while the rest will return to civilian life. **September:** U.S. secretary of state Colin Powell visits Luanda. Angola is elected to the UN Security Council for a two-year term. **October:** An IMF report states that $900 million disappeared from the Angolan government budget in 2001. **November:** The Angolan government presents parliament with a peacetime budget.

Some 77 percent will go to the public sector. Historically, the lion's share of the budget was spent on defense. **21 November:** The Joint Military Commission formed to oversee the April cease-fire is officially disbanded. **28 November:** Angola and the UN High Commissioner for Refugees sign an agreement for the voluntary repatriation of over 400,000 Angolan refugees from neighboring nations. **5 December:** President dos Santos appoints Fernando Dia dos Santos as prime minister. Not related to the president, Prime Minister dos Santos is the first to occupy the position since 1999. The president also announces new ministers for the Govêrno da Unidade e da Reconciliação Nacional (GURN, Government of National Reconciliation). **6 December:** Finance Minister Julio Bessa is fired and replaced by Jose Pedro de Morais. **9 December:** The UN Security Council lifts the nine-year-old sanctions against UNITA. **16 December:** Angola withdraws its last troops from the Democratic Republic of the Congo.

2003   1 January: A global agreement to end the trade in "blood diamonds" takes effect. Blood diamonds are stones mined to help finance rebellion. The agreement is called the Kimberley Process. **6 January:** UNITA formally apologizes for its role in the civil war, stating, "in this context UNITA comes before the people to ask for pardon." UNITA announces its Ninth Ordinary Congress, to be held in June. **15 February:** The UN announces that the UN Mission to Angola (UNMA), having fulfilled its mandate, will end its official presence in Angola. **21 April:** The Ministry of Health, in conjunction with the United Nations Children's Fund (UNICEF), launches the largest health campaign in Angolan history with the aim to inoculate seven million children against measles. **7 May:** U.S. president George W. Bush formally ends sanctions against UNITA. **19 June:** The Angolan government officially closes the Quartering Areas of the ex-UNITA military forces. **24–27 June:** UNITA holds its Ninth Party Congress, the first to be held since the death of UNITA founder Jonas Savimbi. Former foreign secretary Isaías Samakuva is elected president of UNITA. **23 August:** The U.S. State Department drops its long-standing warning that U.S. citizens should stay away from Angola. **December:** The MPLA holds its Fifth Party Congress. Party faithful discuss a possible replacement candidate for Eduardo dos Santos and the timing for the next national elections, scheduled for 2004 or 2005.

Introduction

In Angola, truth is often stranger than fiction. Dominated and exploited by Portugal for almost 500 years, Angola achieved independence in 1975 only to plunge into a 27-year civil war. The civil war became a key element in the Cold War, yet in 1991 the Cold War actors were gone, leaving Angola still mired in civil strife. As of September 2003, peace appeared to be firmly rooted in Angola. The nation faced the monumental process of rebuilding its economic infrastructure and rekindling ties between all Angolans. Angola's natural resources may help pay the way, but much human effort will be needed. The next 20 years should be exciting for Angola and its citizens.

LAND AND PEOPLE

The Portuguese took the name Angola from the title of the Mbundu king, Ngola a Kiluanje. The Portuguese applied the name to the entire colonial possession.

Located in south-central Africa, the Republic of Angola is a country of diverse peoples and a variegated landscape. Namibia is to the south, the Democratic Republic of the Congo (DRC) is to the north, Zambia is situated to the east, and a thin strip of DRC separates the Enclave of Cabinda from Angola. Cabinda is an integral part of Angola, if only because of its petroleum deposits. To the west is the Atlantic Ocean, which provides Angola with 1,025 miles of shoreline. Additionally, the ocean floor contains vast quantities of petroleum, and many consider the waters off Angola to be one of the most lucrative fishing areas in the world.

Angola is located between 12 and 30 degrees south latitude and 18 and 30 degrees east longitude. The area of Angola, including Cabinda, is 481,351 square miles, larger than the U.S. states of California and

Texas combined, or more than twice the size of France. Angola's capital is Luanda. Other important cities include Huambo, Soyo, Lobito, Benguela, Lubango, Malange, and Kuito. Present-day Angola consists of 18 provinces: Bengo, Benguela, Bié, Cabinda, Cuando Cubango, Cuanza Norte, Cuanza Sul, Cunene, Huambo, Huíla, Luanda, Lunda Norte, Lunda Sul, Malanje, Moxico, Namibe, Uíge, and Zaire.

The official language is Portuguese, but, except in Luanda, most Angolans speak Bantu or native languages. Angola has over 60 dialects. The government chose six to be the official educational languages of the nation, namely, Kikongo, Kimbundu, Chokwe, Umbundu, Mbundu, and Kwanyama. Other widely spoken tongues include Ovambo, Luvale, Lucazi, Nyemba, and Rukwangali.

TERRAIN AND CLIMATE

The landscape of Angola is very diverse and has four distinct regions: the northern forests, the central highlands, the coastal plains, and the arid regions in the southwest.

The northern forest region receives an annual rainfall of over 60 inches per year. The area can support agriculture, and the forests provide game for hunters. During the Portuguese era, coffee became a major cash crop in the north. But the civil war destroyed many of the coffee plantations. With the onset of peace, the government hopes to restore Angola's production to 1970s levels. In world coffee production, Angola once ranked third or fourth in coffee production in the world. The industry employed 200,000 Africans, including 10,000 at the country's largest coffee plantation, Fazenda Boa Entrada (Entering Good Farm). Although the forests of northern Angola and Cabinda have barely been harvested to date, they will begin to export valuable hardwoods such as mahogany (pink and white), teak, rosewood, sandalwood, ebony, tola, mulberry, eucalyptus, cypress, pine, and tacula.

A majority of the Angolan population lives in the central highlands. With irrigation available from the many rivers and streams that flow through the area, the region has adequate rainfall to support agriculture. The altitude of the central highlands prevents heavy proliferation of the tsetse fly, allowing for ranching and cattle production. However, because of the prolonged civil war, the tsetse fly is found in 14 of Angola's 18 provinces.

The coastal plain was the site of the initial Portuguese colonization effort. Today, Portuguese culture still heavily influences the region. The Portuguese developed the ports of Luanda and Lobito, but only for the benefit of Portugal, not the native population. The major rail lines all have their termination points on the coastal plain. Farm products in the coastal plain include sugarcane, cotton, and corn, while the fishing industry relies on tuna, sardines, and mackerel.

The arid regions of the southwest lack adequate precipitation to sustain an agricultural economy. The average rainfall is two inches per year in Namibe province. Irrigation is difficult because rivers flow only during the rainy season. The Portuguese called the area Terras do Fim Mundo (Land at the End of the Earth). The lack of consistent rainfall has kept the population small. Most inhabitants are nomadic cattle herders.

Major crops and commodities of Angola include bananas, cabbage, cocoa, coffee, corn, cotton, gums, kale, kapok, manioc, okra, palm kernels, palm oil, peaches, peanuts, peppers, pineapples, plantains, sisal, sugarcane, sweet potatoes, tobacco, tomatoes, vegetables, wax, wheat, and yams. Animal production includes cattle, goats, pigs, and poultry. The Atlantic Ocean provides anchovy, carapau, lobster, mackerel, marlin, red crab, sardines, shark, shellfish, shrimp, stickleback, swordfish, tuna, and whiting.

PEOPLES

The population of Angola is approximately 10,593,171. The annual growth rate is 2.18 percent. The birth rate is 46/1000 of population, while the death rate is 24/1000. Infant mortality is 192/1000. Life expectancy is 44 years. The government began a census (unfinished by September 2003) in 2002—the first since the Portuguese colonial era. The largest ethnic group are the Ovimbundu at 37 percent, followed by the Mbundu at 25 percent, the Bakongo at 13 percent, and other groups making up the remaining 25 percent. Other important ethnic groups include Khoisan (Bushmen), Lunda, Nganguela, and Herero.

RELIGION

Religion plays an important role in Angolan society. Roman Catholics account for 38 percent of the population and Protestants 15 percent. Forty-seven percent hold indigenous beliefs. Frequently, villagers will take components of Christianity and combine these with local beliefs.

Most Angolans believe that magical power resides in many objects. The power is usually neutral, but it can be employed maliciously by witches. If a person has recurrent problems, they may employ a kimbanda, who can determine whether ancestral spirits have been offended or witchcraft is involved. The kimbanda has the ability to communicate with the spirit world. The kimbanda will seek answers, but usually at a price. The better the connection to the spirit world, the higher the charge.

Missionaries played an important role in the liberation struggle. Many of Angola's first generation leaders were the product of missionary schools or received scholarships to study overseas. Portuguese harassment of Protestant missionaries, combined with favoritism toward the Roman Catholic missions, made the Catholic Church suspect to the local population. The United Church of Canada, the United Church of Christ Congregational, the Plymouth Brethren, the Phil African Mission, and the Seventh-Day Adventists were other churches involved in Angola.

Early Movimento Popular de Libertação de Angola (MPLA) policy was hostile toward religious activity, holding that "religion has always been one of the weapons the exploiting classes utilize to divert the exploited ones in the revolutionary struggle for their liberation." Since the early 1990s, the government has softened its position vis-à-vis religious practice. In the late 1990s, cross-religious groups began to advocate an end to the civil war through negotiations. As their numbers grew, the government was obliged to at least pay lip service to the concept of negotiation with UNITA.

EARLY ANGOLAN HISTORY

Knowledge of early Angolan history is imprecise at best. Much of precolonial Angolan history was passed down orally from generation to generation. In addition, the Portuguese kept notoriously poor records and showed little interest in researching the history of the Bantu people. Portuguese historians were more concerned about events in Portuguese Angola than the precolonial era.

The original inhabitants were the Khoisan, or Bushmen. The Khoisan and their forefathers lived in the region as early as 25,000 years ago. One can find examples of Khoisan rock paintings from very early periods in Angola. The Khoisan were hunters–gatherers, the lifestyle still practiced today by their descendants in remote parts of southern Africa. As the Bantu slowly migrated from the north in small groups, perhaps as early as 1000 A.D., the local inhabitants were either assimilated or withdrew into the remote parts of the region.

Most scholars believe the Bantu people arrived in a slow migration from the present-day Nigeria–Cameroon border. This migration of the Bantu would eventually extend to present-day South Africa. Scholars are uncertain what prompted the migration. Prevalent theories include warfare, population expansion, economic development, and desert encroachment. Substantial numbers of Bantu arrived in Angola, probably sometime early in the 13th century. The migration of the Bantu people from northern to southern Africa is one of the great migrations in history. As they moved, the Bantu engaged in traditional hunting and gathering. Once they reached unpopulated areas, they began to establish permanent villages and settlements. Some raised livestock and others farmed, while most combined the two. Taking different migratory routes, the Bantu settled in different regions of the country. They began to develop their own ethnolinguistic character.

In the struggle for land, cattle, women, or slaves, or simply to dominate a neighboring group, conflict began. A number of kingdoms emerged. Some, such as the Bakongo, were very powerful. Others, such as the Mbundu and the Lunda, controlled resources or fertile land. The Monomotapa, based in modern Zimbabwe, controlled much of the trade in the region. The civil war in Angola can be traced, in part, to ethnic conflict that is centuries old.

The Bantu in Angola exhibited limited curiosity about the ocean or sea trade. The ocean might provide some benefits, but the interior of the nation provided land, agricultural produce, game, and trade.

THE PORTUGUESE COLONIAL ERA: 1482–1961

Like other European nations, Portugal aspired to find a sea route to India but knew that exploration would not be easy. Captains might be brave, but the crews were not. Ship captains cut their journeys short rather than face mutiny. Most believed the earth was flat, that monsters roamed the seas, and that once too far away the ship might simply sail into oblivion. Maps either were inaccurate or did not exist.

Portugal's Age of Discovery began in 1415 under the guidance of Prince Henry, the Navigator. Due to the doubts and misgivings of the era, the Portuguese did not reach Angola until 1482, when Diogo Cão reached the mouth of the Congo River. The Portuguese made contact with the Bakongo and exchanged emissaries. Over the next 50 years, a number of Bakongo were sent to Portugal to learn the language and useful skills. In turn, the Portuguese sent specialists, including missionaries, to the Bakongo Kingdom. The era of Brother Kings would reach its height under King Manuel I of Portugal and the Bakongo king, Manicongo Nzinga Mbemba, whose baptized name was Afonso.

King Afonso faced two problems. First, he was torn between his Christian/Portuguese policies and the traditional beliefs and practices that many of his subjects preferred. Second, he was more Christian than the Portuguese, who began to rob and cheat their brother Bakongo. Disturbingly, the buying and selling of slaves became an important commerce to the Portuguese, including the missionaries.

When King Afonso died in 1543, the Bakongo Kingdom was shattered, as various factions tried to assume the throne. The Bakongo Empire would never again achieve the power it held over neighboring princedoms. By 1615, Portuguese influence was nowhere to be found in the Bakongo region. The settlers and missionaries had left.

To the south, the Mbundu people, under the leadership of Ngola, established a kingdom that nearly rivaled the Bakongo. In 1520, the Portuguese sent an expedition under the leadership of Balthasar de Castro to establish ties with the Mbundu. The entourage included merchants and priests. The two African kingdoms began to suffer because of a quarrel over the slave trade, but both also profited from the trade. Finally, in 1556, the Bakongo sent a military expedition to punish the Mbundu. Although both sides had Portuguese soldiers, the Bakongo were defeated at the Battle of the Dande, which further weakened their control.

Several years later, the Ngola Ndambi captured a priest, Father Francisco de Gouveia, and expedition commander Paulo Dias. Dias was detained for five years, and Father Gouveia would perish 15 years later as a prisoner of the Mbundu.

In Lisbon, the capture of the two men led to a review of the Brother King philosophy. The Portuguese realized that their allies in Angola could not deliver upon promises or treaties. First, the diplomacy involved in the Brother King policy needed a pro-Portuguese monarch, which it did not always get. Second, even Angolan princes who profited from the slave trade were ambivalent about it. Finally, myths involving great mineral wealth in the interior of the country made military intervention and even conquest desirable. By 1571, the era of the Brother Kings was over, and it would be replaced by Portuguese military conquest of any group standing in the way of colonial ambitions.

Paulo Dias returned to Luanda in 1575. Between then and 1605, the Portuguese fought a number of inconclusive battles with the Mbundu. The primary mission of the expeditions was to locate the fabulous silver mines of Cambambe. In 1605, Manuel Cerveira Pereira led a force that established a fort in the Mbundu heartland. But after months of searching, the Portuguese were forced to admit that the silver mines were a myth.

Later, Portuguese military actions were designed to increase and protect their interests in the growing slave trade. European conflicts brought Holland into Angola in 1641–48. Portugal became involved in a succession of religious and political conflicts at the behest of Spain. Holland, an enemy of Spain, seized the opportunity to harass the Portuguese territories in Africa. Dutch forces captured Luanda and Benguela in 1641, cementing a series of treaties with the Mbundu and Bakongo, who had tired of Portuguese mistreatment. The Dutch halted the supply of slaves flowing to Brazil. Since the sugar-growing economy of Brazil needed slaves to prosper, wealthy Brazilian colonialists launched a military offensive against the Dutch in Angola. By 1648, the Brazilians had captured Luanda, and the Dutch soon departed from the rest of the country.

The return of the Portuguese had the expected results for the African population. Portugal forced the Bakongo Kingdom to sign a harsh treaty, but the treaty was not enough, and the Portuguese sought to destroy the military power of the Bakongo, which they did on 29 October 1665 at the Battle of Mbwila.

Next came the Mbundu. But eventual destruction of the Mbundu was delayed due to the skilled, dynamic Queen Nzinga. Through her wit and guile she was able to maintain Mbundu sovereignty, despite having been defeated in battle. When she died in 1663, the end was near for Mbundu sovereignty. The king of the Mbundu was not satisfied with his treatment by the returning Portuguese. Warriors of Ngola Ari attacked caravans headed toward the interior. In response, the Portuguese laid siege to his capital at Pungu-a-Ndongo and captured the stronghold in 1671.

Portugal then turned its attention inland to the Ovimbundu. But permanent contact did not occur between the two until the 18th century. From 1774 to 1776, Portuguese forces broke the power of the Ovimbundu. The kingdoms of the Ovimbundu ultimately decided trade would be more beneficial than warfare.

Portuguese military operations broke the power of the prominent Angolan kingdoms, thereby ensuring access to the lucrative slave trade. The Portuguese unknowingly laid the foundations of Angolan nationalism. By dismembering the great kingdoms, the Portuguese allowed the inhabitants to slowly begin to view themselves not as some part of an ethnolinguistic group but as belonging to a greater entity: Angola.

While the slave trade was morally repugnant, Portugal realized an economic boon from it. It is estimated that, from the start of the slave trade until Portugal outlawed it in 1836, three to four million Angolans were sold into slavery from the ports of Luanda and Benguela. Though Portugal did proclaim the end of the slave trade, it was impossible to enforce. Not until 1865 was the slave trade stopped—and it was stopped not by Portugal, but by the British Royal Navy.

With slavery abolished, the Portuguese had to find other profitable ventures. The ivory, beeswax, and rubber trades began. Angolans later exported coffee and cotton. Portugal also began to encourage white migration to Angola. Despite government efforts to encourage migration, the white population of Angola was less than 10,000 in 1900, and many of those were convicts.

Despite its efforts, the Portuguese were never fully able to militarily subjugate Angola. The Dembo nation resided within 100 miles of Luanda. From 1631 until 1919, the Portuguese launched 15 military campaigns against the Dembo. Not until 1919 were the Portuguese able to break the resistance. Renewed resistance from the Ovimbundu and Bakongo had to be crushed. Other ethnolinguistic groups would occasionally revolt, necessitating Portuguese military measures.

The Portuguese exploited the Angolans and the natural resources of the country. Any amenities were for the colonialists. Any economic infrastructure development or improvement was to better furnish Portugal with the wealth of Angola. Little was returned to the population in terms of hospitals, schools, good governance, a participatory political system, or economic benefits. The exportable commodities enriched the colonialists and led to increasingly stifling conditions for the natives.

The end of World War II brought with it the beginning of the end of colonialism. The European powers, with the exception of Portugal, eventually announced that they would forgo their empires. In a 20-year span, most of Africa became independent, except for Guinea–Bissau, Mozambique, and Angola.

Addressing South Africa's whites-only parliament, British prime minister Harold Macmillan remarked on his impression "of the strength of this African national consciousness." He added, "In different places it takes different forms, but it is happening everywhere. . . . The wind of change is blowing through this continent, and, whether we like it or not, this growth of national consciousness is a political fact." Angolans felt the breeze.

The Angolan National Revolution: 1961–1975

On 4 February 1961, supporters of the Movimento Popular de Libertação de Angola (MPLA) (Popular Movement for the Liberation of Angola) attempted to storm several prisons in Luanda. Northern Angola witnessed violence on 15 March 1961 by União das Populações de Angola (UPA) (Union of People of Angola) fighters. These two events marked the beginning of the Angolan national revolution.

The MPLA was formed in 1956 by a merger of several parties, including the Communist Party. Dr. Agostinho Neto was elected president in 1962, and a strong cadre of leaders was chosen. Based in Luanda and surrounding environs, the MPLA recruited the intelligentsia, mestiços, and assimilados into the party. The party viewed itself as the representative of the urban masses.

The UPA had as its goal the restoration of the Bakongo Empire. As such, it was primarily a Bakongo organization led by Holden Roberto, who traveled extensively throughout Africa, Europe, and North America rallying support for the cause. On 27 March 1962, Roberto renamed the UPA as the Frente Nacional de Libertação de Angola (FNLA) (National Front for the Liberation of Angola) in order to broaden the base of its appeal. Also, Roberto created the Govêrno Revolucionário de Angola no Exílio (GRAE) (Angola's Revolutionary Government-in-Exile) to serve as a government-in-exile and also show that only the FNLA represented the Angolan struggle. Jonas Savimbi, an Ovimbundu, was one of the GRAE ministers.

The March attacks in northern Angola were noted for their viciousness not only in the acts of the resistance fighters but also in the reprisals by the Portuguese colonialists. It is estimated that 40,000 Africans and some 400 Europeans were killed. Portugal was stunned by the events and took steps to alleviate the discontent. It improved infrastructure, paved more roads, built schools, assisted struggling farmers, and established protected hamlets for villagers fearing the guerrillas as well as the colonialists. In addition, Lisbon increased troop strength in Angola to 40,000.

By 1968, the MPLA had outpaced the FNLA as the primary insurgency. Surrounded by cronies, Roberto kept the money, supplies, and power. So much so that in July 1964 Savimbi quit the GRAE over Roberto's cronyism. The MPLA, by virtue of its leftist leanings, attracted support from the Soviet Union, the Warsaw Pact, and Cuba. In addition, Tanzania and Zambia allowed weapons for the MPLA to transit across their borders to Angola. Further, the political/military cadre was better able to recruit, train, politically instruct, and control areas under MPLA influence.

Savimbi headed a third nationalist group that emerged in 1966. The União Nacional para a Independência Total de Angola (UNITA) (National Union for the Total Independence of Angola) represented the Angolan peasants. According to Savimbi, the MPLA was too non-African and mestiço/assimilado dominated, while the FNLA was too northern-oriented. UNITA used Maoist methods of indoctrinating the peasants, thus positioning the party as the one best able to defend their interests.

In 1963, the Frente de Libertação do Enclave de Cabinda (FLEC) (Front for the Liberation of the Enclave of Cabinda) was formed in Cabinda through a three-party coalition. The guerrillas called for independence, not only from Portugal but also from Angola.

The three major Angolan liberation movements had limited success against the Portuguese army. Personal, political, and regional jealousies led to the three fighting among themselves as much as against the Portuguese. The colonial authorities resettled over one million villagers into protected villages. Militarily, the Portuguese even employed napalm and chemical defoliants.

During this time, Portugal was fighting a guerrilla war not only in Angola but also in Guinea–Bissau and Mozambique. By 1974, Portugal had lost over 11,000 military personnel in Africa. In Guinea–Bissau, Portugal had 33,000 loyal African and European troops. Mozambique had a combined force of 60,000: 35,000 Africans, 10,000 white Africans from South Africa and Rhodesia, and 15,000 Portuguese. Meanwhile, in Angola, the Portuguese had a combined force of 70,000, of which 40,000 were European. The Portuguese had almost 72,000 troops involved in the three African colonial conflicts. Its overall troop strength was a bloated 250,000.

Portugal, with one of Europe's weaker economies, was beginning to feel the effects. Thousands of youths were rejecting the military call-up by fleeing the nation. Emigration was at a record level, and economic productivity was plummeting. Portugal was not losing its colonial wars, yet it was not winning, and this meant time was on the side of the MPLA, FNLA, and UNITA.

The Portuguese Armed Forces Movement and Angolan Independence: 1974–1975

The Movimento das Forças Armadas (MFA) (Armed Forces Movement) began in August 1973. Many career officers were disgusted with government policies and conduct in the colonial conflicts. *Portugal e o Futuro* (Portugal and the future), written by General António de Spínola, appeared in February 1974. One prevailing subject of the book was the general's belief that Portugal could not successfully conclude its colonial wars. The book became an instant best-seller.

On 25 April 1974, the MFA overthrew the government of Marcelo Caetano. By July 1974, the MFA leadership promised independence to Mozambique, Guinea–Bissau, and Angola. The FNLA, the MPLA, and UNITA met in January 1975 at Mombasa, Kenya, where they acknowledged each other as independent organizations prepared to negotiate with Portugal. Ten days later, the Portuguese and the three liberation movements met at Alvor, Portugal, to discuss Angolan independence.

The Alvor Accords called for an integrated military, a transitional government, and elections for a constituent assembly by October 1975. Portugal would relinquish power on 11 November 1975.

The three movements gathered in the capital city of Luanda to launch preparations for independence. Unfortunately, old animosities surfaced. In June and July 1975, after a series of street battles, the FNLA and UNITA left Luanda, returning to the north and south, respectively.

As the MPLA remained in control of the city, it could proclaim independence under the MPLA banner. In the north, the FNLA, assisted by Zairian troops, began a push to capture Luanda before 11 November. From the south, UNITA and South African forces began a similar drive. South Africans had crossed into Angola to protect their interests in the Ruacana Dam.

Meanwhile, the MPLA began to receive massive amounts of Soviet weaponry as well as substantial numbers of Cuban combat troops. By the end of December 1975, there were 12,000 Cubans and over $200 million worth of Soviet weaponry in Luanda. Controversy remains about the South African–Cuban timeline of intervention. Soviet/Cuban intervention was easier to accept because South Africa was a pariah nation due to its racial policies. The United States began an assistance program to UNITA and the FNLA, but Congress closed the monetary pipeline in December 1975.

The FNLA came within 12 miles of the capital, but was caught in an MPLA/Cuban ambush. Routed, the FNLA forces and the Zairian backers retreated pell-mell to the Zaire border. The FNLA would never again be a significant military force. The UNITA/South African force had farther to travel. MPLA forces destroyed key bridges, slowing the advance.

On 11 November 1975, Agostinho Neto proclaimed the People's Republic of Angola. The new nation was granted immediate diplomatic recognition by Cuba, the Soviet Union, the Warsaw Pact nations, Brazil, and about half of the Organization of African Unity (OAU) members.

Having defeated the FNLA in the north, the MPLA/Cuban forces turned their attention to the south. In a series of clashes throughout December 1975 and January 1976, the two armies fought. South Africa, losing ground, international support, men, and material, announced it would withdraw from Angola by March 1976. UNITA announced it would return to guerrilla warfare against the new colonialists, Cuba and the Soviet Union.

With the war for independence over, it appeared that the MPLA, with its Cuban allies and Soviet weapons, had defeated the Angolan allies of the United States, South Africa, China, and Zaire. In October 1976, President Neto traveled to Moscow, where he signed a 20-year Treaty of Friendship and Cooperation. The FNLA had been extinguished as a military force, but UNITA, while defeated, was not destroyed.

THE ANGOLAN CIVIL WAR: 1975–2002

Savimbi traveled throughout the central provinces, rallying the population and recruiting fresh troops. UNITA lore terms the event the "Long March," alluding to Mao Zedong's march in China. By July 1976, UNITA guerrillas were active in the central provinces, attacking outposts and economic targets.

The MPLA, flush with victory, had publicly pledged, in the name of "socialist solidarity," to assist the Southwest Africa People's Organization (SWAPO) and the African National Congress (ANC) to repel South Africa from Southwest Africa (Namibia) and end the apartheid regime in South Africa. The MPLA government therefore allowed SWAPO and the ANC to establish bases in southern Angola. Soviet and Cuban military instructors would train the guerrilla fighters, who then would filter back into South West Africa or South Africa.

The South African response was immediate. The South African Defense Forces (SADF) began to mount an increasing number of raids against these camps. From a military viewpoint, it made sense to assist UNITA. UNITA guerrillas were antigovernment and consequently useful surrogates to fight the ANC, SWAPO, and the MPLA. As South African commandos killed more enemy forces and captured military hardware, the war booty was given to UNITA to assist their battle against the MPLA. The bounty the SADF provided allowed UNITA to expand its zone of operations into 17 of Angola's 18 provinces. Moreover, the U.S. Congress ended the ban on support to UNITA. Starting in 1986, the Americans began a modest aid program to UNITA, partly in an attempt to woo the rebels away from the stigma of the link with apartheid South Africa.

Cuba and the Soviet Union would not allow their client to be ousted by South Africa. During the 1980s, Cuban troop strength climbed to

50,000, while Soviet weapons deliveries averaged one billion dollars per annum. Twice, South African air and military units kept the MPLA army from capturing Jamba, a city in southeastern Angola that UNITA called the Capital of the Freeland of Angola.

In 1985, the MPLA, Soviet advisers, and Cuban troops drove toward Jamba in force. South Africa responded with air and ground assaults to save the UNITA position. The MPLA column retreated under withering fire with a massive loss of life and equipment. The MPLA and its supporters launched another offensive on Jamba in 1987, with the same results. However, for the first time in the civil war, South African forces followed the retreating MPLA column back toward the city of Cuito Cuanavale. It appeared as if South Africa might move from rescuing UNITA to attempting to win the war on behalf of the rebels.

Initially, Cuban soldiers and the Soviet advisers were airlifted from the city. When Fidel Castro learned that SADF forces were laying siege to the town, he ordered Cuban forces back to hold the town at all cost. After several attempts to capture the city with human wave tactics, the struggle for Cuito Cuanavale settled into a protracted siege. By March 1988, it was evident that Cuito Cuanavale could not be captured by UNITA/SADF. However, it was equally clear to the Soviet Union and Cuba that South Africa would not allow UNITA to be destroyed.

Politically, the world had changed by the late 1980s. The foreign patrons of the MPLA and UNITA were looking for an honorable exit from the Angolan morass. Both sides claimed victory at Cuito Cuanavale. Cuba and the Soviet Union claimed to have saved the town and thwarted further South African maneuvers, while South Africa claimed its intention had been only to protect Jamba. The stalemate at Cuito Cuanavale provided the political cover necessary to initiate negotiations toward ending foreign involvement in Angola's civil war.

Cuba had been substantially involved in Angola since 1975—even earlier in a lesser capacity. Cuban casualties, although unknown to this day, were causing discontent. The Soviet Union, under Mikhail Gorbachev, was seeking to attract Western investment and technology. By actively supporting Third World governments and movements with money, arms, and propaganda, the United States posed the question, "How can the United States monetarily assist the Soviet Union when so many rubles are wasted on the Third World?" Partly in response, Gorbachev initiated the "new thinking" policy, which advocated just solutions for regional conflicts. Finally, the South Africans were tired of the Angolan conflict. Too many soldiers were dying, and weaponry that could not be replaced was being lost. Moreover, internal South African politics were soon to overwhelm foreign policy.

The Brazzaville Protocol was signed in New York City on 22 December 1988 by Angola, South Africa, and Cuba. Under its terms, South Africa would withdraw from South West Africa and grant that nation independence by 1 November 1989. South Africa also agreed to end military support of UNITA. Cuba, in a staged withdrawal, would evacuate Angola by 1 July 1991. Angola agreed to deny bases to SWAPO and the ANC. The Brazzaville Protocol, in essence, ended foreign support for UNITA and the MPLA, perhaps for the first time ever. Angola, a Cold War battlefield, became just another African civil war.

Despite the lack of foreign patronage, both groups had the resources to continue the fight. Throughout the 1980s, petroleum products became a more and more valuable export for the government. Petrodollars allowed the MPLA to purchase the weapons needed to continue the war. UNITA, recognizing South African support was on the wane, began to move its base of operations into Lunda Norte and Lunda Sul provinces. There the rebels began to exploit the diamonds found in the region. UNITA was able to secure hundreds of millions of dollars by selling the gems on the black market. Both the MPLA and UNITA had adequate finances to prolong the conflict.

MPLA forces attempted to capture Jamba in December 1989 without any foreign support. After some early gains, UNITA forces, also without outside assistance, succeeded in defeating the government offensive. Both sides, exhausted, realized that there could not be a military solution to the civil war. UNITA, through Maoist guerrilla tactics, could disrupt and destabilize, but the movement could not capture and hold any major city. Even if the government captured Jamba, UNITA would revert to guerrilla tactics, making destruction of the rebel forces impossible. In April 1990, UNITA and the MPLA government began negotiations toward a peaceful resolution of the hostilities. The peace talks culminated in May 1991 with the signing of the Bicesse Accords. The accords mandated free elections, placement of both armies into cantonment areas, and creation of a Joint Political–Military Commission (JPMC) to oversee implementation of the treaty. The elections were scheduled for September 1992.

The parliamentary vote was decidedly in favor of the MPLA. The presidential contest, however, was much closer and produced no official winner. The Angolan electoral law stipulated that the presidential winner should have 50 percent plus one. Eduardo dos Santos tallied 49.6 percent, Savimbi 40.1 percent. UNITA and other parties complained about fraud and a lack of transparency. The United Nations declared the electoral process to be "generally free and fair." Tension mounted throughout the nation as troops from both armies left the camps.

Through the weekend of 30 October, MPLA soldiers, riot police, and civilians launched a pogrom against UNITA forces and diplomats in Luanda. According to church sources, some 20,000 soldiers and civilians were slain. The UNITA vice president and the chief negotiator were slain. Numerous Bakongo residing in the capital city were also massacred. As a result, the civil war reignited.

Better disciplined and trained UNITA forces emerged from the camps as fully functional units. Many MPLA conscripts had deserted. The remaining MPLA troops were dispirited, undertrained, and poorly equipped and led. Consequently, UNITA forces were able to capture five provincial capitals while laying siege to several others. From November 1992 until approximately June 1993, the military initiative lay entirely with UNITA. Meetings for a cease-fire at Addis Ababa, Ethiopia, and Abidjan, Côte d'Ivoire, proved fruitless. Because of UNITA political intransigence, the United States finally granted diplomatic recognition to Angola in May 1993. As official policy, Washington no longer supported UNITA.

The government of Angola slowly began to alter the dynamics affecting UNITA's military success on the battlefield. As a sovereign nation, the MPLA could legally purchase armaments on the international market. UNITA's supplies came from black-market sources with inflated prices. Funded by petroleum exports, the government of Angola embarked upon a massive purchase of military weapons. In addition, with apartheid ending in South Africa, many white South African soldiers refused to serve under an African National Congress (ANC) government. Some of the veterans formed a mercenary outfit dubbed Executive Outcomes (EO) and sold their expertise to the highest bidder. The MPLA signed two contracts with EO to train the army, pilot government aircraft, and, on rare occasions, fight on behalf of the MPLA.

Beginning in June 1993, the government forces began to recapture towns held by UNITA and break the sieges against the provincial capitals. The UN Security Council enacted economic sanctions against the rebels, depriving them of petroleum and arms. Government armed forces had UNITA on the run by April 1994, culminating in the capture of Huambo in May. UNITA sought negotiations. Meeting in Lusaka, Zambia, UNITA and the MPLA crafted the Lusaka Protocol, once again ending hostilities. The protocol, signed in November 1994, called for the disarmament of rebel troops and for UNITA to enter into the government of Angola as an opposition party. Significantly, neither Savimbi nor President dos Santos signed the document.

From 1994 to 1998, Angola enjoyed relative calm. UNITA did send its parliamentarians and other governmental officials to the capital. However, UNITA dragged its feet on disarming and returning occupied areas to government control. Furthermore, Jonas Savimbi refused to leave Andulo/Bailundo for Luanda. The United Nations, frustrated at UNITA's backsliding, voted further sanctions, trying to force the rebels to obey the Lusaka Protocol. Some UNITA members, living in Luanda, ended their support of Savimbi's leadership and formed UNITA–Renovada.

By 1998, the government's patience was at an end. Government forces attacked the rebel strongholds of Andulo and Bailundo. Although initially repulsed, government forces continued to assault UNITA positions throughout Angola, capturing Andulo and Bailundo and recovering much of the rebels' heavy weapons during the course of 1999. Suffering from losses, defections, and surrender, unable to attack and hold towns or cities, UNITA announced a return to guerrilla warfare.

The Angolan government began a controversial strategy in order to successfully bring the civil war to an end. UNITA practiced Maoist tactics. Mao wrote that "the people are like water and the [guerrilla] army is like fish." To defeat the insurgency, the government drained the ocean. Government soldiers forced hundreds of thousands of people to leave the rural areas for the provincial capitals in order to deprive the rebels of food, laborers, soldiers, and sympathizers. In doing this, however, the government created a humanitarian crisis of enormous proportions.

Except for air transport, the provincial capitals were cut off from assistance. The roads were heavily mined, and the government spent most of its budget on the military, leaving nongovernmental organizations (NGOs) to shoulder the humanitarian crisis. The gambit paid off. UNITA forces, feeling the pinch of UN sanctions combined with the loss of peasant support, finally began to disintegrate.

The coup de grâce occurred on 22 February 2002, when government forces ambushed a column of UNITA troops led by Savimbi. Reportedly, with revolvers firing, Savimbi was killed in a hail of gunfire. The death of UNITA's only president quickly led to a cease-fire that included implementation of the Lusaka Protocol. UNITA forces, some 81,000 soldiers with another 350,000 family members, entered camps to be decommissioned. The relief effort by the government and NGOs was slow, due to the magnitude of the crisis. Many rebel soldiers and family members perished because of starvation. Thousands of peasants emerged from the bush, where they had been hiding from both sides.

UNITA and UNITA–Renovada reunited as the former rebel movement took its place in Luanda as the major opposition party. UNITA party elections took place in June 2003, with Isaías Samakuva elected to replace Savimbi. Since the April 2002 cease-fire, there has been no breach of the agreement.

FUTURE PROSPECTS FOR ANGOLA

If peace can be maintained, Angola has the resources to rebound from the tragic civil war to become a regional power in southern Africa. The nation possesses fertile soil, abundant minerals, huge petroleum reserves, and a people who have persevered.

Yet problems remain. Angola has between two and ten million land mines buried in fields, roads, and trails. Removal will require a major effort in terms of manpower and money. Hundreds of thousands of people remain homeless, living away from their traditional locales. Resettlement will be expensive as the people return to destroyed villages, mined roads, and fields. UNITA soldiers and their families must be reintegrated into civil society. Many rebel troops have known nothing but war. If they are not given the means to become productive citizens, then society risks banditry, lawlessness, and perhaps a return to conflict. In addition, the situation in Cabinda remains unresolved.

Last, but far from least, the government must be willing to share political power with all parties. In many ways, Angola remains a one-party state. The MPLA must have the political will to step down should future election results be unfavorable. Fortunately, Angola's wealth can resolve many of the problems. The key will be the political courage to show leadership while accepting the possibility of having to democratically transfer power in some future election.

The Dictionary

– A –

ABRA A FUNDAÇÃO DA SOCIEDADE (Open Society Foundation). Founded by **Rafael Marques de Morais**, the foundation is one of the most vocal critics of the government. American philanthropist George Soros funds the group. The foundation investigates government corruption, transparency issues with military purchases, and accounting procedures of the **petroleum** industry. *See also* MEDIA.

ABRANCHES, HENRIQUE. Angola's leading political cartoonist, Henrique Abranches created the popular **Movimento Popular de Libertação de Angola** (MPLA) freedom fighter, "Paulo." Although Paulo dates from the 1960s, his adventures, always with a political moral, appeared in the state-controlled *Jornal de Angola* for years. *See also* CULTURE.

AÇÃO DA OBSCURIDADE DA OPERAÇÃO (Operation Dark Action). A government operation launched on 1 December 1998 to capture Andulo, Bailundo, and other areas that **União Nacional para a Independência Total de Angola** (UNITA) had refused to surrender under the terms of the **Lusaka Protocol**. The government suffered heavy losses as UNITA employed tanks and heavy artillery to defend its strongholds. UNITA counterattacked, capturing cities in the **Bié** and **Huambo provinces** and launching a devastating attack against **Kuito**.

ACUTE FLACCID PARALYSIS. A disease that first erupted in Luanda province in 1999. Victims are often under six years of age. The first symptoms are flu-like, but patients also suffer paralysis of limbs and internal organs. Some die due to lung paralysis. It is believed that the disease spread due to people being displaced by the war, a poor sanitation environment, and overcrowded housing. *See also* HEALTH CARE; POLIO.

AFRICAN UNION (AU). The AU replaced the Organization of African Unity (OAU) in July 2002. The proclaimed mission of the union was to "combat poverty, conflict, and corruption, and to promote human rights, democracy, good governance, and development." The OAU was founded in 1963 as an instrument to fight colonialism, apartheid, and foreign interference. The new organization has the same 53-nation membership. The OAU was viewed as inconsequential and powerless. *See also* NEW PARTNERSHIP FOR AFRICAN DEVELOPMENT.

AGE OF MARCH (Tagoma). A movement by inhabitants of northern **Namibia** who seek to move the Angola/Namibia border north to where it stood before being demarcated by the colonial powers. The South West Africa People's Organization (SWAPO) government of Namibia has condemned the movement, and popular support is difficult to ascertain.

AGRICULTURE. Angola's climate is conducive to raising tropical and semitropical crops: bananas, beans, cabbage, kale, cocoa, coffee, corn, cotton, gums, kapok, manioc, okra, palm oil, palm kernels, peaches, peanuts, peppers, pineapples, plantains, potatoes, sorghum, sugarcane, sunflowers, tobacco, tomatoes, sisal, wax, wheat, and yams. Estimates claim that 75 percent of all Angolans depend on agriculture for their livelihood. Popular Angolan foods are *fuba,* a flour dish made from cassava or maize, and *funje,* a manioc flour pudding.

The **civil war**, **land mines**, **internally displaced people** (IDPs), destruction of economic infrastructure and especially roads and **railways**, and disputes of property ownership have turned Angola into an importer of food. In July 2003, it was estimated that 90 percent of the available arable land was not being cultivated.

AIDS/HIV. By September 2003, the Angolan Health Ministry announced that at least 1 million people in Angola were HIV positive.

The number is expected to rise with the end of the **civil war**. Soldiers stationed in Kinshasa or Brazzaville may have come into contact with HIV positive prostitutes. When they returned home, they possibly began to spread the disease to girlfriends and wives. Tribal doctors refer to the disease as "war fatigue" or "slimming sickness." In a 2003 poll taken by United Nations Children's Fund (UNICEF), 32 percent of those polled had never heard of AIDS/HIV. Only 8 percent knew how the virus was transmitted and how to protect themselves. The same poll indicated that Angola had only five testing stations, all of which were located in **Luanda**.

Angola's shortage of trained medical professionals, especially in rural areas, exacerbates the growing crisis. The government has begun programs to increase AIDS/HIV awareness, including one called Viva e Deixe Vivo (Live and Let Live). The **United Nations** has introduced a program called Youth to Youth, a UNICEF program that raises AIDS/HIV awareness by training young people about the disease, then sending them to the provinces to teach their peers about the illness. As of May 2003, 150,000 pamphlets with basic facts about AIDS/HIV produced in **Portuguese** and national languages had been distributed nationwide. Another UNICEF–Angolan government partnership is the Programa Nacional de Luta Contra o Sida (PNLS) (National Program to Fight AIDS), begun in October 2003. The four-year program will project the socioeconomic impact of AIDS in Angola. Also, clinics devoted to AIDS/HIV have been established. The Nigth Clinic was opened in October 2002 to diagnose and treat prostitutes for AIDS/HIV and other sexually transmitted diseases. The project is run by the Instituto Portuguese da Medicina Preventiva (IPMP) (Portuguese Institute of Preventive Medicine), which assisted by Angolan **nongovernmental organizations** (NGOs). The clinic has two physicians, a clinical room, a laboratory, and counseling facilities. The medical post hopes to assist 20 patients per day. There are also recreation and medical information centers, such as the Viana Youth Center, the first of four centers supported by UNICEF, Population Services International, and the Angolan NGO Cuidados da Infancia. The centers feature basketball courts, video and Internet rooms, courses in instructional training, and information on safe sexual practices and AIDS/HIV.

The global scourge was slow to come to Angola, in part, because of the civil war. Myths about the disease include that sex with a virgin is a miracle cure, condoms cause impotence, women cannot get infected with AIDS, and a smelly, root paste will cure the ailment. In Angola, people worry more about **land mines**, starvation, and bandits; AIDS/HIV is at the bottom of the list. In many African societies, the military is the most stable institution. If AIDS/HIV decimates the most stable bureaucratic unit, then chaos will ensue. In the **United States** in 2002, the Pentagon began a million-dollar effort to assist African militaries (including Angola) to understand and control AIDS/HIV.

AIR ANGOLA. An airline company supposedly owned by **Forças Armadas de Angolanas** (FAA) military officers who made millions of dollars through military transportation contracts. With the end of the **civil war**, the company suffered financially and went bankrupt.

ALMEIDA, NDALU DE (1978–). Angolan author who writes under the pen name of Ondjaki and has written seven novels and books of poetry. His works include *Ynari, a Menina das Cinco Trancas* (Ynari, the girl with five braids), *Momentos de Aqui* (Moments from here), and *Acto Sanguineo* (Bloody act), and he won second place in the 2000 Antonio Jacinto competition for new writers. *See also* LITERATURE.

ALMEIDA, ROBERTO DE (1941–). Born in **Bengo province**, Roberto Almeida serves as the speaker of the Angolan parliament. He is also a gifted author who writes under the pseudonym of Jofre Rocha. His works include *Tempo de Cicio* (Time to whisper, 1973), *Assim Se Faz Madrugada* (So it becomes dawn, 1976), *Estórias do Musseque* (Suburban stories, 1976), *Crónicas de Ontem e Sempre* (Chronicles of yesterday and forever, 1985), and *Meu Nome É Moisés Mulambo* (My name is Moisés Mulambo, 2003). *See also* LITERATURE.

ALPHA 5. A mining security firm owned by Agostinho de Matos, brother of former **Forças Armadas de Angolanas** (FAA) chief of staff João de Matos. Alpha 5 protected government and foreign mining interests from the **União Nacional para a Independência Total de Angola** (UNITA) rebels. *See also* TELESERVICES.

ALVES, NITO. In May 1997, Nito Alves and Jose Van Dunem attempted a left-wing coup against the government of **Agostinho Neto**. Alves had been the interior minister before being sacked in October 1996. He had the closest links to the **Soviet Union** among the **Movimento Popular de Libertação de Angola** (MPLA) leadership, but during the attempted coup the Soviets stood idly by while **Cuban** forces assisted the government.

Alves was an African leader in a party that consisted of whites, **mestiços**, and **assimilados**. He advocated "people's power" in the slums of **Luanda**, where he was a hero. The rebels killed Minister of Finance Saydi Mingas, Minister of Finance Garcia Neto, Minister of Economic Affairs at the Foreign Ministry Helder Neto, and **Forças Armadas Populares de Libertação de Angola** (FAPLA) commanders Paulo Mangungo Eugenia Verissimo da Costa, Jose Manuel Paiva, and Eurico Goncalves. The Alves–Van Dunem faction disliked Cuban domination of the army, accused the MPLA officials of being "too light skinned," and rejected Neto's attempts to normalize relations with the West. In the aftermath, the government arrested and imprisoned or executed hundreds. Van Dunem and Alves escaped, but were later captured and executed.

ALVOR ACCORDS. Agreement signed in Alvor, Portugal, on 15 January 1975 by **Portugal**, the **Frente Nacional de Libertação de Angola** (FNLA), **União Nacional para a Independência Total de Angola** (UNITA), and the **Movimento Popular de Libertação de Angola** (MPLA) ending the colonial war. The accord called for a unified army, creation of a transitional government, drafting of a new **constitution**, free **elections** to be held in October, and an immediate cease-fire. "Patriotic acts" committed by both sides during the struggle for independence were granted immunity. Portugal recognized the MPLA, FNLA, and UNITA as "the sole legitimate representatives of the people of Angola." **White settler** political rights were not mentioned. The **Cabinda** Enclave was designated an "unalienable component of Angola." The national army would be composed of 8,000 troops from the MPLA, UNITA, and FNLA, while Portugal would supply 24,000 troops for a total of 48,000. *See also* MOMBASA AGREEMENT; NAKARU AGREEMENT.

AMANGOLA (Amigos do Manifesto Angolano). The proclamation by **Ovimbundu** nationalists in December 1964 calling upon all Angolans to return to their country to prepare the peasants for guerrilla warfare. Later, the group would become a core constituency of **União Nacional para a Independência Total de Angola** (UNITA). *See also* SAVIMBI, JONAS.

AMBO GROUP. In Angola, the term *Ambo* refers to the ethnolinguistic group including the Cafima, Cuamatui, Cuanhama, Evale, and Kyanyama. Comprising about 60,000 people, less than 3 percent of the population, the Ambo reside in south-southwestern Angola in the provinces of **Cuando Cubango**, **Cunene**, and **Namibe**. They also overlap into **Namibia**, where they are the dominant group. They farm and raise cattle.

The Kyanyama played a major role in the early struggle against **Portuguese** colonialism. The last king, Mandume ya Ndemufayo, fought the colonialists almost to a standstill before finally being conquered in 1915. The Kyanyama capital city of Ondjiva was renamed after the conquering Portuguese general, Pereira d'Eca. In 1975, the city was renamed Ondjiva. After ending the final insurrection, the Portuguese allowed no settlers, missionaries, or traders into southwest Angola. Consequently, the Ambo received little education and had little contact with Western values and culture. Nationalism was slow to spread among the Ambo. Ambo nationalism received its start in South West Africa (Namibia), where the **South Africans** and Germans allowed African education and travel.

ANDRADE, MÁRIO PINTO DE (1928–1990). Sometimes referred to as the father of Angolan nationalism. He was the first president of the **Movimento Popular de Libertação de Angola** (MPLA). Born on 21 August 1928 in Golungo–Alto, Angola, he studied in **Portugal** and published a book of poetry in the 1950s before becoming active in Angola's struggle against Portuguese colonialism. In exile, he helped found the MPLA in 1956 and became its president in 1960. Four years later, he gave up leadership to **Agostinho Neto**. He remained active politically but grew disenchanted with the authoritarian nature of the MPLA's leadership. In 1974, Andrade formed a dissident faction called Revolta Activa (Active Revolt). His brother, and MPLA cofounder,

Joaquim remained in Angola to become a leading critic of the government. Mário de Andrade continued disdaining politics and went into exile in Paris and London. He was content to focus upon his work documenting Angola's history. He died on 27 August 1990 in London.

ANDRADE, VICENTE PINTO DE (1950–). Born in **Kwanza Sul province**, Vincente Andrade was educated as an economist. Though a member of the **Movimento Popular de Libertação de Angola** (MPLA), he announced in September 2002 that he would be a presidential candidate in the next elections. Others to announce by August 2003 included Reverend **Feliciano Loa**, **Carlos Contreiras Gouveia**, **Analia Pereira**, and Isaías **Samakuva**.

ANGOLA SELLING CORPORATION (ASCORP). Corporation established on 30 December 1999 in partnership with **Lev Leviev** with a mandate to purchase all of Angola's **diamond** production and to regulate and control the industry from mining to exportation. Beyond Leviev, ASCORP has never revealed its shareholders, leading to concern that powerful individuals in the government and military may be making illegal profits. The **civil war**, **União Nacional para a Independência Total de Angola** (UNITA) diamond efforts, and the *garimpeiros* have made transparency difficult. By Angolan law, ASCORP owns at least 51 percent of every mine.

ANGOLAGATE. Also known as the **Mitterrand**–Pasqua affair. The scandal involved the illegal sale of French arms to Angola. In a highly unusual move, President **Eduardo dos Santos** mentioned the internal affair in accepting the credentials of the new French ambassador to Angola on 23 February 2001. The Angolan president said, "It is not my intent to interfere in internal French matters, but I do have the right to recognize that some people currently involved in judicial proceedings in France made an enormous contribution to the development of friendship and cooperation between France and Angola." *See also* FALCONE, PIERRE; GAYDAMEK, ARKADY; LEVIEV, LEV.

ANGOLAN CENTRE FOR INSTRUCTION IN PEACE. A civil society organization working with the Angolan National Police and

Comité Inter-Eclesial para a Paz em Angola (COIEPA) to rid **Luanda** of the thousands of weapons in the hands of civilians.

ANGOLANNESS (Angolanidade). The concept of what constitutes the Angolan nation. Angolanness is many things to many people, but it implies social consensus about nation-building and norms of governance that embrace all, regardless of background, social standing, political affiliation, or ethnicity. Angola has to create this environment for people to consider themselves Angolan rather than attach loyalty to some other moniker.

ANSTEE, MARGARET. United Nations special envoy to Angola during 1991–93. She oversaw implementation of the **Bicesse Accords**. According to some, she was lax in keeping the parties calm and focused on the **electoral** process. She claimed a lack of resources hurt the peace accord's implementation and was quoted as saying that her mission was like "flying a 747 with only enough fuel for a DC-3."

ANTONOV. Russian-built aircraft used throughout Africa. The twin prop Antonovs are popular for their ability to transport large amounts of freight and to land on virtually any runway. The aircraft are also cheap to maintain and are very durable. In addition, the former **Soviet Union** and the Ukraine, desperate for cash, sell or lease the aircraft at a low price, making the plane even more tempting. Usually flown by Ukrainian or Russian pilots, Antonovs have crashed on a number of occasions in Angola over the past 25 years. Pilots with dubious qualifications, poor traffic control, alcohol, lack of proper maintenance, and **União Nacional para a Independência Total de Angola** (UNITA) guerrilla activity have caused the crashes. Antonovs in service in Angola include the AN-12, 24, 26, 30, and 32 series.

ANTUNES, GABRIELA (1937–). Angolan authoress who won the 1999 Culture Award from the Cultural Foundation of the **Portuguese** Language. Gabriela Antunes, an elementary educator, won for her prominent contribution to preserving the culture of the Portuguese language. Born in **Huambo**, she received a bachelor's degree in linguistics in Germany. Her works include *A Punição de um Dragon: Uma Guia* (The punishment of a dragon: A guide) and *O Jardim de Anita* (The garden of Anita). *See also* LITERATURE.

ARCA DE NOAH DA OPERAÇÃO (Operation Noah's Ark). A government effort to restock Angola's game parks devastated by the **civil war**. The operation was headed by **South African** professor Wouter van Hoven. The first set of 30 elephants arrived in Angola in September 2000. A second set of 50 animals arrived at **Quicama National Park** in September 2001. Along with elephants, the latter airlift consisted of 12 zebras, 12 gnus, 2 giraffes, and 12 ostriches. The 2.9-million-acre park will eventually have over 300 elephants guarded by more than 40 trained game wardens. In September 2002, the South African ship, the *Outeniqua,* delivered a further 200 elephants, roan antelope, eland, reedbuck, waterbuck, and cheetah. The animals were transported in specially designed steel shipping containers.

ARMED FORCES. Since 1975, Angolan soil has been trod upon by the **Movimento Popular de Libertação de Angola** (MPLA), **Forças Armadas Populares de Libertação de Angola** (FAPLA), **Frente Nacional de Libertação de Angola** (FNLA), Exército Popular de Libertação Nacional de Angola (ELNA), **União Nacional para a Independência Total de Angola** (UNITA), **Forças de Libertação de Angola** (FALA), and the three FLEC factions: **Frente de Libertação do Enclave de Cabinda** (FLEC), **Frente de Libertação do Enclave de Cabinda–Forças Armadas de Cabinda** (FLEC–FAC), and **Frente de Libertação do Enclave de Cabinda–Renovada** (FLEC–R). Outside forces have included **Cuban, Soviet**, and Zairian troops, the South African Defense Forces (SADF), and the South West Africa Territorial Forces (SWATF). With the **Bicesse Accords** and the **Lusaka Protocol** came the **Forças Armadas de Angolanas** (FAA), Forças Militares da UNITA (FMU), and the **Namibian** Defense Forces (NDF). In present-day Angola, the FAA consists of a 110,000-man army. The navy has approximately 3,000 members operating small patrol craft, and air force personnel total 7,000 and fly Russian-made fighters and transport aircraft. A small number of FAA personnel remain in the Republic of the Congo and the **Democratic Republic of the Congo**.

ASSEMBLEIA NACIONAL (National Assembly). The National Assembly has 223 deputies elected by popular vote. The president of the National Assembly is the president of the republic. The assembly approves legislation, monitors the executive and other branches of government, approves the state budget, and makes changes to the national constitution. Based on the 1992 elections, the Movimento Popular de Libertação de Angola **(MPLA)** has 129 deputies, **União Nacional para a Independência Total de Angola** (UNITA) has 70, **Frente Nacional de Libertação de Angola** (FNLA) has 5, the Partido Liberal Democrático (PLD) (Liberal Democratic Party) has 3, and the Partido Renovador Social (PRS) (Social Renewal Party) has 6, with the rest held by smaller parties. *See also* CONSELHO DA REPÚBLICA.

ASSIMILADOS. Angolans who, in order to achieve better educational and employment opportunities, abandoned their African culture by learning the **Portuguese** language and social customs. The status of *assimilados* and the legal codes relating to them were formally abolished in 1961.

ASSOCIATION OF AFRICAN OIL PRODUCERS. Created in 1987 with members including Algeria, Angola, Benin, Cameroon, Côte d'Ivoire, the **Democratic Republic of the Congo**, Egypt, Equatorial Guinea, Gabon, Libya, Nigeria, and Republic of the Congo. In a November 2000 meeting, the members agreed to begin the "Africanization of the oil industry," a process started by Angola in 2002. *See also* PETROLEUM.

– B –

BAILUNDOS. Derogatory term used for an **Ovimbundu** manual laborer.

BAIXA DE KASSANJE. Name applied to a massacre of Angolans by the **Portuguese** on 4 January 1961.

BAIXA DE KASSENGE. The king of Baixa de Kassenge, **Kambamjiji Kulaxingu**, petitioned the central government to allow his lands, an area between the **provinces** of **Malange** and **Lunda Norte**, to become the 19th province of Angola. The proposed province would encompass nine districts. The kings' major complaint was the lack of an organized judicial system, a police force, and an economic infrastructure.

BAKONGO GROUP. The third largest ethnolinguistic group in Angola, comprising the Congo, Iacas, Pombo, Sorongo, Suco, Susso, Xikongo, and Zombo. The Bakongo extend into the **Democratic Republic of the Congo**, the Republic of the Congo, and the present-day Angolan **provinces** of **Cabinda**, **Zaire**, and **Uíge**. They speak Kikongo. The Bakongo group formed the Kingdom of the Kongo, an important part of Angolan history. In Angola, the Bakongo number 1.3 million or about 13 percent of the population. The Bakongo had the only centralized monarchy in Angola. The Bakongo king, or *manicongo,* lived in the capital city of Mbanza Kongo. In the 16th century, the capital had a population of over 50,000, and for five centuries the empire was respected and feared by surrounding peoples. For a time, the Bakongo were united and powerful. They farmed, hunted, and **fished**. They also became expert in metallurgy, particularly with iron. Blacksmith was one of the honored professions. In fact, one of the titles of the monarch was the "Blacksmith King." However, after devastating wars and the arrival of the Portuguese, the Bakongo Empire as a dominant force resided mostly in myths, tales, and memories.

From 1690 to 1859, after having displaced the Bakongo Empire, the Portuguese had little presence in Bakongo areas. When the Portuguese reentered the area, modern Bakongo nationalism began. Early political efforts of the Bakongo revolved around attempts to recreate the kingdom. Later, Bakongo nationalists would evolve into Angolan nationalists. *See also* FRENTE NACIONAL DE LIBERTAÇÃO DE ANGOLA; ROBERTO, HOLDEN.

BAMAKOBO. A species of fish that is meek and tasteless. The term is also applied to any African who worked for **Portuguese** settlers.

BANCO AFRICANO DE INVESTIMENTO (BAI) (Africa Investment Bank). A private Angolan investment **bank** opened in November 1997. The BAI began with an initial endowment of $35 million and expanded to $50 million by 2000.

BANCO COMERCIAL ANGOLANO (BCA) (Commercial Bank of Angola). **Banking** services corporation launched in March 1999 intended to serve the business community of Angola. The BCA began with a stock capital of $4 million held equitably by 30 Angolan shareholders whose identities are unknown.

BANCO DE COMÉRCIO E INDÚSTRIA (BCI) (Bank of Commerce and Industry). Opened on 11 July 1992, the **bank** is a semiprivate institution 40 percent owned by the government. The BCI is dedicated to serving the commercial and industrial needs of Angola and has branches in **Luanda**, **Benguela**, **Cabinda**, **Huíla**, **Kwanza Norte**, **Kwanza Sul**, **Lunda Sul**, **Malange**, **Moxico**, and **Zaire provinces**.

BANCO DE POUPANCA E CREDITO (BPC) (Savings and Credit Bank). The BPC has 37 branches and employs 1,500 workers. Some 80 percent of its credit activity is short-term loans to small and medium-sized concerns.

BANCO ESPÍRITO SANTO ANGOLA (BESA) (Holy Spirit Bank of Angola). BESA opened for business in **Luanda** in January 2002. It was the first foreign commercial **bank** with a capitalization of $10 million. Other **Portuguese** banks operating in Angola include **Banco Fomento de Angola** and Banco Portugues do Atlantico.

BANCO FOMENTO DE ANGOLA (BFA) (Promotion Bank of Angola). Opening in June 1999, the BFA became Angola's second largest financial institution. With a staff of over 400, the BFA opened its new **banking** complex in **Luanda** in July 2003. At a cost of $20 million, the state-of-the-art bank is able to provide complete financial services to businesses and individuals. The BFA is active in six Angolan provinces: **Luanda, Huíla**, **Namibe**, **Cabinda**, **Benguela**, and **Bié**.

BANCO REGIONAL DE KEVE (BRK) (Regional Keve Bank). A regional **bank** located at Sumbe in Cuanza Sul province. The institution opened on 5 September 2003, pledging to "provide competitive goods to small and medium agro-industrial enterprises, to the working population and to the informal sector."

BANKING. Banco Nacional de Angola (BNA) is the state-owned central bank, although it continues to illegally intervene in state-owned commercial banks. With the end of the **civil war**, a drive toward capitalism, and the need for **International Monetary Fund** (IMF) and World Bank support, Angola has begun the process of deregulating its financial institutions. Angola has difficulty in securing funding for nonpetroleum projects due to its poor repayment record. Announcements made in 2003 about transparency in Angola's financial accounts may ease the problem.

Still, a number of international banks are establishing branches, mostly in Luanda. Local banks are beginning to employ checking accounts, credit cards, and interest-bearing savings accounts. *See also* BANCO AFRICANO DE INVESTIMENTO; BANCO COMERCIAL ANGOLANO; BANCO DE COMÉRCIO E INDÚSTRIA; BANCO DE POUPANCA E CREDITO; BANCO ESPÍRITO SANTO ANGOLA; BANCO FOMENTO DE ANGOLA; BANCO REGIONAL DE KEVE; CAIXA DE CREDITO AGRO-PECURIA E PESCAS.

BAROTSE PATRIOTIC FRONT. A liberation group led by Imasiku Mutangelwa. The rebels advocate the independence of Barotseland, located in western **Zambia**. The front claims the support of the Kwanggali, Lozi, Mafwe, Masubia, and Mbukushu ethnolinguistic groups. The groups overlap into **Namibia** and Zambia. *See also* CAPRIVI LIBERATION ARMY.

BATIDAS **(strokes).** A term used during the civil war to describe house-to-house searches by government troops in **União Nacional para a Independência Total de Angola** (UNITA) areas that often resulted in rape and plunder.

BATTLE FOR BRIDGE 14. A 9 December 1975 battle between **South African** and **Cuban** forces near Santa Comba, north of **Luanda**. South Africa claimed Cuban losses were between 150 and 200 killed, while the South African Defense Forces (SADF) lost only four. Cuban engineers were attempting to fix a downed bridge when South African artillery opened fire. South African personnel repaired the structure to enable pursuit of the retreating Cuban forces. Cuban versions of this and other engagements are strikingly different. *See also* BATTLE OF CUITO CUANAVALE.

BATTLE OF CUITO CUANAVALE. A dusty, remote city in southeastern Angola that became a pivotal battleground between **Forças Armadas Populares de Libertação de Angola** (FAPLA) and its **Soviet** and **Cuban** allies on one side and **Forças Armadas de Libertação de Angola** (FALA) and its **South African** allies on the other. After the success at the **Battle of Lomba River II**, FALA—the **União Nacional para a Independência Total de Angola** (UNITA) force—and South African Defense Forces (SADF) harassed the retreating Angolan army as it fled toward **Cuito Cuanavale**. For UNITA, such actions were natural; however, for SADF forces, to continue the attack was unexpected. Initially, the Cubans and Soviets were airlifted from the city. On 9 November 1987, in Moscow, **Eduardo dos Santos** and Fidel Castro made the decision to defend Cuito Cuanavale at all costs. Cuban forces returned to the city with the order not to retreat. The Soviet Union replenished Angola's military stocks. Cuban reinforcements arrived from Havana, swelling the numbers to 40,000. In January 1988, UNITA falsely announced the capture of the strategic city. The UNITA/South African forces were unable to capture the city, but the defenders were unable to break out. Twice, UNITA tried a frontal assault against FAPLA/Cuban positions, incurring massive casualties. When South Africa asked for a third assault, UNITA refused. A long siege of the city from December 1987 until March 1988 ensued. Cuito Cuanavale was surrounded by 330,000 land mines.

Finally, with all parties exhausted, they began negotiations supposedly from positions of strength. The South Africans argued they had saved **Mavinga/Jamba** from FAPLA and strengthened UNITA's position in southeastern Angola. But South Africa had taken too many casualties and lost military equipment that, because of sanctions, could not be replaced, and public opinion favored "bringing the boys home." Cuba claimed it had saved Cuito Cuanavale from a South African force determined to install a UNITA government in **Luanda**. Cuba also was searching for a face-saving way out of the Angolan morass, after having been in Angola in force for 13 years. Casualties from battle and disease were mounting. The battle of Cuito

Cuanavale allowed Cuba to negotiate its way out of the entanglement. The Soviet Union, under the leadership of Mikhail Gorbachev, was also seeking an honorable exit. Angola's debt to the Soviet Union was over $9 billion. The Soviet Union, teetering on the brink of economic collapse, was desperate for Western trade and aid. The **United States** pointedly asked why American aid should flow to Moscow when the Soviet Union was selling billions of dollars of weapons to a nation that was not paying. In addition, Washington questioned Moscow's other Third World involvements. Gorbachev began to speak of "**new thinking**" regarding Third World competition with the United States. Cuito Cuanavale was thus a turning point in the Angolan **civil war**. It allowed all the foreign backers of UNITA and the **Movimento Popular de Libertação de Angola** (MPLA) to claim victory, then withdraw. From May until December 1988, South Africa, the United States, Cuba, and the Soviet Union conducted a series of negotiations that resulted in the **Brazzaville Protocol**.

BATTLE OF DEATH ROAD. On 11 November 1975, **Frente Nacional de Libertação de Angola** (FNLA) forces, accompanied by **Central Intelligence Agency** (CIA) agents, **Portuguese** mercenaries, and Zairian troops, approached to within 12 miles of **Luanda**. As the force descended into the Quifangondo Valley, it was ambushed from the far ridge by **Forças Armadas Populares de Libertação de Angola** (FAPLA) and **Cuban** troops employing 122-mm. rockets. Within minutes, some 2,000 shells fell among the FNLA forces. Complete panic ensued as the FNLA and its allies retreated pell-mell toward the Zairian border. FNLA soldiers called the ambush "Nshila wa Lufu" (Death Road). Unknown to all at the time, the FNLA was finished as an effective military force.

BATTLE OF LOMBA RIVER I. The 1985 assault by **Forças Armadas Populares de Libertação de Angola** (FAPLA) in which **Cuban** troops were led by **Soviet** generals against **Mavinga/Jamba**, capital of the Freeland of Angola. The offensive began on 15 August from **Cuito Cuanavale** and Menongue, and by October the rout of the government forces was completed. Each side inflicted heavy casualties on the other, but clearly the armored column of the government was decimated. **Jonas Savimbi** claimed his forces killed 2,300 Cubans and FAPLA soldiers, while destroying 79 vehicles, capturing 52, and destroying 22 aircraft. The **União Nacional para a Independência Total de Angola** (UNITA) admitted to 410 killed and another 832 wounded. UNITA losses were probably higher. UNITA claims were probably exaggerated, but on-the-scene journalists reported equally high numbers. The government had tried for years to capture Mavinga/Jamba, but the 1985 offensive was the largest attempt. A key to UNITA's victory was the intervention of South African air and ground forces. The road into Mavinga is one lane, and the surrounding landscape consists of soft sand not suitable for armored vehicles. South African planes bombed the front and rear of the column, creating a bottleneck leading to the route. During late 1984 and early 1985, the Soviet Union had provided Angola with $1billion in military equipment. Much of it was lost in the sands at the "Land at the End of the Earth." *See also* BATTLE OF LOMBA RIVER II.

BATTLE OF LOMBA RIVER II. The government of Angola used 1986 to recover from the **Battle of Lomba River I** and to prepare for Lomba River II. The **Soviet Union** supplied another $1 billion in military materiel, which was combined with 18,000 **Cuban** and **Forças Armadas Populares de Libertação de Angola** (FAPLA) troops. Soviet general Konstantin Shaganovitch orchestrated the offensive. Once again, the government column was broken by **União Nacional para a Independência Total de Angola** (UNITA) guerrilla attacks, **South African** air power, and South Africa's **32nd Battalion**. UNITA reported that U.S.-supplied **Stinger missiles** and TOW antitank missiles played a crucial role as well. South African sources reported government losses at 2,000 killed with 2,000 seriously wounded. UNITA commanders claimed 1,984 FAPLA troops, along with 27 Soviets and 21 Cubans, killed. Another 5,000 members of the government army were wounded. UNITA claimed its losses as 155 killed and 622 wounded. South Africa reported 19 soldiers lost. The battle was controversial because for the first time South Africa admitted its forces had intervened on behalf of UNITA. **Jonas Savimbi** claimed the victory was by his forces only. Adding to the controversy, as the FAPLA column retreated toward **Cuito Cuanavale**, it was pursued by UNITA and South African forces. Never before had the South African Defense

Forces (SADF) pursued a retreating FAPLA column. When Fidel Castro learned of the South African/UNITA attempt to capture Cuito Cuanavale, he ordered his commanders to hold the city at all costs. The battle for Cuito Cuanavale would set the stage for all international actors to finally find a reason to leave Angola.

BATTLE OF LOMBA RIVER III. On 21 December 1989, **Forças Armadas Populares de Libertação de Angola** (FAPLA) forces, with close air support, launched another offensive against the key **União Nacional para a Independência Total de Angola** (UNITA) center of **Mavinga/Jamba**. An estimated 9,000 FAPLA troops took part in the drive toward UNITA's bases. For the first time, the **Movimento Popular de Libertação de Angola** (MPLA) did not have **Cuban** troops for support, and for the first time UNITA did not have **South African** support. Reportedly, the MPLA column was led by **Soviet** advisers. The battle ended on 8 May 1990, when the MPLA ended the attack. UNITA claimed 139 soldiers killed and 33 captured. It is believed that FAPLA captured the airstrip at Mavinga at one point, but lost it to a **Forças Armadas de Libertação de Angola** (FALA) counterattack. Finally, after 15 years of warfare, in a battle fought without their traditional allies, the MPLA and UNITA realized victory could not be won on the battlefield. Under pressure from the **Soviet Union**, **Portugal**, and the **United States**, the MPLA and UNITA were urged to settle the dispute through negotiation. *See also* BICESSE ACCORDS; ULTIMO ASSALTA DA OPERAÇÃO.

BATTLE OF MBWILA. The battle between **Portuguese** forces and the **Bakongo** on 26 October 1665 that broke the Bakongo Empire as a unified power. The *manicongo,* António I (**Vita Nkanga**), was killed, and his head was returned to **Luanda** in triumph by the Portuguese commander, Luis Lopes de Sequeira.

BEATRICE, DOÑA (Kimpa Vita) (c. 1682–1706). A **Bakongo** prophetess who in the early 17th century preached that Jesus was a Bakongo and Mary was an African. Doña Beatrice was the resurrected Saint Anthony of Padua, and her followers, called Antonians, believed Beatrice could perform miracles. The Antonian Movement attracted broad support throughout the Bakongo region. However,

Beatrice made enemies in the **Catholic Church** and among members of the Bakongo royalty who remained traditional Roman Catholics. In 1706, Beatrice was charged with heresy, tried, found guilty, and burned at the stake. The Antonian Movement was seen as an alternative to the Catholic Church, which supported slavery, and to the Angolan powers that profited from the selling of **slaves**.

BELLA, JOHN (Jorge Marques Bela). A leading Angolan poet who writes of love, female beauty, and peace. His April 2003 work *Cântico Romântico à Paz* (Romantic canticle for peace) contains 30 poems celebrating the anniversary of Angolan peace. He is also author of *Águas de Vida* (Water of life), which earned him the 1996 Galaxy Prize. His other works include *Nzamba—O Rei Sou Eu* (Nzamba, I am the king, 2003), *Madrugada* (Dawn, 2001), and *Caixa Mágica* (Magic box, 2001). *See also* LITERATURE.

BENGO. The **province** that borders the province of **Luanda**. Its capital city is Caxito. The climate is tropical and dry, and the population is estimated at 300,000. Agriculturally, the province grows cotton. Mineral deposits include phosphates and quartz. Ocean **fishing** is also an important source of revenue.

BENGUELA. A **province** located on the southwestern coast. The population is about 600,000. The capital city, Benguela, enjoys a tropical-dry climate. Founded in 1617, Benguela's port played an important role in the **slave** trade. Benguela is the termination point of the **Benguela Railroad. Fisheries** and sisal production are also crucial to the economy.

BENGUELA RAILROAD. Built by the Belgian firm Société Général, the **railroad** runs 1,250 miles from the Angolan seaport of **Lobito** through the heart of Angola to **Zambia** and the **Democratic Republic of the Congo**. Construction began in 1903, and by 1912 the line had reached from **Huambo** to **Lobito**. Completed in 1929 after a quarter century of labor, the railway linked with the central African rail system and the copper belt, totaling 928 miles. The railway in 1973 had 14,000 employees, carried 3.2 million tons of freight, and earned $30 million in revenues. The **União Nacional para a Inde-**

pendência Total de Angola (UNITA) rebels successfully kept the line closed throughout the **civil war**. Reconstruction of the railway will cost many hundreds of millions of dollars.

BERMUDA TRIANGLE. Term used to refer to the Angolan national oil company, the presidential palace, and the National Bank of Angola: places where money can disappear without a trace. The membership of the Bermuda Triangle is thought to be composed of Angola's 100 leading families.

BEYE, ALIOUNE BLONDIN (1939–1998). Alioune Beye was born at Bafoulabe, Mali's first administrative region. He studied law at the University of Dijon in France and international relations at the Hague in the Netherlands. He was a Malian minister who served as the United Nations special envoy to Angola from 1993 to 1998. While traveling to various African capitals to generate support for the Angolan peace process, Beye's chartered aircraft, a Beechcraft 200, crashed on approach to the runway at Abidjan, Côte d'Ivoire. Some diplomats believed that the plane crash was not accidental, but sabotage. According to the speculation, which was never proven, Beye's plane had departed from Lomé, Togo. In 1998, Togo was perhaps the last diplomatic supporter of **União Nacional para a Independência Total de Angola** (UNITA). Togo's president, **Gnassingbé Eyadéma**, facilitated UNITA's **banking** and illegal **diamond** sales. Possibly, Beye's plane was sabotaged prior to takeoff from Lomé. He was temporarily replaced by Major Kofi Obeng of Ghana, who had headed the UN peacekeeping forces in Angola since April 1998. Later, **Issa Dialo** was named permanent replacement.

BICESSE ACCORDS (Estoril Accords). The cease-fire and peace treaty between the **Movimento Popular de Libertação de Angola** (MPLA) and **União Nacional para a Independência Total de Angola** (UNITA), signed on 31 May 1991 at Bicesse, Portugal. The agreement called for a combined national army of 40,000 soldiers, cantonment of both the MPLA and the UNITA armies, establishment of a Commissão Conjunto Político–Militar (Joint Political–Military Commission) (JPMC), creation of a Commissão Mista de Verificação e Fiscalização (Joint Verification and Monitoring Commission)

(JVMC), and elections to be conducted in September 1992; the **United States** and the **Soviet Union** would no longer militarily supply their clients, and the **United Nations** would organize and conduct the elections. The negotiations were conducted over 13 months of intense and tortuous bargaining. On 16 June 1991, UNITA representatives returned to the capital city to begin legal, political activity. It was the first official presence of UNITA in **Luanda** since 1975. On 30 September, **Jonas Savimbi** returned to the capital, declaring, "I am here in Luanda."

BICUAR NATIONAL PARK. Located in **Huíla province**, the park is being restocked with wildlife to reverse effects of the **civil war**. *See also* ARCA DE NOAH DA OPERAÇÃO.

BÍE. A **province** located in central Angola and with a temperate climate. The capital city is **Kuito**, sometimes called the "Martyred City" because of the extensive damage inflicted during the **civil war**. Bíe possesses a temperate climate and a population of about 800,000. **Agricultural** products include rice and coffee, while iron and manganese are important minerals.

BILATERAL CONSULTATIVE COMMISSION. A group established in September 1999 that allows the **United States** and Angola to discuss issues of concern. Usually, the meetings revolved around political events, economic issues, trade and investment opportunities, and social and humanitarian topics. The commission meets on an irregular basis. The second commission meeting was held in **Luanda** in May 2000. The third meeting was convened in Washington, D.C., in October 2000. No further meetings have been convened.

BIRTH RATE. In Angola, the birth rate is extremely high at 7.1 **children** per woman, the fourth highest in the world. One newborn child in seven does not reach 12 months of age, and one newborn in four does not reach the age of five years. Angola has the third highest under-five mortality rate behind Afghanistan and Sierra Leone. Maternal mortality is also high, estimated to be 1,850 per 100,000 live births. Midwives perform most deliveries. They typically inject a drug used to expel the afterbirth. However, they often misuse the drug, injecting it too early, which causes the birth canal to constrict, killing the child. Aid workers say that pregnant women are last in line for meals. In traditional Angolan culture, pregnant women can become severely malnourished because they perform most of the labor and eat only after the males have been served. Other cultural norms require pregnant women to eat a vegetarian diet that deprives them of calcium and iron. Technically, medical care is provided by the state, but in reality, proper medical assistance requires bribery. For example, patients are billed between $250 and $400 for a caesarean section, although government policy says patients should not be charged. The charge for a normal birth is usually $50, while an abortion is $200. *See also* WOMEN.

BIZIMUNGU, AUGUSTIN. General Bizimungu, wanted for participating in the 1994 Rwandan genocide, was discovered in a **União Nacional para a Independência Total de Angola** (UNITA) demobilization camp in August 2002. The International War Crimes Tribunal for Rwanda sought the general, one of their eight most wanted suspects, on charges of genocide and crimes against humanity. During the 1994 massacres in Rwanda, more than one-half million were slain, most of them Tutsis.

BLOOD DIAMONDS. Diamonds mined by rebel groups in Angola and Sierra Leone that were sold illegally to finance war against the governments of those nations were sometimes also called "gemocide," "conflict diamonds," or "death stones." *See also* GLOBAL WITNESS; KIMBERLEY PROCESS.

BLOODY FRIDAY. Term used by **Bakongo** living in **Luanda** to describe the January 1993 massacre of Bakongo by military, police, and armed civilians. *See also* HALLOWEEN MASSACRE; NINJA.

BOA VISTA (Good View). A shantytown located in **Luanda**. The government evicted longtime residents to a location outside of Luanda in 2001 in order to construct an upscale area for Luanda's elite. The 13,000 families were moved to a tent city 25 miles from Luanda. Boa Vista borders the exclusive residential area of **Miramar** and the open-air market of **Roque Santeiro**. The value of the land in Boa Vista is estimated to be in the millions of dollars. Boa Vista provides a beautiful view of Luanda's harbor and the Atlantic Ocean. According to plans, the Angolan government intends to construct a residential area with restaurants, bars, swimming pools, and supermarkets and install cable television. In the initial stages of forcibly removing the residents, two were killed and four were wounded.

BOERE. A slang term voiced by **Forças Armadas Populares de Libertação de Angola** (FAPLA) and the South West Africa People's Organization (SWAPO) to describe **South African** and South West African Territorial Force (SWATF) personnel.

BOERS. Groups of Afrikaner trekkers arrived in Angola fleeing British rule in 1879–1905. They introduced their ox-driven wagons to the region, modernizing transportation. However, the Boer people remained independent, rejecting attempts by the **Portuguese** authorities to assimilate them into Portuguese Angolan culture. In 1928, most of the Boers departed Angola for South West Africa.

BONGA. Regarded as Angola's Bob Marley, Bonga is known for his danceable **music** with a political conscience. During the 1970s, his music was so political that **Portugal** issued a warrant for his arrest. He fled Europe. His discography includes *Paz Em Angola* (1991), *Angola* (1993), *Angola 72* (1997), *Angola 74* (1997), *Swinga Swinga!* (1999), *Katendu* (1999), *Semba Angola* (2000), *Mulemba Xangola* (2001), *Bonga Wanga* (2001), *Mulemba Xangola* (2001), and *Sana* (2002).

BOUT, VICTOR (1967–). Ukrainian born in Tajikistan who also goes by the name of Victor Boutov and who was accused by the **United Nations** of supplying arms to **União Nacional para a Independência Total de Angola** (UNITA) through his air transport company Air Cess. Bout also employed Air Pass, Cessavia, IRBIS, and Central Africa Airways to smuggle goods to the rebels. He served in the KGB during the **Soviet** era. It is believed he carries five passports, including two from Russia and one from Ukraine. Bout controls his empire from the United Arab Emirates, where he has links to more that 12 trading companies in Eastern Europe, Africa, and Central Asia. *See also* FOWLER COMMISSION REPORT.

BP-5. A high energy, high protein biscuit. One half biscuit, or 250 grams, covers the minimum daily adult requirement of vitamins, minerals, and proteins and exceeds the requirements for a **child**. The BP-5 works well with severely malnourished people. The biscuit contains soy protein concentrate and wheat protein. During the manufacturing process, the BP-5 is not heat treated, ensuring that the milk and soy protein remains high. Further, the lack of heat makes possible inclusion of vitamins C and A and other needed amino acids. The BP-5 biscuit has been used extensively in Angola. *See also* MÉDECINS SANS FRONTIÈRES.

BRAÇAS AOS HOES (Arms to Hoes). A program begun in Mozambique in 1995 that collects weapons in exchange for such items as hoes, sewing machines, bicycles, machetes, and other economically necessary instruments. From 1995 to 2002, over 500,000 weapons were collected in Mozambique under the program. The Angolan Council of Churches asked the Mozambican Christian Council for advice and guidance in bringing the program to Angola.

BRAZIL. One of the first nations to recognize the **Movimento Popular de Libertação de Angola** (MPLA) government in 1975, Brazil plays a growing role in Angola's **economy** and **culture**. Brazil has the largest black population outside of Africa. Brazilian culture is exported through television soap operas such as *Clone*. Angolans covet Brazilian fashion, films, and **music**. Brazil was Angola's fourth largest trading partner in 2002, when the latter imported $142 million in Brazilian goods. Several large Brazilian companies operate in Angola, including the state-owned oil firm, Petrobas. *See also* CAPOEIRA; PASTINHA, GRAND MESTRE.

BRAZZAVILLE PROTOCOL (New York Accords). An agreement by **South Africa**, Angola, and **Cuba** first signed on 13 December 1988, then formally signed in New York City on 22 December 1988. The Brazzaville Protocol stipulated a general truce effective immediately. Beginning 1 April 1989, Cuban forces would start withdrawal from the Angola–**Namibia** border, to be completely withdrawn in a staged process by 30 June 1991. By 1989, Cuban forces in Angola totaled some 52,000 soldiers. South African troops would leave **Namibia** by the end of 1989. The **United Nations** would oversee the Cuban and South African withdrawal with a force of 7,500 policemen and observers. The UN would also supervise the Namibian elections scheduled for 1 November 1989. South Africa agreed to cease assistance to **União Nacional para a Independência Total de Angola** (UNITA), while the **Movimento Popular de Libertação de Angola** (MPLA) was forced to make a similar concession regarding the African National Congress (ANC) and the South West Africa People's Organization (SWAPO). Negotiations on the Brazzaville Protocol lasted from May until December 1988. During that time, the principals held 22 meetings in seven different nations. The Brazzaville Protocol was the direct result of the **Battle of Cuito Cuanavale**. Right or wrong, the Cubans, Angolans, and South Africans all claimed victory in a war from which they sought to extricate themselves. By claiming victory, they could argue that they were not retreating or abandoning their clients. For the first time since their inceptions, UNITA and the MPLA would have no foreign patrons. UNITA was not mentioned in the protocol, nor were talks between the MPLA and UNITA guaranteed. More fighting would be necessary before the two realized a military victory was unlikely. *See also* BATTLE OF LOMBA RIVER II; CUBAN WITHDRAWAL FROM ANGOLA.

BRUSSELS CONFERENCE. Donors Round Table meeting held in Belgium on 25–26 September 1995 where Angolan president **Eduardo dos Santos** and **União Nacional para a Independência Total de Angola** (UNITA) leader **Jonas Savimbi** pledged to cooperate, and the international community agreed to commit $700 million for Angola's reconstruction. Due to the political/military uncertainties in Angola in the 1990s, no money was ever delivered. *See also* LUSAKA PROTOCOL.

– C –

CABINDA. Angola's oil-rich **province** is separated from Angola by a thin land strip of the **Democratic Republic of the Congo**. It was first occupied by **Portugal** in 1491 and became a major port for the slave trade. At the Madrid convention of 1786, Cabinda became integrated into the Kingdom of Angola. The Conference of Berlin drew the current boundaries in 1885. Cabinda remained a backwater until the discovery of **petroleum** in 1966. It is sometimes called "the New Kuwait" or "the Kuwait of Africa." The capital city is also called Cabinda. The population is a mere 100,000. Cabinda's climate is equatorial and resources include crude oil, gold, timber, and uranium. Agriculturally, cocoa is the major crop. Many Cabindans have never accepted the fact that they are Angolan. Cabinda has three active liberation movements, though none proved capable of defeating government forces. In October 2002, the **Forças Armadas de Angolanas** (FAA) launched a major counterinsurgency throughout Cabinda that was highly successful. Many believed the government, from a position of strength, would now begin negotiations with the Cabindan factions. The conflict in Cabinda drags on because of basic irreconcilable differences. The Cabindans seek a complete secession from Angola, while the government of Angola is willing to discuss greater autonomy, but nothing more.

Two problems exist. First, Angola must find a Cabindan leadership who can negotiate for all Cabindans and who will accept the negotiated results. Second, if Cabinda is granted special privileges, other Angolan provinces might make similar requests. The **nongovernmental organization** (NGO) **Open Society Foundation** in July 2003 held a two-day civil society conference on the future of Cabinda that was attended by local leaders, **church** officials, and foreign nationals. The Angolan government condemned the meeting as outside interference in Angola's affairs. *See also* FRENTE DE LIBERTAÇAO DO ENCLAVE DE CABINDA; FRENTE DE LIBERTAÇÃO DO ENCLAVE DE CABINDA–FORÇAS ARMADAS DO CABINDA; FRENTE DE LIBERTAÇÃO DO ENCLAVE DE CABINDA–RENOVADA.

CAETANO, MARCELLO (1906–1980). Marcello Caetano received a doctorate in law from the University of Lisbon (1931) and taught there for a number of years. He served in different posts under **António Salazar** and eventually became prime minister of Portugal in 1968 after a stroke felled **Salazar**. Caetano continued the policies of his predecessor, especially the colonial wars in Africa. Members of the **Movimento das Forças Armadas** (MFA) overthrew his government in April 1974. He was exiled to Madeira and later to **Brazil**.

CAIXA DE CREDITO AGRO-PECURIA E PESCAS (CCAP). One of the first Angolan **banks** to be declared insolvent. The bank collapsed under a mountain of bad loans, many of them made to prominent government and military figures. Under pressure from the **International Monetary Fund** (IMF), the Angolan government closed the bankrupt institution on 1 May 2001.

CAMAFUCA–CAMAZAMBO DIAMOND MINE. The Camafuca–Camazambo mine went into operation in late 2002. A consortium of the state-owned **diamond** company ENDIAMA, the Angolan company Comica, the Canadian firm Southern Era Resources, and the Israeli firm Minex jointly operate the mine. Expectations were for the mine to produce gems valued at $4.7 million per month. The mine is a **kimberlite** mine, one of only two in Angola. The other kimberlite mine is **Catoca**.

CAMPAIGN AGAINST WAR IN ANGOLA. An initiative begun by the **Catholic Church** and the **Open Society Foundation** in September 2001 urging all armies to agree to a cease-fire for the good of every Angolan. The head of the Catholic Church in Angola, Archbishop **Zacarias Camuenho**, strongly urged **União Nacional para a Independência Total de Angola** (UNITA), the **Movimento Popular de Libertação de Angola** (MPLA), the Angolan government, and the Angolan people to support the campaign. *See also* COMITÉ INTER-ECLESIAL PARA A PAZ EM ANGOLA.

CAMUENHO, ZACARIAS. The bishop of the southern Angolan city of Lubango and a key person in the **Comité Inter-Eclesial para a Paz em Angola** (COIEPA). Archbishop Camuenho has dedicated his life to bringing peace to Angola. In October 2001, he was awarded the Sakharov Prize for Freedom of Thought, a human rights prize awarded annually by the European Parliament. The award included a 50,000 Euro monetary prize. *See also* CAMPAIGN AGAINST WAR IN ANGOLA.

CANCER DA OPERAÇÃO (Operation Cancer). A government effort in August 1996 to expel West African and Lebanese immigrants engaged in "speculative activities." The government expelled 165

Malian, Sierra Leonian, and Gambian immigrants. Nationwide, the operation led to the arrest of 748 illegal immigrants from 26 nations.

CANCER DOIS DA OPERAÇÃO (Operation Cancer Two). A police sweep in 1999 against the same immigrant groups targeted by **Cancer da Operação**. Over 50 Senegalese were deported for "indulging in illicit trade of industrial goods."

CANDONGO. A term used for informal trading, smuggling, or black marketeering.

CÃO, DIOGO. In 1483, this **Portuguese** mariner landed at the mouth of the Congo River. The captain took four **Bakongo** as ambassadors and left four Portuguese as representatives to the court of the *manicongo*. When Cão made a return voyage, he brought gifts, messages of hope that the Africans would renounce their idols to accept Christianity, and the four Africans. The four Africans astounded the Bakongo with tales of strange dress, customs, culture, weapons, and religion.

CAPOEIRA. A dance that is a fusion of martial arts and gymnastics that began in Africa, evolved in **Brazil**, and is returning to Angola. Originally devised to break the depression of enslavement in Brazil, the **music** was played to teach the rhythm and memory of Africa. To the **slave** owners, *capoeira* seemed to be playful dancing. Eventually, the slavers realized the meaning of the dance and forbade it under penalty of death. For almost 400 years, *capoeira* was taught and practiced in secret. The person best known for preserving the *capoeira* tradition was **Grand Mestre Pastinhas**. The *capoeira* begins with dance movements close to the ground. The Berimbau, a steel-stringed bow instrument with a gourd to resonate the sound, plays the music. The Berimbau is accompanied by the Pandeiro (tambourine), the Atabaque (a conga-like drum), and the Agogo (African bell). *See also* CULTURE.

CAPRIVI LIBERATION ARMY. A Namibian group, supported by **União Nacional para a Independência Total de Angola** (UNITA) during the **civil war**, that demanded the Caprivi Strip be freed from **Namibian** control. The group also received support from the **Barotse Patriotic Front**. The leaders of the army were Mishake Muyongo and the chief of the Mafwe ethnolinguistic group, Boniface Mamili. Several members of the army had served in the South West African Territorial Force (SWATF). For UNITA, disruption in the Caprivi Strip would have brought into question Namibia's support for the Angolan government. The Caprivi Liberation Army is believed to have had 2,500 fighters, members, and sympathizers.

CARAVANEROS. The name given to **União Nacional para a Independência Total de Angola** (UNITA) policemen prior to the 1992 national elections. The police were named for the new General Motors vans they drove.

CARDOSO, FREDERICO (a.k.a. Roderick Nehone). Angolan writer who published *Tempos sem Véu* (Times without veil) in July 2003. The 38-year-old author is a lecturer at the **Agostinho Neto** University and also wrote *Trabalhos Do Genesis* (Genesis works). He also serves as vice president of the Angolan Writers Union (UAE). *See also* LITERATURE.

CARNATION REVOLUTION. The term used to describe the **Movimento das Forças Armadas** (MFA) revolution in **Portugal** in 1974. During the turmoil, young women placed pink carnations in the rifle barrels of the soldiers. *See also* SPINOLA, ANTÓNIO DE.

CARREIRA, HENRIQUE TELES "IKO" (1933–2000). Angola's first defense minister, Iko Carreira, was a veteran **Movimento Popular de Libertação de Angola** (MPLA) militant serving as head of security during the war of liberation against **Portugal**. After the death of President **Agostinho Neto**, Carreira's star waned. He was appointed ambassador to Algeria and later served as a military attaché to Spain, where he was stationed at the time of his death.

CARVALHO, EMILIO MIGUEL DE. First African bishop to be named the president of the Council of Bishops of the United Methodist Church. De Carvalho was also an early advocate for the

Catholic Church to pose as a "third force" as an alternative to the **Movimento Popular de Libertação de Angola** (MPLA) and **União Nacional para a Independência Total de Angola** (UNITA).

CARVALHO, RUY DUARTE DE (1941–). Born on 22 April 1941 in Santarém, **Portugal**, Ruy Carvalho migrated early in life to southern Angola, where he became an author. His books include *Os Papéis do Inglês* (The English papers, 2003), *Actas da Maianga* (The Maianga minutes, 2003), *Hábitos da Terra* (Customs of Earth, 1988), *Ondula Savana Braca* (The waves of the Branca Savanna, 1981), *Exercício de Crueldade* (Cruel exercise, 1978), *Como Se o Mundo Não Tivesse Leste* (As if the world were lost, 1977), and *A Decisão da Idade* (The time of decision, 1976). *See also* LITERATURE.

CASA MILITAR. The presidential guard unit that answers directly to the president and is separate from the **Forças Armadas de Angolanas** (FAA) command and control structures.

CASSAMBA ATTACK. The first attack by **União Nacional para a Independência Total de Angola** (UNITA) forces, led by **Jonas Savimbi**, against the **Portuguese** colonial army, in 1966. Savimbi described the attack as "an army of 12 people with knives."

CATETE GROUP. An organization that consisted of Africanist **Movimento Popular de Libertação de Angola** (MPLA) members. The group resented **Soviet–Cuban** domination and the **assimilado/ mestiço** leadership of the party. From the early 1980s, it favored a more laissez-faire **economy**, a nonaligned foreign policy, and a willingness (though unspoken) to negotiate with **União Nacional para a Independência Total de Angola** (UNITA). However, the black Africanists, who included **Iko Carreira**, Manuel Pacavira (former secretary for production), and Agostinho Mendes de Carvalho (former health minister), never had the numbers to influence official party policy.

CATHOLIC CHURCH. The Roman Catholic Church has played a vital yet complicated role in Angolan history. Seen by many Angolans as the religion of the oppressor, the church has worn many hats. After all, the **Portuguese** arrived in Africa with a message of "commerce, civilization, and Christianity." During Angola's war for independence, the Catholic Church was the **Portuguese** colonial regime's most important ally. The church played a more vital role during the **civil war**. While tending to people's religious needs, it also became the supplier of goods and services, in effect, becoming a surrogate state bureaucracy. In the latter stages of the war, the church helped people find their voice in opposing the continuation of the conflict. President **Eduardo dos Santos** decided to send a representative to the **Congresso da Paz** only after the church added its name to the Congress. *See also* RADIO ECCLESIA.

CATOCA MINE. Located 22 miles northwest of **Saurimo**, the capital of **Lunda Sul province**, Catoca is the largest **diamond** mine in Angola. It produced 1.2 million carats in 1999, 1.5 million in 2000, and 2.0 million in 2001. The value of 2 million carats is approximately $165 million. If the Catoca mine can increase production to 2 million carats, it will become the world's fourth largest diamond mine. It is one of two producing kimberlite mines in Angola. During the **civil war**, the mine was guarded by a **Forças Armadas de Angolanas** (FAA) regiment, with an on-site, 400-man security force. A high security location, Catoca has its own 116-acre farm that includes livestock, vegetable gardens, a dairy operation, and an irrigation system. Ore from the open pit is crushed, washed, and x-rayed to extract the stones. The kimberlite deposit has a depth of 1,968 feet and a 40-year estimated lifespan. The four owners of the mine are ENDIAMA, Russia's Almazi Rossii-Sakha, Brazil's Odebrecht, and **Lev Leviev**'s Daumonty Financing. In 2002, $40 million was spent to open a second pit and supply the accompanying equipment to search for diamonds.

CATUMBELA RIVER. Its headwaters rising in the central highlands, the river flows westerly into the Atlantic near **Benguela**. Biópio and Lomaum dams supply power to **Lobito**, Benguela, and the Cubal–Ganda industrial region.

CENTRO DE DESENVOLVIMENTO E DEMOCRACIA PARA ANGOLA (CDDA) (Center for Democracy and Development in Angola). A Lisbon-based **União Nacional para a Independência**

Total de Angola (UNITA) office cited in the **Fowler Commission Report** as a violation of **United Nations sanctions**. The UNITA offices closed in **Portugal** in 1998 after the UN tightened sanctions. However, UNITA representation continued in Portugal under a new moniker, the Commissão de Justica, Paz e Reconcilição em Angola (CJPRA) (Commission for Justice, Peace, and Reconciliation in Angola).

CHILDREN. Angolan children suffered enormous hardships from the 27-year **civil war**. The importance of this is highlighted by the fact that 54 percent of the population is under 18. Only 27 percent of Angola's children are fully immunized against preventable diseases. Angola is one of the world's worst nations in terms of immunization coverage. Preventable diseases include **polio**, tetanus, whooping cough, acute respiratory infection, **malaria**, diphtheria, meningitis, pneumonia, and **measles**. Angola's **children** also suffer from a severe form of malnutrition called kwashiorkor. This condition is caused by protein deficiency, and initial symptoms are irritability, lethargy, and apathy. Later signs include failure to grow, mental deficiency, increased susceptibility to infection, and edema. Health agencies have discovered a large number of Angolan babies with marasmus. This is a severe form of malnutrition resulting from protein deficiency and causing extreme deterioration in infants. The infant first does not gain weight, then begins to lose weight. Brain and skeletal growth continue, resulting in a long body and large head in proportion to weight. The skin of the infant sags and appears loose. Poor sanitation, unavailability of drugs, and lack of access to clean water makes a bad situation intolerable. Also, Angola has one of the world's worst under-five mortality rates, with 25 percent of children perishing before their fifth birthday. Forty-five percent of Angola's children suffer from chronic malnutrition. A shortage of qualified medical personnel plays a key role in the failing health sector. One million Angolan children, or 44 percent, do not attend school. The nearly three-decade-long civil war has devastated childhood development. Many children who fought for the rebels or government or were separated from their relatives will be mentally, physically, and emotionally affected for years. In 2003, over 45,000 children were returned to relatives by the Angolan government. All children, and most adults, have never known peace. Consequently, their outlook is often clouded, without hope. Many children exhibit symptoms of trauma, including lack of sleep, nightmares, thoughts of war and death, and general insecurity. **Luanda** is overrun with street children: orphans, abandoned or displaced. They sleep where they can and survive by washing cars, guarding parked cars, or doing other odd jobs for money. Often, the children form **street gangs** to assist and protect one another. With the end of the civil war, international donors expect the government of Angola to spend more oil and **diamond** revenue on social development projects, repairing infrastructure, demining **agricultural** fields, rebuilding schools, funding hospitals, and providing **internally displaced people** (IDPs) and demobilized soldiers adequate resources to begin life anew. Unless the government takes significant steps in that direction, international donors may close the checkbook. Such a development would be a crushing blow to the future of all Angolans. *See also* HEALTH CARE.

CHILDREN'S PARLIAMENT. The **United Nations** Children's Fund (UNICEF) and the Angolan government, in conjunction with the Day of the African Child, held the first Angolan **Children**'s Parliament from 14 to 16 June 2000. At the **Assembleia Nacional** in **Luanda**, 287 children, aged 10–17 and representing every **province**, participated in plenary sessions, working groups, and parliamentary caucuses. Some of the recommendations put forward by the parliament included expanded educational opportunities. The delegates viewed **education** as the key to development. They suggested that schooling be provided to all children and that teachers receive fair compensation. **Health care** must be provided for all Angolan citizens. Infant and child mortality must be reduced. Other recommendations related to sports, culture, child rights, and leisure.

CHILUBA, FREDERICK (1943–). President of **Zambia** from 1991 to 2001. It was during this era that relations between **Luanda** and Lusaka soured, as Angola accused the Chiluba government of directly assisting the **União Nacional para a Independência Total de Angola** (UNITA) rebels or turning a blind eye toward those government ministers involved in such activity. At one point, Angola was on the verge of attacking Zambia, before tensions relaxed. *See also* INDENI PETROLEUM REFINERY; KAUNDA, KENNETH; ZAMBIA INITIATIVE.

CHITUNDA, JEREMIAS KALANDULA (1942–1992). Jeremias Chitunda was born in Chimbuelengue to Emilio Chitunda and Rosalina Kalombo. He completed his primary schooling at Chimbuelengue and Dondi Mission, Bela Vista. He attended secondary school at Dom João de Castro College and at the **Huambo** National Secondary School. After harassment by **Portuguese** colonial police, Chitunda fled Angola to Zaire. Later, he obtained a scholarship to the University of Arizona. Joining **União Nacional para a Independência Total de Angola** (UNITA) in 1966, Chitunda served as representative to the southwestern **United States**. He obtained a degree in mining engineering and worked for several mining companies in North America. In 1976, he was appointed UNITA representative to the United States, a position he held until 1986. At the **UNITA VI Party Congress** in August 1986, Chitunda was promoted to vice president. He remained in **Luanda** after the 1992 election in order to negotiate the modalities for the second round presidential runoff. Trapped in the capital city over the weekend of the **Halloween Massacre**, Chitunda was murdered at close range. The **Movimento Popular de Libertação de Angola** (MPLA) government allowed a Portuguese television crew to film the remains of Chitunda and Elias Salupeto Pena. The government never returned the bodies to UNITA, making them martyrs for the rebel cause.

CHIVUKUVUKU, ABEL EPALANGA (1957–). Born on 11 November in Luvemba, Abel Chivukuvuku is the son of Pedro and Margarida Chivukuvuku. His primary **education** was at Dondi Mission, Bela Vista, and he completed his secondary education at **Huambo** National Secondary School. He enrolled in **União Nacional para a Independência Total de Angola** (UNITA) in 1974 and joined **Forças Armadas de Libertação de Angola** (FALA) in 1976. He was sent from Angola in 1979 as UNITA's representative to Africa. Later, he would serve in **Portugal** and Great Britain. He returned to Angola in 1992 and ran as a UNITA candidate for parliament. Wounded in the **Halloween Massacre**, Chivukuvuku remained a prisoner until 1997, when the UNITA parliamentarians finally arrived in **Luanda**. Slowly splitting from the military wing of UNITA, he maintained his independence from all factions of the party. In October 1998, he was elected chief UNITA parliamentarian, a position he held until September 2000, when a **UNITA–R** member replaced him. By 2003, it was expected that he would seek the UNITA presidency. Handsome and charismatic, he is popular throughout the party, although his long stay in Luanda might alienate him from those who remained in the bush. At the **UNITA IX Party Congress**, he chose not to run for president of the party.

CHOKWE GROUP. The Chokwe ethnolinguistic group includes the Cacongo, Chokwe, Lunda, Lunda-lua-Chindes, Lunda-Ndembo, Mai, and Mataba. They overlap the Angolan borders with **Zambia** and the **Democratic Republic of the Congo** and can be found in **Bié, Cuando Cubango, Lunda Norte, Lunda Sul**, and **Moxico** provinces. In Angola, the Chokwe number 400,000, or about 8 percent of the population. Chokwe became traders of ivory, rubber and beeswax during the 19th century. Hunting was especially important to Chokwe culture, but **agriculture** also played a key role. The group is famous for its carved figures and ritual masks.

Portuguese colonialists had little or no contact with the Chokwe until 1930. Like the Bakongo, early nationalist sentiment had overlapped into neighboring nations. Not until 1959 did Angolan Chokwe form a political organization.

CIVIL WAR. The Angolan **civil war**, according to some sources, began in August 1975 when the **Movimento Popular de Libertação de Angola** (MPLA) forcibly evicted **União Nacional para a Independência Total de Angola** (UNITA) and the **Frente Nacional de Libertação de Angola** (FNLA) from **Luanda**. The conflict ended in February 2002 with the death of UNITA leader **Jonas Savimbi**. There were periods of peace during the 27-year conflict, but they were never long enough for the peace process to take root. From 1975 to 2002, the Angolan **civil war** was internationalized, as **Cuba**, the **Soviet Union**, **South Africa**, Zaire, the **United States**, China, **Portugal**, the Warsaw Pact nations, **Brazil**, France, Algeria, **Zambia**, **South West Africa/Namibia**, North Korea, Gabon, Côte d'Ivoire, and the Republic of the Congo played a variety of roles. The war went from ethnic conflict to Cold War battle zone back to ethnic conflict. In the end, it was the **Forças Armadas de Libertação de Angola** (FALA) and the **Forças Armadas de Angolanas** (FAA) that came to terms to end the long-running war. It will take years of serious effort and hundreds of millions of dollars for Angola to recover from the devastation. Over 1 million Angolans died during the fighting, and hundreds of thousands were wounded. Families were torn apart. The war created thousands of orphans and amputees, and an estimated 2.6 million people were displaced. The political/economic/cultural infrastructure was reduced to virtual nonexistence. Fortunately, Angola has the resources to eventually recover and prosper, thanks to **petroleum**, **diamonds**, rich farmland, and other natural resources that can provide the funding to rebuild.

CLARK AMENDMENT. An amendment to the 1976 Defense Appropriations Bill sponsored by Senators Dick Clark (Democrat–Iowa) and John Tunney (Democrat–California). Passed on 19 December 1975, the amendment ended Central Intelligence Agency (CIA) monetary assistance to the **Frente Nacional de Libertação de Angola** (FNLA) and the **União Nacional para a Independência Total de Angola** (UNITA). The amendment froze $28 million destined for the Angolan factions, but $8.2 million "in the pipeline" was delivered. The amendment remained in effect until 1985. On 11 June of that year, the U.S. Senate repealed the Clark amendment by a vote of 63-34. The House voted 236-185 to lift the ban on 11 July. The repeal did not include funding for UNITA, which would not be provided until 1986. *See also* REAGAN DOCTRINE.

COALITION FOR RECONCILIATION, TRANSPARENCY AND CITIZENSHIP. During September 2002, civil society groups participated in a conference titled "The Agenda for Peace and Reconciliation in the Republic of Angola" conducted by the coalition. Trade unions, **churches**, and nongovernmental organizations (NGOs) expressed concern about **União Nacional para a Independência Total de Angola** (UNITA) and **Movimento Popular de Libertação de Angola** (MPLA) domination of the peace process. The groups issued a statement questioning the legitimacy of the Angolan government. Also, the statement called for a cease-fire in **Cabinda**. *See also* COMITÉ INTER-ECLESIAL PARA A PAZ EM ANGOLA; CONFERÉ NCIA EPISCOPAL DE ANGOLA E SÃO TOMÉ.

COBRA MILITIA. The name of Republic of the Congo forces loyal to former president Denis Sassou-Nguesso. Fighting erupted on 5 June 1997 between the Cobras and forces loyal to President Pascal Lissouba when government troops attempted to disarm the Cobras before scheduled presidential elections. Tensions had simmered since the 1992 legislative elections, which Sassou-Nguesso accused Lissouba of rigging. The fall of Zaire's president Mobutu Sese Seko emboldened Sassou-Nguesso, whose Cobras received assistance from new Zaire (**Democratic Republic of the Congo**) leader **Laurent Kabila** and from Angola. The Angolan government had accused Lissouba of allowing arms for **União Nacional para a Independência Total de Angola** (UNITA) to transit through the Republic of the Congo port of Pointe Noire. By October 1997, the Cobras, with assistance from Angolan armored units and air strikes, overthrew the Lissouba government. In less than one year, the Angolan army had overthrown the legally elected president of the Republic of the Congo and had assisted in the removal of a long-time dictator, Mobutu, by indigenous rebel forces. The government of Angola was not content to allow the **United Nations** to stumble through the peace process. The government took upon itself the task of removing supporters of UNITA in southern Africa.

COCA-COLA. The soft drink giant entered the Angolan market in June 2000 with the 140th bottling plant in Africa. Located in Bom Jesus, about 75 miles from **Luanda**, the factory has a capacity of 1,000 cases per hour. The Coca-Cola Company brought the first foreign direct investment in Angola not related to oil or **diamonds**. The factory was a joint venture between the government of Angola and Coca-Cola Incorporated called Coca-Cola Bottling Luanda. In 2001, Coca-Cola opened a second factory, in Lubango.

COFFEE. Production of coffee in Angola began in the 1830s. Coffee quickly became an important cash crop. Most of the coffee grown is robusta grade, which is used in many blends, due to its lower cost as compared to arabica grade. Coffee is grown in **Luanda**, **Uíge**, **Cuanza Norte**, and **Cuanza Sul provinces**. In the early 1970s, Angola competed with Côte d'Ivoire for the title of Africa's largest coffee producer. Angola exported 5.2 million 132-pound bags of coffee in 1974. By 1975, it had over 2,000 coffee plantations, mostly owned by **Portuguese** settlers. The abandonment of Angola by the Portuguese devastated the coffee region. The plantations were overgrown by elephant grass and jungle creepers. By 1984, the country's production placed 26th internationally at 283,000 bags, or 5 percent of the colonial level. Exports fell to a low of 48,780 bags in 1993. Over 400 agronomists left for Brazil during this period. With the end of the **civil war**, the government hopes to revive the industry to colonial levels. In July 2000, the International Coffee Organization donated $8 million for a pilot program to regenerate a number of coffee plantations. By 2003, the National Coffee Institute director estimated total rehabilitation costs would be $230 million. Most of Angola's coffee bushes are over 40 years old, well past prime production years. New bushes would be expensive, and they would take three years before producing beans. *See also* AGRICULTURE; LIANGOL COFFEE FACTORY.

COMBÓIO PARA A VIDA (Convoy for Life). A program launched in 2003 and sponsored by the Angolan Health Ministry, the World Heath Organization (WHO), the U.S. Agency for International Development (USAID), and the United Nations Children's Fund (UNICEF). The goal is to educate the population about the steps to be taken to avoid **malaria**, such as use of mosquito nets and insecticide.

COMISSÃO INTERSECTORIAL DE DESMINAGEM E ASSISTÉ NCIA HUMANITÁRIA ÀS VITIMAS (CNIDAH) (Intersectoral Commission for Demining and Humanitarian Assistance). The government of Angola has sought to consolidate and reorganize the coordination of all **land-mine** activities in Angola under CNIDAH. CNIDAH serves as government contact for **nongovernmental organizations** (NGOs) and donor agencies and works with the **United Nations** Development Program (UNDP). The agency formerly responsible for these activities, the Instituto de Removação de Obstáculos e Engenhos Explosivos (National Institute for the Removal of Explosive Obstacles and Ordinance), was transformed into the National Demining Institute (Instituto Nacional de Angola Demining, INAD) with responsibility for operations, logistics, and technical training, including incorporation of military personnel into demining brigades. By October 2002, critics complained that the CNIDAH had no office space, had no permanent staff, and had issued no formal policy statements.

COMITÉ INTER-ECLESIAL PARA A PAZ EM ANGOLA (COIEPA) (Interdenominational Committee for Peace in Angola). A cross-section of civic groups campaigning for peace in Angola founded in April 2000. Led by the Reverend **Daniel Ntoni-Nzinga**, COIEPA urged a cease-fire and the resumption of peace negotiations. Thirty-five civic organizations make up COIEPA, including the Council of Angolan Christian Churches, the Angolan Evangelical Alliance, and the **Conferência Episcopal de Angola e São Tomé** (CEAST) (Bishops Conference of Angola and São Tomé). The first March for Peace was held in **Luanda** in June 2000, when 5,000–10,000 people gathered to call for a cease-fire. In June 2001, thousands of **children** marched through Luanda demanding respect for their rights and the end of the use of children soldiers in the **civil war**. In August, the **churches** announced a month of prayer for peace in Angola. *See also* CAMPAIGN AGAINST WAR IN ANGOLA; GRUPO ANGOLANO DE REFLEXAO PARA PAZ; REDE DA PAZ.

COMMITTEE OF FRIENDS FOR ANGOLA. A **United Nations** group begun in July 1999, consisting of the People's Republic of China, Côte d'Ivoire, France, Gabon, Russia, Morocco, **Namibia**, Nigeria, the United Kingdom, the **United States**, **Brazil**, Canada, **Portugal**, and Zimbabwe.

COMMUNAUTÉ ÉCONOMIQUE DES ÉTATS AFRICAINS CENTRAUX (CEEAC) (Economic Community of Central African States). Founded in 1984, the CEEAC includes Angola, Burundi, the Central African Republic, Chad, the Republic of the Congo, the **Democratic Republic of the Congo**, Equatorial Guinea, Gabon, Rwanda, and São Tomé and Príncipe.

COMMUNIDADE DOS PAÍSES DE LÍNGUA PORTUGUESA (CPLP) (Community of Portuguese-Speaking Countries). An organization designed to foster better economic, cultural, and political ties between **Portuguese**-speaking nations. The CPLP includes **Por-**

tugal, Angola, **Brazil**, Mozambique, Guinea–Bissau, East Timor, Cape Verde, and São Tomé and Príncipe.

COMPANHIA ANGOLANA DE DISTRIBUIÇÃO ALIMENTAR. A private company established in the Virgin Islands to conduct oil for arms swaps and to transfer money from Angola as a future nest egg for high military and **Movimento Popular de Libertação de Angola** (MPLA) officials.

COMPAORÉ, BLAISÉ. President of Burkina Faso accused by the **United Nations** of assisting **União Nacional para a Independência Total de Angola** (UNITA) in breaking international sanctions. Burkina Faso supplied UNITA with fuel, while **Jonas Savimbi** contributed money to Blaisé Campaoré's political campaigns. *See also* EYADÉMA, GNASSINGBÉ; KAGAME, PAUL.

CONFERÉNCIA EPISCOPAL DE ANGOLA E SÃO TOMÉ (CEAST) (Bishops Conference of Angola and São Tomé). A **Catholic Church** organization that advocated a peaceful resolution to the **civil war**. According to CEAST, peace could be achieved by dialogue, tolerance, and reconciliation. *See also* COMITÉ INTER-ECLESIAL PARA A PAZ EM ANGOLA; GRUPO ANGOLANO DE REFLEXAO PARA PAZ; REDE DA PAZ.

CONGRESSO DA PAZ (CCP) (Peace Congress). A meeting of representatives of the *Church*, members of parliament, ambassadors accredited to **Luanda**, international aid organizations, and some government officials held in Luanda from 18 to 21 July 2000 to urge **União Nacional para a Independência Total de Angola** (UNITA) and the government to resume peace negotiations. Over 250 people participated and a letter from **Pope John Paul II** was read asking all parties to "take bold and courageous decisions." At the conclusion of the congress, the Angolan Roman Catholic Church called for an immediate cease-fire.

CONSELHO DA REPÚBLICA (Council of the Republic). Consultative body to the president consisting of the prime minister, speaker of the parliament, attorney general, leaders of political parties with seats in the **Assembleia Nacional**, and 10 citizens appointed by the president.

CONSTITUTION. In February 2002, the Angolan **Assembleia Nacional**'s Constitutional Affairs Committee published a draft document that would serve as the basis of the country's new constitution. Included were provisions that Angola would have a multiparty system, human rights would be respected, and the **economy** would be based on a free market and free enterprise. The executive, legislative, and judicial branches of government would be politically independent and elections would be held on a regular basis. The nation's symbols would be decided by a public competition. Angola would be a secular state. A clause in the constitution would define who is an Angolan, and **Portuguese** would be the official language. The various ethnic, religious, linguistic, and cultural identities would be cherished and protected. The state's natural resources were recognized as existing for the good of all Angolans. Finally, the constitution would be supreme over the county's laws and institutions. As of October 2003, the constitution had not been adopted by the Assembleia Nacional.

CONSTRUCTIVE ENGAGEMENT. A policy developed in the early 1980s by Assistant Secretary of State for African Affairs Chester Crocker. The policy became the framework for U.S. policy in southern Africa during the **Ronald Reagan** administration. Rather than condemn **South Africa** for its apartheid policies, the United States sought to work with South Africa over an array of issues ranging from **Namibia**, **Cuban** troops in Angola, U.S.–South African relations, and apartheid. Critics claimed U.S. policy was really turning a blind eye to South African aggression throughout southern Africa.

COSTA, GUSTAVO. Angolan journalist who wrote an article titled "Corrupção Faz Vítimas em Angola" (Corruption makes victims) for the Portuguese newspaper *Expresso* in April 1999. The piece charged chief presidential adviser José Leitão with embezzling state funds. The Angolan Supreme Court gave Gustavo Costa an eight-month jail sentence, suspended for two years, with a fine of $2,000. Costa was charged both with *difamação* and *injúria*. *See also* MEDIA; MORAIS, RAFAEL MARQUES DE; SANTOS, AGUIAR DOS.

COUTINHO, ANTONIO DE ALVA ROSA. In 1974, Admiral Coutinho became the **Portuguese** high commissioner for Angola. He openly supported the **Movimento Popular de Libertação de Angola** (MPLA) and allowed **Soviet** cargo ships to unload vast quantities of arms and ammunition. Coutinho was known as the "Red Admiral" for his support of the then Portuguese prime minister, the Communist Party's General Vasco Gonçalves. **Holden Roberto, Jonas Savimbi**, and Zaire's president Mobutu Sese Seko were so critical of Coutinho for his support of the MPLA that Portugal replaced him with General Silva Cardoso. Admiral Coutinho was especially disliked by the settler population, who fled Angola to Portugal. They likened him to an "assassin" and demanded his execution.

COUTOS. See QUILOMBOS.

CROWN AGENTS. British firm hired by the Angolan government in December 2000 to take over operation of Angola's customs service. The firm was hired with the idea that Angola's profits would dramatically increase under foreign management.

CUANDO CUBANGO (Kuando Kubango). A **province** in the southeastern part of the country in an area the **Portuguese** once termed the "Land at the End of the Earth." The capital city is Menongue, but the province also includes **Mavinga** and **Jamba**, made famous by the **civil war** battles that occurred there. The climate is tropical-dry and temperate. This province is Angola's second largest in terms of area, yet it has a population of only about 140,000. Corn, beans, and cereals are important crops, and **diamonds** provide mineral resources.

CUANGO (Kuango). A town in the **diamond** heartland of northeastern Angola. Cuango played an important role during the **civil war**, as both **União Nacional para a Independência Total de Angola** (UNITA) and government forces attempted to seize and hold the city. Cuango is situated in the Cuango River Valley of **Lunda Norte province**, the richest diamond area in Angola. UNITA surrendered the town to the government on 30 September 1997 as part of the **Lusaka Protocol**.

CUANZA CONFERENCE. Held in 1976, this **União Nacional para a Independência Total de Angola** (UNITA) conference was called to discuss the military and political strategy against the **Cuban–Soviet** intervention following the retreat from the cities in 1975–76.

CUANZA NORTE (Kwanza Norte). A **province** in eastern Angola with a population of about 400,000. The capital city is N'Dalatando. The climate is tropical-humid, which facilitates the growth of sugarcane and **coffee**. Mineral resources include iron and calcareous.

CUANZA SUL (Kwanza Sul). A **province** on the central coast with a tropical-dry and temperate climate. The population is about 580,000; Sumbe is the capital city. Coffee and pineapples are the major crops, and quartz production and **fisheries** also provide economic stimulus.

CUBA. Cuba has had a long relationship with Angola and the **Movimento Popular de Libertação de Angola** (MPLA) dating back to the early 1960s. Some reports indicate that Che Guevara trained MPLA fighters in 1965, and **Agostinho Neto** visited Cuba in 1966. Cubans also served as guards for Neto early in the struggle against **Portugal**. As the **Alvor Accords** unraveled into a swirl of violence, Cuban soldiers began to land in **Luanda** in large numbers through **Operation Carlotta** on 25 July 1975. As the **civil war** intensified, the number of Cuban troops climbed to 12,000. Cuban forces firing Soviet-supplied 122-mm rocket launchers destroyed the advancing **Frente Nacional de Libertação de Angola** (FNLA) column in the **Battle of Death Road**. A debate has raged as to whether Cuba was acting upon its own initiative or was a proxy warrior for the **Soviet Union**. Evidence is strong on both sides, but, at any rate, Cuban involvement helped secure victory for the MPLA over **União Nacional para a Independência Total de Angola** (UNITA) and FNLA. Fidel Castro initially wanted to withdraw Cuban forces from Angola in 1976. However, as UNITA revived and continued the guerrilla war, the number of Cuban forces escalated to the 50,000–60,000 range. Cuban soldiers contracted African diseases and returned home to infect the local population. Dengue fever, **malaria**, renal and intestinal schistosomiasis, leishmaniasis, and meningitis struck the Cuban forces. By the late 1980s, **AIDS/HIV** had become a major concern. During the **Nito Alves** attempted coup in 1977, the Cuban forces remained loyal to President Neto, ensuring the failure of the coup. For its part, the Soviet Union was ambivalent about the attempt.

Angola paid Cuba $40 per day for each Cuban soldier. In addition, Angola paid $600 a month for every Cuban schoolteacher. Eventually, world events forced Cuba to seek an honorable exit from Angola; the **Battle of Cuito Cuanavale** provided the face-saving pretext. The 1988 **Brazzaville Protocol** paved the way for **Cuba's withdrawal from Angola**. The number of Cuban casualties may never be known. Estimates range from 2,000 to 15,000. Ironically, at one point in the Angolan civil war, Cuban troops protected U.S. oil installations in Angola from UNITA attack. The **United States** was then officially arming UNITA and had no diplomatic relations with either Cuba or Angola. With the end of the Cold War, Cuban–Angolan relations remained cordial, but clearly Angola has turned from socialism toward capitalism.

CUBAN WITHDRAWAL FROM ANGOLA. Under the terms of the **Brazzaville Protocol**, **Cuba** was required to withdraw in stages. Between December 1988 and 1 April 1989, **Cuba** withdrew 3,000 soldiers from Angola. By 1 August 1989, all Cuban troops were north of the 15th parallel, which ran through **Cuito Cuanavale**. On 1 November 1989, the day of the **Namibian** elections, all Cuban forces were north of the 13th parallel, or the **Benguela Railroad**. Also by that date, 50 percent of Cuban forces had departed Angola. By 1 April 1990, 66.7 percent were gone. The total on 1 October 1990 was 75 percent. By 1 January 1991, Cuban numbers were 12,000 or less. Finally, by 1 July 1991, all Cuban forces were gone from Angola. The Cuban withdrawal was completed with only minor glitches.

CULTURE. Probably the best representative of Angola's cultural heritage is the Chokwe Thinker. The most recognizable piece of Angolan art, it expresses harmony and symmetry. Other notable pieces of Angolan artwork include the *kalelwa* and *mwnaa-pwo,* masks worn by male dancers during circumcision and puberty rituals, respectively.

As in most of Africa, dancing is an important component of culture. The *kabetula* is a traditional dance style of Angola performed as a series of fast waddles accompanied by acrobatic leaps. Another dance is the *semba,* which is characterized by drumbeats and instruments known as *tarolas* and *dilongas.* Semba dancers move their bodies — oscillating the legs — to the rhythm of the drumbeats. The *kazukuta* dance involves slow tap dancing followed by wild arm swinging. One area where Angolan culturally lags is drama. Since independence, only 23 plays by nine authors have been published. Jose Mena Abrantes leads with 12 productions. There is no professional theater in Angola. Amateurs such as the Experimental Theatre Group, JULU, Oasis, **Horizonte Nzinga Mbande**, and the Makotes keep the genre alive by taking part in festivals both in and out of Angola. JULU is a theater troop that performs plays on civil, cultural, **economic**, political, and social topics. *See also* CAPOEIRA; MUSIC; MUSICAL INSTRUMENTS.

CUNENE. A **province** located in the southwest part of the nation with a population of about 200,000. The capital city is Ondjiva. The climate is tropical-dry and arid. Farm products include corn and cereals; iron and copper are mineral resources produced there.

CUNENE RIVER. A river that begins in the central highlands, flows south, then veers west, where it forms the Angola–**Namibia** border before emptying into the Atlantic. The river has hydroelectric dams—the Matala, Gove, Matunto, Ruancana, and Calueque—that provide more power than the area presently needs. The Gove was almost destroyed during the **civil war**. Another dam is planned, although Namibia and Angola disagree as to the final placement. Namibia wants the dam at Epola Falls, while Angola favors an area near the Byanes Mountains. The Cunene River has the capability to provide an enormous power supply not only to Angola but also to Namibia and **South Africa**. There has been criticism from human rights and environmental groups who oppose any more dam construction, arguing that valuable acreage will be flooded and traditional living areas of the local residents will be destroyed. The Himba people believe that "Epola Falls is God's Creation." The Himba traditional leader and his people believe that "When God made the falls, He left his footprint in the rock below."

– D –

DEFAMATION. *See DIFAMAÇÃO.*

DEGRADADOS. Exiled convicts sent from **Portugal** to Angola. The *degradados* were a substantial portion of Angola's white population through the 20th century.

DELL, CHRISTOPHER WILLIAM. U.S. Ambassador to Angola since June 2001. A career foreign service officer, William Dell had been the senior U.S. diplomat in Kosovo's provincial capital Pristina since February 2000. Previously, he served as deputy chief of mission in Maputo, Mozambique, and Sofia, Bulgaria.

DEMBO, ANTÓNIO SEBASTIÃO (1944–2002). António Dembo, born in Nambuangongo, **Luanda province**, was the son of Sebastião and Muhemba Kabuko. He completed his primary schooling at Muxaluando and Quimai Methodist schools. His secondary education was at El Harrach and the École Nationale d'Ingénieurs et Techniciens d'Algérie in Algeria. Dembo joined **União Nacional para a Independência Total de Angola** (UNITA) in 1970. After traveling throughout Africa on behalf of UNITA, Dembo returned in 1982 to become commander for the Northern Front and later the Northern Front chief of staff. In 1992, after the death of **Jeremias Chitunda**, he became UNITA's vice president and the general in charge of UNITA's Special Commandos, the Tupamaros. As the war turned against UNITA in 2001 and 2002, Dembo's forces were constantly on the run from government troops. After the death of **Jonas Savimbi**, Dembo became UNITA president, although only briefly. In February or March 2002, Dembo, according to different reports, died from either complications of diabetes, starvation, or wounds received in battle.

DEMOBILIZATION CAMPS. Established after the **Memorandum of Understanding** was signed in April 2002, the camps quickly became a potential flashpoint. So many **União Nacional para a Independência Total de Angola** (UNITA) soldiers and their families appeared at the camps so quickly that provisions, housing, hospitals, and schools were inadequate. As a result, dissatisfaction grew along with death and deprivation. The Angolan government, UNITA, the **United Nations**, and **nongovernmental organizations** (NGOs) appealed to the international community for assistance. Ultimately, over 85,000 troops and 300,000 family members assembled at the camps. At first, soldiers were given one kilo of rice, a small tin of fish, a small piece of dried fish, and a half kilo of maize. The allotment was to last 10 days. Food to soldiers' families was hit-and-miss. The Foro de ONGs Angolanas (FONGA) (Angolan Forum of Nongovernmental Agencies) was barred from the camps in May 2002. By 2003, the situation had improved, but the potential for troops to leave the camps to engage in banditry remained. *See also* HUMANITARIAN SITUATION.

DEMOCRATIC REPUBLIC OF THE CONGO (DRC). The DRC was known as **Zaire** during the rule of Mobutu Sese Seko. Mobutu seized power in 1965, and until his ouster in 1997 effectively plundered his own nation. His personal wealth at one time exceeded $4 billion. Opponents of Mobutu's one-party rule formed the Union for Democracy and Social Progress, whose leaders were harassed and imprisoned. The **United States**, a long-time supporter of Mobutu during the Cold War, ended military and economic aid because of alleged corruption and human rights abuses. During the genocide in Rwanda in 1994, some 1.3 million ethic Hutus fled into eastern Zaire. In October 1996, Zaire ordered the expulsion of ethnic Tutsis encamped in eastern Zaire, leading them to revolt. Led by **Laurent Kabila** and supported by several adjoining nations, the rebels advanced on the capital city, Kinshasa. With rebels about to enter the capital, Mobutu fled on 16 May 1997. On 7 September 1997, Mobutu died of cancer while exiled in Morocco. Laurent Kabila's government was corrupt, inefficient, and unresponsive to the needs of the people. Almost immediately after Kabila secured power, Congolese rebels launched a civil war attempting to overthrow the regime. As the rebels neared the capital city of Kinshasa, Angolan armored units intervened to rescue the Kabila government. Angola reported sending 2,500 troops into the Democratic Republic of the Congo. After the assassination of Laurent Kabila in 2001, Angola sent an extra 2,000 soldiers to ensure the continued rule of Kabila's son, Joseph. *See also* ZAIRIAN CIVIL WAR.

DIAKITE, JOSEFINA PITRA. Pitra Diakite became Angola's ambassador to the **United States** on 23 March 2001. She is the third Angolan ambassador to the United States since the two nations established diplomatic relations in 1993. Ambassador Diakite received a law degree from **Agostinho Neto** University, and she served as a member of the Ministry of External Affairs from 1991 until her U.S. appointment.

DIALO, ISSA. The **United Nations** envoy who replaced **Alioune Blondin Beye** in August 1998. Issa Dialo was born in Conakry, Guinea, in 1939. He graduated from the University of Paris with a degree in international relations and political science and received a doctorate from the Graduate Institute of International Studies at the University of Geneva.

DIAMONDS. Top quality gems were discovered in Angola and by 1971, Angola was mining 2.4 million carats. When **Portugal**'s African empire collapsed in 1974, so did Angola's production. The **União Nacional para a Independência Total de Angola** (UNITA) moved into the diamond region of **Lunda Norte** and **Lunda Sul** in the mid-1980s as **South African** support for UNITA began to ease. UNITA used the profits to purchase black-market weapons, food, and **petroleum** products. In 1986, the Companhia de Diamantes de Angola (DIAMANG) was liquidated due to excessive operating losses. It was replaced by the state-owned Empresa Nacional de Diamantes de Angola (ENDIAMA). In 2002, Angola produced 2.7 million carats, with a value of $329 million. Through the first half of 2003, 2.1 million carats with a value of $303 million were mined. Analysts believe that Angola could eventually mine over 6 million carats per year. According to one economist, Angola, "has the finest reserve of 2-carat, gem-quality diamonds in the world." After the civil war ended, the Angolan government hired the South Africa firm Mintek to develop not only the diamond sector but also other extractable minerals. *See also* ANGOLA SELLING CORPORATION; GARIMPEIROS; KIMBERLEY PROCESS.

DIAS, LÁZARO (1921–2003). Lázaro Dias was a long-standing member of the Assembleia Nacional (National Assembly) as a member of the **Movimento Popular de Libertação de Angola** (MPLA). During his service, he held the positions of justice minister and first vice speaker of the assembly.

DIAS, PAULO DE. Grandson of Bartolemeu Dias. In 1559, Paulo de Dias was sent by the **Portuguese** crown to be the representative to the **Mbundu** ruler. On Dias's arrival in 1561, the Mbundu promptly placed him under arrest and held him for four years. Upon returning to Portugal, he was instrumental in the policy to discard the Brother Kings philosophy in favor of military conquest. He arrived back in **Luanda** in 1575 as *donatário*. By the time of Dias's death in 1589, his forces had pushed only 10 miles into **Mbundu** territory.

***DIFAMAÇÃO* (defamation).** Article 46 of the Press Law makes it illegal to defame someone either in print, orally, or by any means of publication by imputing to that person a fact that is offensive to his/her dignity. If the person defamed is the president of Angola, proof of the facts attributed is not admissible. Violation of the law is a criminal offense punishable by one year in prison. In practice, a journalist is guilty if a prosecutor files charges. *See also INJÚRIA;* MEDIA.

DISLOCADOS. People displaced by the **civil war**.

DOCTORS WITHOUT BORDERS. See MÉDECINS SANS FRONTIÈRES.

DONATÁRIO. During the 16th century, land holdings in **Portuguese** colonies were given to nobles who were called *donatário,* or proprietors, the first of whom was **Paulo de Dias**. The *donatário* had administrative and fiscal responsibility for their areas.

DONOR FATIGUE. This signifies that international donors to humanitarian crises no longer contribute, because they have become weary of repeated appeals for donations. In Angola's case, international donors voiced concern that the Angola government, with **petroleum** and **diamond** revenues, was not doing more to assist its own people. Allegation of government corruption also made donors hesitant. Donor fatigue in Angola comes at a very crucial juncture, because so many lives are directly in the hands of international donors and aid agencies.

DUTCH INTERREGNUM (1641–1648). Portugal, at the insistence of Spain, became involved in a number of religious and political wars on the European continent during the first half of the 17th century. Spain's enemies, including Holland, became Portugal's enemies. The

Dutch began harassing Portugal's African empire, capturing
Benguela and **Luanda** in 1641. The Portuguese were unable to dis-
lodge the Dutch, who ended the **slave trade** to **Brazil**, severely affecting that economy. Brazilian colonists raised an army, sailed to
Angola, and forced the Dutch to surrender. Later, the Dutch abandoned the rest of their holdings wrested from Portugal.

– E –

ECONOMY. **Portugal**'s African colonies were meant to provide goods
and services to the Metropole, not to ease the Angolans' plight. What little economic progress and infrastructure existed was removed, sabotaged, or destroyed by the Portuguese when the **white settler** population
withdrew in 1974–75. Angola's flirtation with socialism, combined with
the disastrous effects of the **civil war**, further deteriorated the economic
state of the nation. However, the large deposits of **petroleum** and **diamonds**, combined with the government's turn toward free-market capitalism, provide reason for optimism. Subsistence **agriculture** is practiced by 85 percent of the population. Consequently, most of the food
requirements must be imported. Oil production and the attendant **industries** account for 90 percent of the gross domestic product (GDP).
The GDP totaled $16.9 billion in 2002. Beyond oil and diamonds, An-
gola is rich in natural resources, with gold, **timber**, and **fisheries**.

To fully take advantage of these resources, the government must
continue to reform its economic policies. Inflation has been brought
down from 325 percent in 1999 to 106 percent in 2002, but the government, as of September 2003, had failed to make sufficient progress
on reforms suggested by the **International Monetary Fund** (IMF),
such as increasing foreign exchange reserves and promoting greater
transparency in government and oil revenue financial accounts. Also
worrisome is Angola's external debt of $9.9 billion in 2002. Unem-
ployment and underemployment affect more than half the population,
with purchasing power parity at $1,600 in fiscal year 2002. Further
economic indicators, such as per capita income, population below
poverty, and numbers for unemployed and underemployed are not reliable. The **United States** is Angola's largest trading partner, accounting for 44.2 percent of its exports, totaling $8.6 billion in 2002. *See*

also NOVA VIDA; PROGRAMA DE AÇÃO GOVERNO; PROGRAMA DE ESTABILIÇÃO E RECUPERÇÃO ECONÔMICA DE MEDIO PRAZO 1998–2000; PROGRAMA ECONÔMICO E SOCIAL PARA1994; SANEAMENTO ECONÔMICO E FINANCIERO.

EDUCATION *(instrução)*. Angolans received little, if any, education from the **Portuguese** during the colonial era. Assimilated Angolans, along with *mestiços*, had some opportunity. The only available option for Angolans was through the missionary schools.

During the **civil war**, over 20,000 classrooms were destroyed. The classrooms that are still functioning report class sizes as large as 90 students. Over 70 percent of Angola's children do not attend school. The lack of classrooms combined with a shortage of educational professionals, **land mines**, poor **health**, lack of funds, displacement, and needed identity papers make school attendance difficult. Only 34 percent of the children who attend school reach the fifth grade. University education is accessible only to the elite. While public education is free, few parents can afford to send their children to school. Children start school late or leave early in order to enter the job market. Children leave school to take care of the home and siblings while the parents attempt to work or find work. As a result, by 2002, more than 2 million children were not in school, and illiteracy had climbed to over 60 percent. In July 2003, the Angolan government announced plans to spend $800 million on new schools, to rehabilitate schools, and to hire and train more teachers. The program, to be completed by 2015, is funded by the Angolan government, **Brazil**, the **African Investment Bank**, and others.

In November 2002, the Angolan government announced plans to construct universities across the nation. Science and technology schools would be built in the mineral-rich **provinces** of **Namibe**, **Lunda Sul**, **Uíge**, **Cabinda**, and **Benguela**. Medical schools would be built in **Bié**, **Huambo**, and **Huíla provinces**. Finally, an agricultural university would be constructed in **Malange**, with general learning institutions in **Kwanza Norte**, **Kwanza Sul**, **Bié**, Namibe, **Lunda Norte**, Lunda Sul, and **Malange**. In 2003, Angola had only three state universities, all located in **Luanda**: **Agostinho Neto** University, the **Universidade Catholic de Angola**, and the **Universidade Independente de Angola**.

ELECTIONS *(eleição).* The Angolan national elections held in September 1992 were the first free, fair elections ever conducted in the former **Portuguese** colony. Voters elected a parliament and the president. Voter registration was 4.8 million out of approximately 5.5 million people eligible to vote. Preelection violence was only sporadic, but complaints of voter registration irregularities, combined with only a partial troop demobilization, led to some concern. Eleven people campaigned for the presidency, but the two major presidential candidates were **Eduardo dos Santos** and **Jonas Savimbi**. Eighteen parties campaigned for parliamentary seats. There were 5,905 polling stations for the 4,828,468 voters. The **United Nations** provided only 400 monitors and civilian police in a nation the size of Texas and California combined. In **Namibia**, which has only 1.5 million citizens, the UN had sent 1,700 monitors. As early returns were tallied showing dos Santos and the **Movimento Popular de Libertação de Angola** (MPLA) with large presidential and parliamentary leads, Savimbi complained of fraud and threatened a return to war.

On 5 October, **União Nacional para a Independência Total de Angola** (UNITA) pulled its soldiers out of the newly established Angolan army. The final election results issued 16 October showed dos Santos with 49.6 percent of the vote, compared to Savimbi's 40.7 percent. Under the electoral law, because no candidate had won a majority, a runoff election was required to be held within 30 days. In the 223-seat parliamentary contest, the MPLA won 129 seats to UNITA's 70, with the rest being won by smaller parties. After one month of belligerent rhetoric by both the MPLA and UNITA, the **civil war** resumed in November 1992. No further elections have been held, but with peace in Angola, elections are being discussed for 2004 or 2005. Potential candidates announced by August 2003 included **Vicente Pinto de Andrade, Carlos Contreiras Gouveia, Analia Pereira**, and **Isaías Samakuva**.

EMPREGO DO CIDADÃO (Citizen Employment). A program begun in August 2002 designed to employ demobilized soldiers and youth.

ESTADO NOVO (new state). By 1933, **António Salazar** had consolidated political power in **Portugal**. He wrote a new colonial act, and a new constitution was drafted under which Portugal became a new state. Overseas territories were to be referred to as provinces, which were to become fully integrated into Portuguese culture, economy, and politics. In Angola, the reality was a centralization of the economy, severe repression of nationalistic tendencies, and press censorship. After World War II, the new state encouraged more Portuguese emigration to Angola. *See also* LUSOTROPICALISM.

ESTAMOS CONTIGO (We Are with You). A government–Chevron–Texaco program to reincorporate **União Nacional para a Independência Total de Angola** (UNITA) soldiers into private life through **education** and job placement. The classes will study electricity, **agriculture**, construction, masonry, carpentry, and water works.

EXECUTIVE OUTCOMES (EO). A **South Africa**–based **mercenary** company formed in 1989 that signed several multimillion dollar contracts with the Angolan government beginning in 1993. EO was hired to recapture Soyo from **União Nacional para a Independência Total de Angola** (UNITA) rebels. The first two contracts called for $7.5 million. The next contract hired EO to train the 16th Brigade, a brigade that had been virtually destroyed by South African forces in the 1980s. Later, the 16th successfully drove UNITA rebels from the rich **diamond**-producing areas of Angola. Ironically, since the South Africans had seen combat on behalf of UNITA rebels, they were well aware of rebel capabilities, tactics, strategy, and force deployments. Eventually, EO would have 2,000 employees in Angola working under a $40 million contract. The company hired South Africans, **Brazilians, Portuguese**, white **Namibians**, and Israelis. However, most Executive Outcomes personnel came from **South Africa**'s **32nd Battalion**, the Reconnaissance Commandos (Reccies), the Parachute Brigade (Parabats), and the South West African paramilitary unit **Koevoet** (Crowbar). The mercenary outfit admitted to losing 11 personnel dead and another seven missing in Angola. On 31 December 1998, Executive Outcomes stopped operating from South Africa after parliament enacted a law making it illegal for South African citizens to participate in other nations' wars.

EYADÉMA, GNASSINGBÉ. The president of Togo accused by the **United Nations** of assisting **União Nacional para a Independência**

Total de Angola (UNITA) to break sanctions by preparing phony paperwork to cover illegal arms purchases from Bulgaria. *See also* COMPAORÉ, BLAISÉ; KAGAME, PAUL.

– F –

FALCONE, PIERRE. A French national also holding Angolan citizenship who through his company, Brenco International, purchased arms for the government of Angola from 1993 to 2002. With his partner, **Arkady Gaydamek**, he shipped helicopters, MIG aircraft, and other weapons purchased through the Czech firm ZTS–Osos to Angola. French law in 1993 stated that France could sell neither to the Angolan government nor to the **União Nacional para a Independência Total de Angola** (UNITA). For French authorities, the problem was not with purchasing the arms or transporting the weapons to Angola, but stemmed from the financing of the sale. French investigators explored whether the government-owned export firm Sofremi had handled either money or paperwork. Further, Falcone owns three companies— Pro Dev, Naphta, and Falcon Oil—that have stakes in two of Angola's most promising deepwater oil exploration blocks. The questions raised included: Were the **petroleum** stakes a payoff to Falcone? and How high in the **Eduardo dos Santos** administration did the corruption rise? The French investigators in 2001 requested to interview members of the president's strategic cabinet. President dos Santos rejected the French request. On 26 September 2003, the Angolan government appointed Falcone as its minister–counselor to the United Nations Educational, Scientific and Cultural Organization (UNESCO), located in Paris. The action provided Falcone with diplomatic immunity. Angolan opposition parties denounced the appointment as "criminal." *See also* ANGOLAGATE; LEVIEV, LEV; MITTERRAND, JEAN-CHRISTOPHE.

FAMILY RECEPTION AREAS. The name given to camps for **União Nacional para a Independência Total de Angola (UNITA)** soldiers and their families. Over 80,000 soldiers and 300,000 dependents entered the camps. There, the soldiers were disarmed, demobilized, and given national identity cards. The government also provided a kit for the soldiers, which included clothing, domestic and agricultural tools, and approximately $100 in cash. The government intended to offer educational and vocational–technical courses to assist the soldiers in learning trades. Finally, the government transported the soldiers, with their families, to their native villages with the promise of land.

FATAL TRANSACTIONS. The international campaign by four **non-governmental organizations** (NGOs) to halt the illegal mining and selling of **diamonds** to **União Nacional para a Independência Total de Angola** (UNITA). *See also* GLOBAL WITNESS.

FAZENDA **(farm).** Large tracts of property once owned by **Portuguese** absentee owners. More recently, the *fazendas* have been owned by important members of the government and military. To revitalize the **agricultural** sector, the farms need to be subject to a land reform effort to provide land for peasant ownership. *See also* COFFEE.

FEIRA INTERNACIONAL DE LUANDA (FILDA) (Luanda International Trade Fair). The annual marketing event held by the government to lure international investors to Angola. The fair has been held 20 times with increasing participation from international industries and businesses. The 2003 fair, titled "Door to Africa—Window to the World," opened with 503 foreign and national exhibitors representing 21 nations. The most visible were **Portugal**, **South Africa**, **Brazil**, Spain, Germany, Botswana, and Zimbabwe. The **United States**, **Cuba**, Norway, China, Ghana, Russia, Cape Verde, Sweden, Poland, Israel, Holland, Austria, **Namibia**, and Italy also were represented. Businesses included those involved in food and beverages, telecommunications, industrial equipment, consultancy, construction and public works, and pharmaceuticals.

FEMALE GENITAL MUTILATION (FGM). An African practice widely condemned by international health experts as both physically and psychologically damaging. FGM is still practiced in remote areas of **Moxico province**. *See also* HEALTH CARE.

FISHING INDUSTRY. Angola is geographically situated where the cold **Benguela** current meets the warm Agulhas current, making the coastal waters one of the richest fishing regions on the globe. As with other aspects of the Angolan **economy**, the departing **Portuguese** in 1975 left little of the industry behind, taking most of the fishing vessels, destroying fish processing facilities, and withdrawing their expertise. Still, Angola's fishing catches have increased over the past several years. According to the Fisheries Ministry, 157,148 tons of fish were harvested from the ocean in 1998. The figure rose in 1999 to 169,799 tons, in 2000 to 232,350 tons, and in 2001 to 243,350 tons. The ministry attributed the increase to the application of new laws and more private initiative. However, there are problems looming in the future. Commercial drag fishing is harming the livelihood of local fishermen. The European Union (EU) has fishing treaties with many African nations, including Angola. The EU agreement with Angola does not place a limit on the amount of fish that can be netted. Overfishing is thus becoming a problem. Ships from other African nations, Europe, Asia, and Russia fish off Angola's shore. Local and commercial catches have increased 37 percent since 1999, and fish stocks in the Atlantic Ocean are a quarter of what they were 50 years ago. If trends continue, Angola's waters will suffer the same fate as those of the North Atlantic and will become overfished. Angola has purchased speedboats, trained inspectors, and launched a $33 million Monitoring and Control of Fishing Activities Project that allows Angolan officials to monitor the position, route, and cruising speed of international industrial-sized fishing vessels.

FITINHAS **(drugged, or drunk).** The word used to describe irregular soldiers who participated in the **Halloween Massacre** of October 1992.

FOLHA 8. A biweekly **newspaper** in **Luanda** edited by **William Tonet** and often very critical of government policies or perceived corruption.

FOOD FOR WORK. A program employed by many **nongovernmental organizations** (NGOs) to wean people away from handouts so they can achieve self-respect by working for food. **Refugees** or **internally displaced people** (IDPs) are put to work in schools, homes, and hospitals or at digging wells. The programs restore a sense of worth to the individual, help restore infrastructure destroyed by the war, and begin to transform the participants from relief agency cases to productive citizens.

FORÇAS ARMADAS DE ANGOLANAS (FAA) (Armed Forces of Angola). The FAA was created by the 1991 **Bicesse Accords**, which disbanded the **Forças Armadas Populares de Libertação de Angola** (FAPLA) of the **Movimento Popular de Libertação de Angola** (MPLA) and the **Forças Armadas de Libertação de Angola** (FALA) of **União Nacional para a Independência Total de Angola** (UNITA). The agreement called for a combined army of 52,600 soldiers, with the MPLA and UNITA each providing half of the force. By the time the **Govêno do Unidade e da Recociliação** (GURN) was inaugurated, UNITA had supplied only 7,000 of the required 26,300 soldiers. For the national police, only 300 of the 5,500 rebel members joined.

FORÇAS ARMADAS DE LIBERTAÇÃO DE ANGOLA (FALA) (Armed Forces for the Liberation of Angola). The name of the **União Nacional para a Independência Total de Angola** (UNITA) guerrilla army. Today it no longer exists, as some 5,000 FALA members were incorporated into the **Forças Armadas de Angolanas** (FAA) following the cease-fire of April 2002. During the late 1970s and most of the 1980s, FALA, commanded by **Jonas Savimbi**, may have been the best guerrilla army in the world. Disciplined, dedicated, and well commanded, FALA operated in 17 of Angola's 18 **provinces** and even occasionally ventured into the suburbs of **Luanda**. FALA had six types of forces: special, regular, semiregular, compact, intelligence, and dispersed. Special forces were trained in reconnaissance and sabotage. Regular forces were the conventional military units. Semiregular forces roamed certain areas, deployed as the need arose. Compact troops were the true guerrilla portion of FALA and employed Maoist warfare techniques. Military intelligence was handled by Service de Intelligencia Militar. The dispersed forces, whose main function was as porters or in food production, were poorly trained. UNITA also made valuable use of Hunter (Caçador) Units. To thwart a mechanized attack, UNITA placed recoilless rifles on four-wheel drive vehicles, usually Toyota Land

Cruisers, and employed them as highly mobile, lethal tank killers. At one point, FALA numbered approximately 110,000 troops, although reliable figures do not exist. **United Nations sanctions**, combined with a shift in government military tactics, finally defeated FALA.

FORÇAS ARMADAS POPULARES DE LIBERTAÇÃO DE ANGOLA (FAPLA) (Popular Armed Forces for the Liberation of Angola). The name of the **Movimento Popular de Libertação de Angola** (MPLA) army, which fought during the late colonial period against the **Portuguese** and later against **União Nacional para a Independência Total de Angola** (UNITA). FAPLA was often poorly trained and led, and its morale suffered for years. Usually unpaid and forcibly recruited, FAPLA troops performed poorly until mercenary firms such as **Executive Outcomes** began to train the army. FAPLA would be merged into the **Forças Armadas de Angolanas** (FAA) in 1992 under the **Bicesse Accords**.

FOREIGN RELATIONS. Angola's colonial power, **Portugal**, was a member of the North Atlantic Treaty Organization (NATO) after World War II. Most NATO members, including the **United States**, disapproved of Portuguese policy toward its African possessions. However, the logic of the Cold War muted excessive criticism. **South Africa**'s policy of apartheid was similarly overlooked, as Portugal and South Africa were viewed as bastions against African communism.

From 1975 until 1989, Angola was closely aligned politically and militarily to the **Soviet Union** and **Cuba**. Since the **Movimento Popular de Libertação de Angola** (MPLA) **Third Party Congress**, Angola has steered sharply toward the West, improving relations with the United States and Europe. Angola has also sought to expand contacts with the Portuguese-speaking world. African policy has seen Angola flex its military muscle in the **Democratic Republic of the Congo** and the Republic of the Congo, where it overthrew pro-**União Nacional para a Independência Total de Angola** (UNITA) governments. With the end of the **civil war**, Angola has taken the lead in the **Southern African Development Community** (SADC), making successful overtures to **Namibia**, South Africa, and Zimbabwe, and Angolan–**United Nations** relations have remained steady. Angola worked for years to have the **United Nations Security Council** enact and enforce sanctions against UNITA. Present-day Angola is a member of the UN, the African Union (AU), the World Health Organization (WHO), and the International Monetary Fund (IMF), to name but a few.

4 DE FEVEREIRO CAMPO DE AVIAÇÃO (February 4th International Airport). The **Luanda** international airport. The name refers to 4 February 1961, the date of the Luanda uprising by the **Movimento Popular de Libertação de Angola** (MPLA) partisans, who attacked the prisons of São Paulo and Casade Reclusão, trying to release political detainees.

FOWLER COMMISSION REPORT. Robert Fowler served as Canadian ambassador to the **United Nations** and as the chairman of the United Nations Sanctions Committee on Angola. His report, issued on 14 March 2000, accused **Togo** of allowing **União Nacional para a Independência Total de Angola** (UNITA) to use the country as a political base. Togo's president **Gnassingbé Eyadéma** provided money to **Jonas Savimbi**'s family members and helped ship weapons to the rebels. Burkina Faso was accused of sending fuel to UNITA, and Burkina Faso's president **Blaisé Compaoré** was termed **Jonas Savimbi**'s closest friend among African leaders. Rwanda was charged with breaking United Nations sanctions by assisting UNITA aircraft to refuel. Gabon was also accused of shipping fuel to UNITA and of allowing the refueling of aircraft destined for UNITA territory. Bulgaria was accused of selling weapons to UNITA. In addition, it trained the rebels on how to operate the weapons. Belgium purchased undocumented **diamonds** from the rebels. **South Africa**, **Zambia**, Côte d'Ivoire, Morocco, and Belgium were identified as having lax sanctions, allowing UNITA personnel to move freely. Military equipment was secured by the South African brothers, the De Deckers, and the president of Zaire, Mobutu Sese Seko, also assisted. The **United States**, France, Germany, **Portugal**, and Switzerland were criticized for allowing UNITA to maintain offices.

The Fowler Commission recommended the following: the **Southern African Development Community** (SADF) should establish a regional air-control network to better track illegal aircraft, and the

United Nations Security Council should publicly list nations and individuals assisting the rebels, impose sanctions against those nations breaking Security Council resolutions, and establish a monitoring mechanism to follow up on the Fowler Commission Report. *See also* MONITORING MECHANISM'S FINAL REPORT ON SANCTIONS AGAINST UNITA.

FOXBAT COLUMN. Toward the end of August 1975, **South Africa** agreed to establish two training bases in Angola: one for **União Nacional para a Independência Total de Angola** (UNITA) at Calombo and another for Daniel Chipenda's **Frente Nacional de Libertação de Angola** (FNLA) unit at Mapupa. The Calombo force was led by a South African colonel with 18 instructors. They assisted UNITA in stopping the **Movimento Popular de Libertação de Angola** (MPLA) advance on **Huambo**. Later, South Africa reinforced its troops with six armored cars, allowing UNITA to secure the central plateau. *See also* OPERATION ZULU.

FRANÇA, ANTÓNIO DOS DANTOS (1938–). António França was born on 9 April 1938 in Mupa, **Cunene province**. Trained as an **agricultural** engineer, he studied both in Angola and abroad. He was appointed to the **Movimento Popular de Libertação de Angola** (MPLA) Central Committee in 1974 and became a member of the Political Bureau in 1977. His career has been impressive: he served as commander of the Presidential Regiment, chief of staff of the Angolan Armed Forces from 1982 to 1990, and first vice minister of defense. In diplomatic service, França served as chief of the Angolan delegation for Peace in Southern Africa (the **Brazzaville Protocol**), chief of the Military Commission of the Delegation for the **Bicesse Accords**, and head of the government delegation on the Joint Political/Military Commission for Compliance with the Bicesse Accords. He was appointed as Angola's ambassador to the **United States** and served from 1996 to 2001.

FRENTE DE LIBERTAÇÃO DO ENCLAVE DE CABINDA (FLEC) (Front for the Liberation of the Enclave of Cabinda). **Cabinda** is separated from Angola by a thin strip of the **Democratic Republic of the Congo**. However, the Organization of

African Unity (OAU) recognized Cabinda as an integral part of Angola. As independence neared in 1975, the **Movimento Popular de Libertação de Angola** (MPLA), **União Nacional para a Independência Total de Angola** (UNITA), and **Frente Nacional de Libertação de Angola** (FNLA) agreed that Cabinda was part of Angola. However, Cabinda had a liberation organization, FLEC, that argued for an independent Cabinda. Three movements coalesced to form FLEC: the Movimento de Libertação do Enclave do Cabinda (MLEC) (Liberation Movement of the Enclave of Cabinda), the Comité de Accão da União Nacional de Cabinda (CAUNC) (Action Committee of the National Cabindese Union), and the Alliance du Mayombe (ALLIAMA) (National Alliance of the Mayombe). Founded in 1963 by Ranque Franque, FLEC believed that Cabinda had been incorporated into Angola by the **António Salazar** regime in 1958 in violation of the Treaty of Simulambuco. In 1885, Cabindan chiefs had signed an agreement with the **Portuguese** granting Portugal trading rights in Cabinda in return for protection against territorial encroachments by the Congo Free State of King Leopold II of Belgium. After the **Movimento das Forças Armadas** coup in 1974, FLEC was optimistic that Cabindan independence would be granted. The Portuguese governor of Cabinda, Brigadier General Temudo Barata, lent his support to FLEC. However, after two days of battles between the MPLA and FLEC, the Portuguese military intervened, arresting Barata. Portuguese intervention allowed the MPLA to gain dominance in the **petroleum**-rich **province**. Since 1975, FLEC has maintained a low-level insurgency. Cabinda's drive for independence has been undermined by the split of FLEC into the Frente de Libertação do Enclave de Cabinda–Renovada (FLEC–R) and the Frente de Libertação do Enclave de Cabinda–Forças Armadas de Cabinda (FLEC–FAC).

FRENTE DE LIBERTAÇÃO DO ENCLAVE DE CABINDA–FORÇAS ARMADAS DO CABINDA (FLEC–FAC) (Front for the Liberation of the Enclave of Cabinda–Armed Forces of Cabinda). Formed by a split in the Frente de Libertação do Enclave de Cabinda (FLEC) in 1975, FLEC–FAC is led by Henrique Nzita Tiago. FLEC–FAC operates inside **Cabindan** territory, while the

Frente de Libertação do Enclave de Cabinda–Renovada (FLEC–R) operates as a government-in-exile.

All three groups maintain popularity in Cabinda, but all lack funds and arms. In October 2002, the Angolan army claimed to have captured the rebel group's chief of staff, General Francisco Lwenba, and the minister of defense, Estanislau Boma, a claim denied by FLEC–FAC. The report was ultimately proven false. However, further offensive actions by the Angolan army led to the surrender of FLEC–FAC army chief Lwenba and six other high-ranking rebels in June 2003. Lwenba joined the Angolan army in October 2003 with the rank of lieutenant colonel.

FRENTE DE LIBERTAÇÃO DO ENCLAVE DE CABINDA– RENOVADA (FLEC–R) (Front for the Liberation of the Enclave of Cabinda–Renewed). Formed by the split in the **Frente de Libertação do Enclave de Cabinda** (FLEC) in 1975, FLEC–R is led by Antonio Lopes. FLEC–R acts more as a government-in-exile than as a liberation movement. However, all three **Cabindan** factions enjoy strong local support but lack financial and military resources. *See also* FRENTE DE LIBERTAÇÃO DO ENCLAVE DE CABINDA–FORÇAS ARMADAS DO CABINDA.

FRENTE NACIONAL DE LIBERTAÇÃO DE ANGOLA (FNLA) (National Front for the Liberation of Angola). Modern **Bakongo** nationalism initially sought to restore the Bakongo Kingdom. In 1957, the União das Populações do Norte de Angola (UPNA) (Union of People of North Angola) was founded. Later, UPNA decided to send a representative abroad to present its case to the world community. The person chosen was **Holden Roberto**, nephew of UPNA president Manuel Barros Necaca. While at the First All-African People's Conference (AAPC) in Ghana, Roberto changed the name of UPNA to União das Populações de Angola (UPA) (Union of People of Angola). Single-handedly, Roberto transformed the group from a sectionalist to a nationalist organization. At various times, Roberto was urged to merge with the **Movimento Popular de Libertação de Angola** (MPLA), but he rejected the notion.

On 15 March 1961, UPA guerrillas launched an uprising in northern Angola that led to the deaths of hundreds of white settlers and thousands of Africans. Many Angolans fled to the Congo, where they were recruited into the UPA. UPA merged with the Partido Democrático de Angola (PDA, Democratic Party of Angola) on 28 March 1962 to form the FNLA. One month later, the Govêrno Revolucionário de Angola no Exílio (GRAE) (Angola's Revolutionary Government-in-Exile) was formed. As the date for independence approached, most observers believed that the FNLA had the strongest militarily of the three movements. The FNLA had been trained and armed by the Chinese and had the largest military contingent. But the FNLA was decimated in the **Battle of Death Road** and never achieved prominence again. Roberto spent considerable time in Kinshasa, Zaire, and was eventually challenged for the party leadership by **Lucas Ngonda** in 1999. The FNLA held its Second Congress in 1999 and elected a 288-member Central Committee. Holden Roberto was awarded the post of honorary chairman, an offer he declined. In 2003, Roberto and Ngonda met to mend fences and try to revitalize the party. *See also* MATADI ROYALISTS.

FRONT LINE STATES. These included Angola, Botswana, Nigeria, Mozambique, Zimbabwe, Tanzania, and **Zambia**. The original intention was for the states to provide support to one another in the face of aggression by apartheid **South Africa**.

FUNDAÇÃO EDUARDO DOS DANTOS (FESA) (Eduardo dos Santos Foundation). The philanthropic and cultural organization founded by Angola's president in 1996. Much of the foundation's money comes from international **petroleum** firms eager to stay in the president's good graces. In July 2003, FESA opened a Canadian office with its local partner, Canadaide, seeking to gain experience in community development, **AIDS/HIV**, and technological development. Critics deride FESA as the "ultimate fruit" of state privatization. The group has offices in **Brazil**, Spain, Egypt, and Hong Kong.

FUTUNGO MARKET. Located south of **Luanda**, the bazaar is the largest handicraft market in Angola. Open only on Sunday, the market hosts mostly **Mbundu** and **Bakongo** traders, though other ethnolinguistic groups are also represented. Bands play traditional Angolan songs, and more mundane supplies can also be purchased.

– G –

***GALO NEGRO* (black cockerel).** The black rooster is a party symbol of **União Nacional para a Independência Total de Angola** (UNITA).

GAMBARI, IBRAHIM. The **United Nations** secretary-general's special adviser on Africa. He was named to lead the United Nations Mission to Angola (UNMA) from September 2002 until February 2003. He was replaced in December 2002 by **Erick de Mul**. Gambari became nonresident representative until February 2003.

GANGUELA GROUP. Twenty ethnolinguistic groups make up the Ganguela. They are the Ambuela, Ambuila–Mambumaba, Avico, Bunda, Cangali, Camachi, Econjeiro, Ganguila, Gengista, Iahuma, Lovale, Luena, Luimbe, Lutchazi, Mbande, Ncoia, Ndungo, Nhemba, Nhengo, and Ngonoielo. The economy of the Ganguela is based upon hunting, **agriculture**, and **fishing**. Fishing was especially important because the Ganguela group is located in eastern Angola, where many well-stocked rivers are found. The 20 groups together make up 7 percent of Angola's population.

***GARIMPEIROS* (gold washers).** Freelance **diamond** diggers working the diamond-rich **provinces** of Angola. Estimates of the number of diggers range from 100,000 to 200,000. It is estimated that the informal diggers mine diamonds worth $240 million per year. *See also* ANGOLA SELLING CORPORATION.

GASOSAS. Literally, this means "soft drink," but the word is commonly used to describe a bribe.

GAYDAMEK, ARKADY. Paris-based arms dealer accused of illegally selling weapons to the Angolan government, in partnership with **Lev Leviev** of Israel and **Pierre Falcone**. Arkady Gaydamek is reported to have French, Israeli, Angolan, and Canadian citizenship. *See also* ANGOLAGATE; MITTERRAND, JEAN-CHRISTOPHE.

GAZETA CRUZ VERMELHA (Red Cross Gazette). A booklet published by the Cruz Vermelha de Angola (CVA) (Angolan Red Cross) and begun in 2002 in an attempt to reunite relatives separated by the civil war. Copies were distributed in Angola, **Namibia**, **Zambia**, and the **Democratic Republic of the Congo**. The *Gazette* will be updated every four months. If relatives recognize a family member, they notify the CVA or the International Committee of the Red Cross (ICRC), which assist in the reconnection. The information is also on the ICRC website for Angolans living abroad. By October 2002, 175 children had been reunited with their relatives. The *Red Cross Gazette* is the first of its kind on the African continent. *See also* MEDIA.

GBADOLITE DECLARATION. On 2 June 1989, **União Nacional para a Independência Total de Angola** (UNITA) president **Jonas Savimbi** shook hands with Angolan president **Eduardo dos Santos** in Gbadolite, Zaire. Gbadolite, the hometown of President Mobutu Sese Seko, was the site of a luxurious palace called the "Versailles of the Jungle." The meeting was the first ever between Savimbi and dos Santos. The handshake, witnessed by 17 African leaders, was supposed to signify a meeting of minds, but any agreement arrived at was sketchy at best. Most of the details were deferred to a later date. The meeting was the work of President Mobutu of Zaire; in attendance were leaders from Angola, Botswana, Burundi, Cameroon, the Cape Verde Islands, Chad, the Central African Republic, Côte d'Ivoire, Gabon, Mali, Mozambique, Nigeria, Sao Tomé and Príncipe, Tanzania, Zaire, **Zambia**, and Zimbabwe. Part of the agreement called for a cease-fire to begin on 24 June. Another section, later disputed, called for Savimbi to go into either internal or external exile. Savimbi's future status immediately caused a firestorm. The **Movimento Popular de Libertação de Angola** (MPLA) argued that UNITA had agreed to be incorporated into the MPLA with an offer of some governorships and cabinet posts. UNITA countered that continued negotiations were the legacy of Gbadolite. Almost immediately, both sides reported cease-fire violations. By 25 August, the Gbadolite Declaration was a dead letter. What had happened? The Gbadolite Declaration was so vaguely worded that it was open to multiple interpretations. Another problem was Mobutu. In order to be a successful mediator of the 14-year-old **civil war**, Mobutu told Savimbi and dos Santos what he thought they wanted to hear. Later, it was learned that the UNITA and MPLA delegations had never sat in the same room. Instead, Mobutu floated from room to room, reassuring delegates, but neither asking for nor receiving any proposals or concessions. The peace process limped along for a few more months, but the MPLA and UNITA were never able to make it back to the handshake stage, much less forge a formal peace agreement, until 1991. President Mobutu's mediation value was crippled as neither side trusted him, and thus the war continued.

GLOBAL OIL DEAL. Proposal by the **nongovernmental organization** (NGO) Christian Aid that would oblige oil companies and countries to publish details and revenues from **petroleum** production and sales. In a report titled *Fuelling Poverty: Oil, War and Corruption* released in 2003, Christian Aid alleged a direct link between exploitation of petroleum resources and indicators of high poverty rates, such as low spending for **health** services, low school attendance rates, poor adult literacy, and high **child** malnutrition. The NGO called for a global commission to create regulations to reverse the effect. In the case of Angola, Christian Aid asserts that the national oil revenues are not disclosed in the state budget and that no mention is made of how the revenue is spent. *See also* GLOBAL WITNESS.

GLOBAL WITNESS. An advocacy group based in London that has investigated **União Nacional para a Independência Total de Angola** (UNITA) black-marketing of **diamonds** as well as the government's lack of transparency involving **petroleum** revenues. In 1998, Global Witness published *A Rough Trade: The Role of Companies and Governments in the Angolan Conflict.* The report accused major diamond dealers of knowingly purchasing stones from UNITA, thereby allowing the rebels to rearm and resupply. It was estimated that from 1992 to 1998 UNITA sold $3.7 billion worth of diamonds illegally. Global Witness also accused several countries and companies of breaking **United Nations sanctions** against the rebel group. The diamond report was followed in 1999 by the report titled *A Crude Awakening.* This report detailed government corruption in the Angolan oil industry and how top government officials skimmed funds off the top. The report was also highly critical of international **petroleum** companies and banks. In a 2002 report titled *All the President's Men,* Global Witness probed even deeper into government corruption.

GOUVEIA, CARLOS ALBERTO CONTREIRAS. President of the Partido Republicano de Angola (PREA) (Angolan Republican Party) who announced in March 2003 that he would stand as a candidate for the Angolan presidency.

GÔVERNO DA UNIDADE E DA RECONCILIAÇÃO NACIONAL (GURN) (Government of National Unity and Reconciliation). After two cancellations, the GURN was formally established on 11 April 1997, after **União Nacional para a Independência Total de Angola** (UNITA) parliamentarians arrived in **Luanda** to take their positions. The GURN was composed of 29 ministers and 56 vice ministers drawn from all political parties represented in the **Assembleia Nacional** (National Assembly). **Jonas Savimbi** was given legal status as "leader of the largest opposition party." He was also allocated a home, a salary, and personal bodyguards paid for by the government. Savimbi never returned to Luanda. The **Movimento Popular de Libertação de Angola** (MPLA) government, frustrated at the slowness of the peace process, suspended UNITA from the GURN on 31 August 1998. The government cited UNITA's "dubious attitude" toward the **Lusaka Protocol** as the reason for this move. Later, the MPLA government would allow **União Nacional para a Independência Total de Angola–Renovada** (UNITA-R) members to serve in the government.

GRUPO ANGOLANO DE REFLEXAO PARA PAZ (GARP) (Angolan Group for the Reflection of Peace). A peace group founded on 2 April 1999 by **Daniel Ntoni-Nzinga**, a theologian; Carlinhos Zassala, a professor at **Agostinho Neto** University; Filomeno Viera Lopes, an economist; Francisco Tunga Alberto, general secretary of the FONGA; and **Rafael Marques de Morais**, a journalist. The group called on the **Movimento Popular de Libertação de Angola** (MPLA) and **União Nacional para a Independência Total de Angola** (UNITA) to stop fighting and place the Angolan people first. The platform called for an end to international mediation, which had not worked, and a beginning of Angolan mediation to resolve differences between the two warring parties. The overall goal of all Angolans, according to the group, should be peace. *See also* COMITÉ INTER-ECLESIAL PARA A PAZ EM ANGOLA; REDE DA PAZ.

GUERRA DA INDEPENDÊ NCIA (War of Independence). The war against **Portuguese** colonialism, which lasted from 1961 until 1975.

GUERRA DA MATO (War of the Bush). The second phase of the war in Angola, the phase between Angolan liberation movements during which they were assisted by their foreign sponsors. It lasted from 1975 to 1991.

GUERRA DAS CIDADES (War of the Cities). The third phase of the war in Angola, which lasted from late 1992 until late 1994.

GUICHET ÚNICO DA EMPRESA (GUE) (One Stop Shop). Started in August 2003, the GUE is a menagerie of government offices located at one site. The GUE hopes to make interaction between the government and population more user friendly.

– H –

HALLOWEEN MASSACRE. Term applied to events in **Luanda** over the weekend of 30 October to 1 November 1992. After **União Nacional para a Independência Total de Angola** (UNITA) questioned the validity of the Angola national **elections**, both sides increased their war rhetoric. Despite continued negotiations toward the second round of presidential elections, the **Movimento Popular de Libertação de Angola** (MPLA) partisans, army, and police attacked UNITA positions throughout Luanda during Halloween weekend. UNITA vice president **Jeremias Chitunda**, top negotiator Elias Salupeto Pena, and party secretary Aliceres Mango were killed. **Abel Chivukuvuku**, the UNITA foreign affairs spokesman, was seriously wounded and **Arlindo Chenda Pena, Forças Armadas de Libertação de Angola** (FALA) chief of staff, was also wounded but escaped. **Church** sources later reported that 25,000–30,000 UNITA and **Frente Nacional de Libertação de Angola** (FNLA) supporters were killed over the weekend and during the following days. *See also* BLOODY FRIDAY; NINJA.

HARE, PAUL. A U.S. special representative to Angola under President Bill Clinton who helped negotiate the **Lusaka Protocol** in 1994.

Later, he served as chairman of the **U.S.–Angola Chamber of Commerce**.

HAVEMOS DE VOLTAR (We Will Return). A theater and dance troupe funded by the Lutheran World Federation (LWF) and Action by Churches Together (ACT) that uses skits, dancing, and drumming to teach people about **AIDS/HIV** and other community issues. All the members of the troupe, which was founded in 1990, were displaced by the **civil war**.

HEALTH CARE. The **civil war**, government spending priorities, **refugees**, **internally displaced people** (IDPs), and poverty have combined to make Angola's health care system one of the world's worst. Over 1,500 hospitals and clinics were destroyed or severely damaged. There is a lack of medicines and trained medical personnel. Several easily treatable diseases are rampant. One malady, endemic goiter, which is caused by insufficient use of iodized salt, affects over 2 million Angolans. Another is leprosy, of which Angola has one of the highest infection rates in southern Africa, with the number of patients doubling from 2001 to 2002. If not treated, leprosy can lead to deformities and blindness. Lymphatic filariasis is a disease clinically known as elephantiasis. In the provinces of **Lunda Norte** and **Lunda Sul** infection rates exceed 40 percent. The **nongovernmental organization** (NGO) World Vision launched a campaign in 2003 to treat the disease. Finally, pellagra is a skin disease caused by a vitamin B deficiency. Health care NGOs provide peanut butter to help provide needed nutrients. Angola also faces a medical crisis with **AIDS/HIV** and **malaria**. Less serious are **measles** and **polio** because they can be easily prevented by vaccination. Less than half the population uses government medical facilities when they are ill because of long waits, lack of medicines, the poor quality of care, and the imposition of unofficial fees. Only 40 percent of the population has access to safe drinking water and sanitation. The average life expectancy is only 44 years. In 2002, measles, tuberculosis, and malaria accounted for 70 percent of the deaths in Angola. The **United Nations** Children's Fund (UNICEF) estimated that in 2002 chronic malnutrition levels were 46 percent. *See also* CHILDREN.

HEINBECKER, PAUL. A Canadian appointed by the **United Nations Security Council** in August 2000 to replace Robert Fowler as the chairman of the Committee to Investigate **União Nacional para a Independência Total de Angola** (UNITA) violations of UN Sanctions.

HERERO GROUP. The Herero people are known by such names as Chavicuas, Chimbas, Cuanhocas, Cuavales, Dimbas, Dombes, Guendelengos, and Hacavonas. Historically, the Herero were pastoralists. They occupy the present-day **provinces** of **Huíla**, **Benguela**, and **Namibe**. Related groups are also located in **Namibia**.

HEXÀGONO DA OPERAÇÃO (Operation Hexagon). Government military effort launched in April 2000 to complete destruction of **União Nacional para a Independência Total de Angola** (UNITA) conventional military units. During the attacks, the **Forças Armadas de Angolanas** (FAA) captured Cangumbe, Cangonga, Chicala, Cuemba, and Munhango. UNITA suffered heavy losses in men and war materiel. The operation ended in August 2000. *See also* CIVIL WAR.

HIGH DIAMOND COUNCIL. The High Diamond Council was accused by the **Fowler Commission Report** of knowingly purchasing **União Nacional para a Independência Total de Angola** (UNITA) **diamonds**. The Diamond Council, based in Antwerp, Belgium, is the industry group that promotes and oversees Belgium's $20 billion per year industry. Antwerp is the world's largest diamond trading center, accounting for 85 percent of the trade in rough diamonds and 50 percent of the trade in polished stones. Israel and India are also prominent diamond centers.

HORIZONTE NZINGA MBANDE. Angolan theater troupe founded in 1986. The goal of the actors is to acquaint the nation with the poetry and prose of its citizens. Productions of the group include *Risos Diluidos* (Diluted laughs), *A Madrasta* (The stepmother), *O Padrasto* (The stepfather), *Fabiana* (Fabian), and *Lueji—Nascemento de um Império* (Lueji: the birth of an empire). The troupe is supported by the Angolan Writers Union (UEA) and performs every Friday. *See also* CULTURE.

HOSTAGES. As part of **União Nacional para a Independência Total de Angola** (UNITA) strategy to weaken the government economically, the rebels began to capture hostages, march them hundreds of miles to **Jamba**, then release them before the international press. Hostages from friendly nations such as **Portugal** or the **United States** were released relatively quickly. Hostages from unfriendly nations such as Great Britain or the **Soviet Union** were held indefinitely. Captured **Cubans** were usually executed on the spot. Most of the hostages said UNITA treated them well, and some expressed admiration for the movement. But all complained about the long marches, some hundreds of miles, and that life in Jamba was boring. **Jonas Savimbi** admitted to capturing hostages to place economic pressure on the government, but he also maintained that the hostages would be returned when the war was over. He also employed hostage taking as a way to legitimate UNITA in European eyes. Often, the only way UNITA would release a European was if a diplomat from the person's nation traveled to Jamba to ask for the release.

HUAMBO. Once called Nova Lisboa, or New Lisbon, Huambo is a **province** and the name of its capital city. Huambo city was founded in 1912. Located in the central highlands, the province has a population of about 750,000. The climate is temperate, allowing for the growth of potatoes, rice, fruits, and olives. Mineral resources include gold and tungsten. It was once noted for its architecture and flowering tropical plants that were exported. Huambo city stands on a high plateau and serves as a road, **rail**, and air transport hub for central Angola. Before the war, its railway repair shops were among the largest in Africa. On 6 March 1993, **União Nacional para a Independência Total de Angola** (UNITA) forces captured the city after a 55-day siege. Most of the 400,000 residents fled into the bush. An estimated 15,000 were killed. The capture of the city was important because it is located in the heart of UNITA territory. **Jonas Savimbi** was so intent on capturing Huambo that he ordered human wave tactics in the latter stages of the battle to overwhelm government positions. The **Catholic Church** in the city described the battle as "one of the bloodiest battles in African history." The government was able to reorganize and reequip its army. In June 1994, government troops initiated a nationwide offensive to recapture cities and ground held by the rebels. The siege of **Kuito** was broken. Finally, on 9 November, government forces recaptured Huambo city. UNITA, despite deploying a large number of troops, could not halt the offensive, and it made a tactical error by attempting to protect a stationary target with guerrilla forces against a force equipped with heavy armor, artillery, and air power. Many of the government soldiers were residents of Huambo who had been forced from their homes in the earlier battles. Government troops also benefited from training by **Executive Outcomes** and other mercenary firms.

HUÍLA. A **province** in southwestern Angola and the capital city of the same name. With a population of about 450,000, the area produces wheat, cereals, and livestock in a temperate climate.

HUMANITARIAN SITUATION. After the **Memorandum of Understanding** was signed in April 2002, **nongovernmental organizations** (NGOs) had the opportunity to work in areas they previously were barred from. In the "newly accessible areas," the NGOs discovered truly horrific conditions. Mortality and malnutrition rates were five to 10 times above emergency threshold levels. Some 200,000 people were suffering from advanced malnutrition. Critical malnutrition rates were reported throughout the nation. Basic **health care**, sanitation, potable water, essential nonfood items, and identity cards did not exist. The NGOs reported that, unless massive amounts of food and medicines arrived, hundreds of thousands of Angolans would soon perish. The medical NGO **Médecins sans Frontières** said the humanitarian crisis in Angola was the worst in Africa in a decade. In October 2002, the **United Nations** called the situation in Angola "one of the worst in the world." According to one NGO, half a million people faced imminent starvation. Civilians were targets during the civil war. The government forced them to leave the rural areas to prevent them from supporting the **União Nacional para a Independência Total de Angola** (UNITA), while the rebels needed the civilians for various military duties. Consequently, many people fled or were forced by the warring parties to be on the move constantly. As a result, no one could plant or harvest crops. When the war ended, the civilians had nowhere to go. Another unforeseen problem was that, once people were receiving adequate daily nutrition, they were urged to return to their home areas.

Unfortunately, the areas were not prepared for an influx of people. There were no seeds, tools, medical facilities, or housing available. **Land mines** also made internal travel by **internally displaced people** (IDPs) or aid agencies difficult. Consequently, many IDPs quickly faced a serious nutrition problem. Questions were raised as to whether the government that had won the war was now on the verge of losing the peace. The United Nations Development Program warned that, despite the war's end, food shortages were increasing and would not ease until returning refugees made their first harvest. The report further stated that 60 percent of Angolans lived below the poverty level, earning less than $1.68 per day. *See also* DEMOBILIZATION CAMPS.

HYDROELECTRIC POWER. Angola possesses a number of rivers that can provide a substantial amount of hydroelectric power. The Cunene, **Cuango**, Cubango, and **Kwanza** Rivers either have already been or are scheduled to begin producing electricity. Most of the expertise and capital were provided by **Portugal** and **South Africa**. The Gove Dam on the Cunene River was meant to provide power to **Huambo**. However, **União Nacional para a Independência Total de Angola** (UNITA) rebels destroyed the generators and almost destroyed the dam itself. While several of the dams need reconditioning or modernizing, power lines and distribution facilities are in poor condition and there is a lack of homes capable of receiving electricity. For now, the current generating capacity is far more than needed. Thus Angola can sell excess electricity to **Namibia**, Botswana, and South Africa to earn much needed foreign exchange.

– I –

IMPARCIAL FAX. The first daily independent **newspaper** licensed by the government, in February 1994. The paper had only 300 subscribers, but thousands of daily readers. Founded by Jaime Goncalves, it was edited by **Ricardo de Melo**, who was assassinated by unknown assailants in 1995. The night de Melo was killed, two of his reporters were also assaulted. *See also* MEDIA.

INDENI PETROLEUM REFINERY. Zambia's only oil refinery was nearly destroyed in May 1999 by a fire that broke out under mysterious circumstances. Angola had accused the Zambian government of harboring **União Nacional para a Independência Total de Angola** (UNITA) rebels, a charge the Zambian government denied. On 11 May, the intelligence and defense ministers of Angola and Zambia met in Swaziland to discuss the growing tension between the two nations. The talks broke down the same day. Exactly one week later, the refinery incident occurred. The governments of Zaire and the Republic of the Congo were replaced by the **Forças Armadas de Angolanas** (FAA) because of their support for UNITA, and the refinery blaze was seen as a warning to Zambia from Angola to end all support for UNITA. The refinery is of strategic importance to Zambia because it is the main supplier of fuel to the country's copper mines. Two days earlier, a fire at the main **petroleum** storage facility in Côte d'Ivoire was destroyed by arson of unknown origin. Côte d'Ivoire had also been a strong supporter of UNITA. In December 2000, the Indeni refinery, which cost $12 million to repair, resumed production after 18 months.

INDÍGENAS. An African without *mestiço* or *assimilado* status: under **Portuguese** rule such a station meant uncivilized. When the distinctions were abolished in 1961, 99 percent of all Africans were still categorized as *indígenas*.

INDUSTRY. As with most of Angola's economic infrastructure, when the **Portuguese** left in 1975 they destroyed, disabled, or took most of the industrial capability. For example, in 1974 Angola had nearly 4,000 manufacturing entities employing 200,000 people and producing $650 million in goods and services. By March 1976, there were approximately 280 industrial companies left in Angola. The **Movimento Popular de Libertação de Angola** (MPLA) nationalized most of the economy, which led to shortages of parts, machinery, and expertise. The **civil war** destroyed what remained. In 2004, if peace has truly arrived, the government must invest a substantial sum to reinvigorate industry. This will mean not only rebuilding and rehabilitating but also improving internal transportation—**rail** and roadways—as well as developing an internal market that for too long has been accustomed to imported goods.

INFORMAL MARKETS. The Angolan **economy** has never been able to provide the population of **Luanda** with needed goods and services. Bureaucratic inertia, the effects of state planning, and the **civil war** combined to make day-to-day living in the capital a struggle. A number of informal markets arose to provide the basic necessities and some luxury items for the population. The government normally turns a blind eye to the illegal markets. Among the more prominent markets are São Paulo, **Futungo Market**, Congolenses, Rocha Pinto, Asa Blanca, Neves Bendinha, Kinaxixe, Estalagem, and the most famous, **Roque Santeiro**. A study in 2002 found the Kinaxixe market to include 346 vendors, 146 greengrocers, 200 hawkers, and more than 60 kitchens. The infrastructure was severely degraded, with no potable water or functioning bathroom available. São Paulo market was restored and enlarged in 2002. Presently, the market has 729 vendors. Rocha Pinto (Young Rock Chicken) is a shantytown outside of Luanda with a large black market in the town square. The population consists of **refugees** fleeing the **civil war**.

INJÚRIA **(injury).** Under Article 46 of the Press Law, *injury* is defined as defaming someone without imputing to him/her a specific fact, but by gesture, orally, in writing or drawing, or by any other means of publication harming the person's reputation. Injury is also a criminal violation with a maximum prison sentence of one year. In practice, a journalist is guilty of the crime if the prosecutor files charges. *See also* DEFAMATION; MEDIA.

INTERNALLY DISPLACED PEOPLE (IDPs). People who have either abandoned their homes voluntarily or have been forced out due to the **civil war**. IDPs wish to return home, which places a burden on **nongovernmental organizations** and the Angolan government. The civil war created one of the world's largest displaced populations. Already high in 1999 at 2 million, the total was 4 million by 2002 and remained high into 2003. *See also* REFUGEES.

INTERNATIONAL MONETARY FUND (IMF). Angola joined the IMF and the World Bank on 19 September 1989. In order to gain admission, Angola promised to devalue the national currency, the **kwanza**, separate the function of the central bank from commercial banks, reduce the number of state-owned enterprises, and expand private enterprise. In April 2000, the IMF and the government of Angola signed a nine-month agreement that called for revision of tax laws, adjustment of tariffs, completion of an audit of the **petroleum** sector, reduction of state spending, accelerated privatizations, liberalization of foreign trade, expansion of investment in the infrastructure, ending of extrabudgetary expenditures, and establishment of greater transparency in public accounting. An internal report of the IMF was leaked in October 2002 that concluded that the Angolan government could not account for over $4 billion from 1997 to 2001 and $1 billion in 2002. The report was especially critical of the state-owned oil company, Sonangol (**Sociedade Nacional de Combustíveis de Angola**). The company placed oil revenues in offshore accounts, not in the Angolan central bank as required by law, and had not been independently audited. Angola, blaming shoddy accounting practices, claimed the money was not missing. The $1 billion reported missing in 2002 was three times the amount of humanitarian aid to Angola. *See also* BANKING; ECONOMY.

IONA NATIONAL PARK. A park located in southern **Namibe province**. In August 2003, the Angolan and **Namibian** governments signed a memorandum to link Iona National Park with Namibia's Skeleton Coast Park.

IRAQ. Name given to a slum in **Luanda**. It is one of numerous areas in the region filled with **internally displaced people** (IDPs). Iraq has no potable water and no latrines, and families reside in cardboard boxes.

ISLAM. According to the Islamic International News Agency, Muslims represented 25 percent of Angola's population in 1999. Many Angolans converted to Islam while **refugees** in neighboring Islamic nations. Muslim businessmen from West Africa also have increased the number of converts. There are various theories about the rapid spread of Islam through non-Arab Africa. Islam is able to respect and absorb African traditions. In return, African religions have influenced Islam. For example, the practice of Islam is more mystical in Africa than it is in other parts of the world. The mystical, spiritual world is central to African religions.

– J –

JAGA. Term applied to any invader of the coastal areas from the interior of Angola during the 16th and 17th centuries. Some of the Jaga were members of the Imbangala group or simply roving bands of brigands.

JAMBA. The **União Nacional para a Independência Total de Angola** (UNITA) major base located in deep southeastern **Cuando Cubango province**. The Portuguese called the area the "Land at the End of the World." Once described as the "Capital of the Free Land of Angola," it was attacked in 1985, 1987, and 1990. At the height of UNITA's power, Jamba was a showcase for Westerners enamored with UNITA and **Jonas Savimbi**. Jamba was captured by government forces in December 1999. The name means *elephant* in **Umbundu**.

JANGA. A thatched, circular meeting hall found in rural villages.

JEICHANDE, MUSSAGY. A Mozambican appointed by **United Nations** secretary-general Kofi Annan as head of the **United Nations Office in Angola** (UNOA) on 4 August 2000. The office, no longer involved in the settlement of the **civil war**, would be concerned with humanitarian assistance, promotion of human rights, and maintaining liaison with political, military, police, and other civil authorities.

JOHN PAUL II, POPE (1920–). The pope visited Angola for a week in June 1992. He celebrated the **Movimento Popular de Libertação de Angola** (MPLA) break with Marxism and urged reconciliation among the Angolan people. While in Angola, the pontiff met with both **Jonas Savimbi** and President **Eduardo dos Santos**. The pope was 72 years of age on his 55th voyage since assuming the papacy in 1978. On 9 July 1997, the Vatican established diplomatic relations with Angola.

JOINT DECLARATION OF ANGOLAN POLITICAL PARTIES. On 2 October 1992, eight opposition parties protested electoral fraud in a document titled the Joint Declaration of Angolan Political Parties. The document claimed that the **Movimento Popular de Liber-**

tação de Angola (MPLA) had used intimidation tactics through deployment of riot police near voting stations, nonobservance of electoral rules concerning distribution of party propaganda near voting sites, failure to provide voter registration lists to opposition parties, and unexplained changes in previously announced voting results. Despite these and other problems, the **United Nations** declared the Angola vote to be "generally free and fair." *See also* ELECTIONS.

JOVENS JUSTICEIROS (Justice of the Juveniles). Groups of **Movimento Popular de Libertação de Angola** (MPLA) supporters as young as 15 who were given weapons to be used against **União Nacional para a Independência Total de Angola** (UNITA) supporters in the **Halloween Massacre** of October 1992.

JUDICIAL SYSTEM (Sistema Judicial). In June 2003, the International Bar Association (IBA) noted that only 23 of 168 municipal courts in Angola were operating. Most cases were sent to **provincial** courts, which led to delays and a large backlog of cases. Due to a shortage of judges and attorneys, detainees could spend up to three years in jail before trial. The IBA reported that many government lawyers also practiced privately, creating the potential for conflict of interest. The IBA suggested raising the salaries of government lawyers, barring them from private practice, improving courthouse working conditions, and computerizing court records. Further, the IBA urged the Angolan government to increase the number of attorneys by offering financial assistance and lowering the age when students could begin a law program. Currently, the maximum age is 25 years for day school and 35 years for night school. In August 2003, Angola's Justice Ministry signed an agreement with the U.S. Department of Commerce to modernize Angola's judicial system. The agreement calls for an exchange of experiences between judges, lawyers, clerks, and other specialists. Also, the U.S. Commerce Department will teach archiving techniques, train personnel, and assist in computerization of court records.

JUVENTUDE DO MOVIMENTO POPULAR DE LIBERTAÇÃO DE ANGOLA (JMPLA) (Popular Movement for the Liberation of Angola Youth). The JMPLA was founded in 1962. Before independence, it was employed as a political organizing tool. Since 1977, the only path to **Movimento Popular de Libertação de Angola** (MPLA) membership has been through the JMPLA. Members are expected to participate in the Directorate of People's Defense Organization and in political study groups. *See also* ORGANIZAÇÁO DE MULHER ANGOLANA.

– K –

KABILA, LAURENT-DÉSIRÉ (1939–2001). The former president of the **Democratic Republic of the Congo**. He overthrew Zairian dictator Mobutu Sese Seko in 1997 with military assistance from Angola, Rwanda, and Uganda. However, the former allies fell out, and Rwanda and Uganda backed rebels opposed to Kabila, while Angola, **Namibia**, and Zimbabwe helped maintain Kabila in power. On 16 January 2001, Kabila was assassinated by one of his bodyguards. He was succeeded in office by his son, Joseph. As of October 2003, there had been a partial settlement of the civil war that had become one of Africa's deadliest conflicts.

KAGAME, PAUL (1957–). President of Rwanda accused by the **United Nations** of allowing planes destined for **União Nacional para a Independência Total de Angola** (UNITA) areas to refuel and fly over Rwandan territory. Rwanda was also accused of allowing UNITA to freely operate in the capital city of Kigali. *See also* COMPAORÉ, BLAISÉ; EYADÉMA, GNASSINGBÉ.

KALUANDA. Derogatory term used by **União Nacional para a Independência Total de Angola** (UNITA) to describe the elite of **Luanda**.

KAUNDA, KENNETH (1924–). President of **Zambia** during Angola's independence struggle. Kaunda repeatedly called for a negotiated solution to the civil war, referring at one point to Moscow and Havana together as "a plundering tiger with its deadly cubs." Later, Zambia's government recognized the **Movimento Popular de Libertação de Angola** (MPLA) as the sovereign government of Angola.

KHOISAN GROUP. The original inhabitants of Angola, the Khoisan ethnolinguistic group is also known as the Bushmen, Hottentots, Kung,

Kxoe, Khoi Khoi, Ovahimba, San, Vatua, and !Xu. At present, the Khoisan number only several thousand located in southern Angola and the Kalahari Desert. The Khoisan refer to themselves as the "harmless people." However, when the Bantu, and later the **Portuguese**, arrived, their numbers and living area were sharply reduced through warfare and disease. The group leads a nomadic life and survives by hunting and gathering. Later, the Portuguese and **South Africans** employed Khoisan as trackers against the guerrilla fighters of South Africa and **Namibia**. The Khoisan currently number 3,600 in Angola and speak !Kung.

KIKONGO. The language spoken by the **Bakongo** people. Lingala is one of the many dialects of Kikongo.

KIMBANDA. A diviner who has inherited or acquired the skills to communicate with the spirit world. Many Angolans believe that magical power resides in many things. The power is neutral but can be used for malevolent purposes by witches. The *kimbanda* can contact the ancestral spirits to learn if they have been offended and, if so, how to remedy the matter. *Kimbanda* charge for their services; the greater their ability, the higher the cost.

KIMBERLEY PROCESS. Term applied to an international effort to crack down on the illicit trade in **diamonds**. The Kimberley Process, named after the **South African** mining town, is designed to determine the country of origin of the stone when it passes through customs. The agreement came into effect on 1 January 2003. The new regulations require that all shipments of rough diamonds be sent in tamper-proof containers accompanied by certificates guaranteeing the origin and contents. The importing nation must acknowledge receipt of the diamonds, certify they have not been tampered with, and reject any shipment that does not meet the requirements. Diamonds lacking the proper paperwork cannot be purchased by the 56 signatories to the agreement. By July 2003, Angola had met the criteria for participation in the process, and by 7 November 2003, the 46 major diamond-producing nations had entered into compliance with the Kimberley Process. *See also* BLOOD DIAMONDS.

KIMBERLITE MINES. Kimberlite mines require sophisticated technology to reach the **diamonds** embedded in volcanic rock. The

Camafuca–Camazambo mine in northeastern Angola was drilled to a depth of 500 feet and began production in late 2002. The only other mine producing kimberlite in Angola is **Catoca**, also located in the northeast.

KIMBUNDU. The language spoken by the **Mbundu** group.

KINGUILAS. Illegal street moneychangers in **Luanda**, usually **women**. The Kinguilas offer better exchange rates than the **banks**.

KIOSA, JOSE DOMINGOS BERNARDO (1925–2002). Kiosa was an Angolan nationalist who later served as the **Movimento Popular de Libertação de Angola** (MPLA) vice president. He also assisted the Organization of African Unity (OAU) in creating the African Movements of Liberation, which was the OAU umbrella organization for all liberation movements. In 1991, Kiosa returned home after 32 years in exile. He was appointed a member to the **Conselho da República** (Council of the Republic) and later served as Angolan ambassador to the Vatican.

KISANGWA. A maize beverage preferred by the **Ovimbundu**.

KISSAMA FOUNDATION. Foundation created to help restock Angola's national parks with elephants and other animals from **South Africa** and Botswana. *See also* ARCA DE NOAH DA OPERAÇÃO.

KOEVOET (crowbar). A South West African Territorial Force (SWATF) unit that operated in Angola and **Namibia** against South West Africa People's Organization (SWAPO) guerrillas. Koevoet was a counterinsurgency unit using many of the tactics employed by its foes. Koevoet gained a reputation for brutality. The unit operated on a bounty policy that paid soldiers for dead guerrillas or captured equipment. At maximum strength, the group had 250 white officers and 750–800 Ovambo troops.

KPMG. To produce more transparency in the **petroleum** industry, the Angolan government hired the British firm KPMG to perform an oil diagnostic. The initial report, entitled *The Evaluation of the Angolan*

Petroleum Sector, was released in July 2003. The report contains allegations of billions of missing dollars. It is highly critical of Sonangol (**Sociedade Nacional de Combustíveis de Angola**), the state oil company; the central bank, **Banco Nacional de Angola** (BNA); and the government treasury, in particular, concerning how these institutions record transactions with one another. According to KPMG, the major problem stems from use of different exchange rates between the **kwanza**—the local currency—and the U.S. dollar, used by the petroleum industry. Because of the practice of keeping books in both dollars and kwanzas, KMPG found it "difficult and sometimes even impossible" to reconcile discrepancies in the books. The British company found no clear case of fraud or corruption but warned that poor accounting practices create the opportunity for such crimes. *See also* INTERNATIONAL MONETARY FUND.

KROLL AND ASSOCIATES. A multinational company experienced in international intelligence and security matters. In April 2001, Kroll and Associates was hired by the **United Nations** to assist a committee in monitoring sanctions against **União Nacional para a Independência Total de Angola** (UNITA). The assigned task was to trace the flow of **diamonds** used by UNITA to purchase military equipment. The hiring of Kroll and Associates was unusual because the United Nations normally gathers intelligence from governments, not from private investigators.

KUDIBANGUELA. A clandestine organization that distributed antigovernment leaflets in urban areas of **Luanda** during the **civil war**.

KUITO. Capital of **Bié province**. Sometimes referred to as the "Martyred City" or "Angola's Stalingrad" because of its near total destruction during the **civil war**. An estimated 30,000 people, at least one-third of the population, perished in the city during the nine-month **União Nacional para a Independência Total de Angola** (UNITA) siege. Kuito has the highest concentration of amputees in the world. In a last desperate attempt to take and hold Kuito, UNITA and government forces battled in hand-to-hand combat in June 1994. Reportedly, UNITA was on the verge of a major victory. A gap had been created in government positions, and UNITA tanks and armor were on the cusp of entering the city. However, fuel supplies, a major problem throughout the war for UNITA, ran out. The heavy equipment, and with it any hope of capturing the city was abandoned. When the civil war reignited in 1998, UNITA again made a concerted push to capture the city using heavy artillery and tanks.

KULAXINGU, KAMBAMJIJI. The king of Baixa de Kassenge who in 2002 wished to establish a 19th Angolan **province** that would have included parts of **Malange** and **Lunda Norte** provinces.

KWACHA. Derogatory term used by the government to describe members and supporters of **União Nacional para a Independência Total de Angola** (UNITA).

KWACHA DOT COM. The **União Nacional para a Independência Total de Angola** (UNITA) website operated from Ireland by Leon Dias. The other **Kwacha** Internet site was based in Bailundo but stopped posting messages before Bailundo fell to government forces. As of August 2003, the **UNITA–Renovada** site also stopped postings. With the reunification of UNITA completed, a new website may emerge.

KWANDA BASE. Petroleum company camp for offshore/onshore workers in **Cabinda**. The modern facility has every Western convenience. Workers, if they choose, can have little or no contact with the local population.

KWANZA. The monetary unit of Angola, launched on 8 January 1977. The kwanza, named for the **Kwanza River**, replaced the escudo. After using the titles of "new kwanza," "adjusted kwanza," and "kwanza-KZ," the government reverted to using the term *kwanza* in 2000. In September 2003, one U.S. dollar equaled 80 kwanzas. *See also* ECONOMY.

KWANZA RIVER (Cuanza River). The largest of Angola's rivers. The Kwanza's headwaters are in the central highlands and flow north and west into the Atlantic 40 miles south of **Luanda**. The Cambambe dam, though damaged during the **civil war**, provides energy for the capital city and most of northern Angola.

KXOE. A 3,000-strong **Khoisan** people living in **Namibia**'s Caprivi Strip. When Namibia allowed the **Forças Armadas de Angolanas** (FAA) to conduct military operations against **União Nacional para a Independência Total de Angola** (UNITA) from Namibia in 2000, the Kxoe began to be harassed and in some cases murdered. During the **South African** occupation of Namibia, the Kxoe had been employed by the South African Defense Forces (SADF) as trackers against the African National Congress (ANC), the South West Africa People's Organization (SWAPO), **Forças Armadas Populares de Libertação de Angola** (FAPLA), and the **Cubans**. To the FAA and the Namibian army, the Kxoe were UNITA sympathizers or worse.

– L –

LAND MINES. A big challenge for the reconstruction of Angola is presented by the massive amount of land mines scattered throughout the nation. Angola is infested with 76 different types of mines manufactured in 22 nations and planted by **Portugal**, the **Soviet Union, South Africa, Cuba**, Zaire, the South West Africa People's Organization (SWAPO), the African National Congress (ANC), the various **Frente de Libertação do Enclave de Cabinda** (FLEC) factions, **Forças Armadas de Angolanas** (FAA), **Frente Nacional de Libertação de Angola** (FNLA), **Forças Armadas de Libertação de Angola** (FALA), and **Forças Armadas Populares de Libertação de Angola** (FAPLA). Very few maps were drawn of the fields where mines were planted. Consequently, finding the mines is not only difficult, but it is also a dangerous, labor-intensive job. There is one land mine for every 415 Angolans. There are more than 70,000 mine-disabled Angolans, and mine-attributed deaths are at 30,000. The number of mines varies, but most estimates place it between 2 and 10 million. As of 2003, three quarters of land-mine accidents had involved **internally displaced people** (IDPs). In returning to their home areas, the IDPs are the most likely to walk in areas of unknown safety. Land mines also hamper agricultural production and food distribution by **nongovernmental organizations** (NGOs). In 2003, only 2 percent of the land was arable. Halo Trust, a British charity founded by two ex–British army officers, has been involved in land-mine removal from Angola since 1995. Their mine removal teams wear Plexiglas visors to shield their faces, heads, and necks and Kevlar vests over their torsos and trunks. The job is painstakingly slow and dangerous. A small square can take two hours to clear. Other mine removal groups include the Norwegian People's Aid and Mines Advisory Group. Most of the land mines are small and designed to maim and demoralize. The Italian-made Valmara, VS-69, is set off by a trip wire; its blast rises to chest height and sprays 1,200 4-mm steel cubes. Anyone within 100 feet is torn apart. Some mines are as small as a can of tuna. Mines were used as defenses around towns or key sites such as power pylons or bridges. Mines can be manufactured for as little as $3, but cost as much as $1,000 to remove. Angola ratified the Ottawa Convention on Landmines in July 2002, but did not begin implementation until 2003. A partial list of land-mine types that have been found in Angola with their nation of origin includes NR409 (Belgium), PSM-1 (Bulgaria), Type/72B (China), PP/MI/SR (Czech Republic), M59 (France), PPM-2 (Germany), M14 (India), VS/69 (Italy), M/966 (Portugal), Mon/100 (Russian Federation), No.8 (South Africa), Mark/7 (United Kingdom), M18A1 (**United States**), Prom/1 (Yugoslavia), and Rap/2 (Zimbabwe). *See also* CIVIL WAR.

LANGUAGES. The languages spoken in Angola include Akhoe, Bolo, Chokwe, Diriku, Fiote, Holo, Kikongo-San Salvador, **Kikongo**, **Kimbundu**, Kung-Ekoka, Kung-Tsumkwe, Kwadi, Kwangali, Kwanyama, Lingala, Lucazi, Luimbi, Lunda, Luvale, Luyana, Maligo, Mbangala, Mbukushhu, **Mbundu**, Mbundu-Loanda, Mbwela, Ndombe, Ndonga, Ngandyera, Nkangala, Nkhumbi, Nsongo, Nyaneka, Nyemba, Nyengo, Oung, Ovambo, **Portuguese**, Ruund, Sama, **Umbundu**, Xun, Yaka, Yauma, Yombe, and Zemba. Rukwangali is a **Namibian** dialect spoken in southern Angola. Bantu languages are spoken from Cameroon through east and central Africa to all of southern Africa. Over 220 million people speak a Bantu language, the largest number of which speak Swahili.

LEVIEV, LEV. An Israeli citizen and the owner of a large **diamond**-purchasing company in Angola. Leviev and an associate, Sylvain Goldberg, are believed to be in business with **Isabel dos Santos** to sell diamonds on the international market. *See also* ANGOLAGATE; FALCONE, PIERRE; GAYDAMEK, ARKADY; MITTERRAND, JEAN-CHRISTOPHE.

LIANGOL COFFEE FACTORY. The Liangol factory was once Angola's main **coffee** factory. **Portugal**'s Delta Café rehabilitated the factory, which resumed operation in 2000 after being dormant since 1986.

LIMBEZA **(cleansing).** A term used to indicate ideological cleansing. Systematic political killings carried out by armed civilians and special police loyal to the **Movimento Popular de Libertação de Angola** (MPLA) and by **União Nacional para a Independência Total de Angola** (UNITA) rebels. UNITA employed the term to describe events such as the **Halloween Massacre** in Luanda in October 1992. *See also* CIVIL WAR.

LIQUIFIED NATURAL GAS (LNG). In 2001, foreign **petroleum** companies began to make plans to market Angola's liquefied natural gas instead of flaring the gas at the wellhead. Chevron/Texaco corporation has estimated that Angola's reserves of LNG range from 9.5 trillion cubic feet (TCF) to over 25 TCF. So far, the LNG deposits have been found in blocks 15, 17, and 18. Texaco, Exxon/Mobil, British Petroleum, TotalElfFina, and Sonangol (**Sociedade Nacional de Combustíveis de Angola**) are the major operators in the blocks. Consequently, they will incur most of the expense. Plans call for export of LNG by 2005 employing four to six tankers. Demand for LNG has risen in recent years as natural gas prices have soared in the **United States**. LNG is environmentally friendly and can be shipped via tanker. Sonangol has pledged to end flaring by 2006, aiming instead to export the gas to the United States, South America, and Europe.

LITERATURE. Luanda, with its mix of European, *assimilado*, *mestiço*, and African peoples, has always been the core of Angola's rich and vibrant **culture**. The first novel published by an Angolan author was *O*

Segredo da Morta (The secret of the dead), written in 1935 by Antonio Assis Jr. The next generation brought such figures as **Agostinho Neto**, Antonio Jacinto, and Viriato da Cruz. Working through the magazine *Mensagem,* these authors attempted to awake Angolans to the need to resist **Portuguese** domination and to encourage Angolan nationalism. Later, writers such as Oscar Ribas, Uanhenga Xitu, **Arnaldo dos Santos**, and Mario Antonio authored works tailored toward Angolans and everyday life. After 1975, the Angolan government became the sponsor of literature through the creation of the União dos Escritores Angolano (UEA) (Angolan Writer's Union). State sponsorship boosted the publishing industry, bringing such authors as **Pepetela**, **Ruy Duarte de Carvalho**, **Henrique Abranches**, David Mestre, and **Manuel Rui Monteiro** to the public's attention. The new generation of writers includes José Sousa Jamba, Boaventura Cardoso, Roderick Nehone, Alberto Oliveira Pinto, and Jacques Arlindo dos Santos. Angola's poets include Botelho de Vasconcelos, João Melo, Paula Tavares, José Luis Mendonca, and Lopito Feijoo. Their themes revolve around relationships, love, and the complexities of life. A problem for authors in Angola is that books are a luxury few Angolans can afford. Citizens need money for basic necessities. The cost of a book varies from 750 to 1,500 **kwanzas** (one U.S. dollar equals 80 kwanzas). Editorial Nzila is a publisher located in Luanda that publishes Angolan authors.

LIVESTOCK. The Bantu people have been herdsmen from time immemorial. The **Portuguese** helped make livestock an industry by digging wells for water and successfully eradicating the tsetse fly, which carries **trypansomiasis**. However, when the Portuguese left Angola in 1975, many of them destroyed the ranches, cattle processing facilities, and cattle. Cattle vaccination programs virtually ceased, and because of the war, eradication efforts against the tsetse fly stopped. The southern **provinces** can sustain cattle, but not so the northern ones, where the tsetse fly is found. The end of the **civil war** combined with financial support could see Angola become a net exporter of beef in the future. *See also* AGRICULTURE.

LOA, FELICIANO DE CARVALHO (1956–). Loa was born in October 1956 in Bembe, **Uíge province**. He received a Ph.D. in religious sciences at a university in Germany. He served as chairman of the Congregational Christian Church for Africa–European Friendship. On 20 August 2003, Reverend Loa announced his candidacy in the presidential contest to be held in 2004/2005. He will run as an independent. In his press conference, Loa announced that "Angola is made up of several peoples who should be given the opportunity of building a federal state."

LOBBYING. *See* PUBLIC RELATIONS.

LOBITO. Founded by the **Portuguese** in 1843, **Lobito** is Angola's most important port city after **Luanda**. The city serves as the western terminus of the **Benguela Railroad**. Completion of the railroad in 1929 led to Lobito's rise as a commercial center. The harbor, protected by a sandbar, is among the best on the west coast of Africa. However, the **civil war** disrupted rail traffic, lessening the city's commercial viability.

LONG MARCH (strategic march). After **União Nacional para a Independência Total de Angola** (UNITA) abandoned conventional warfare against the **Movimento Popular de Libertação de Angola** (MPLA) and **Cuban** forces, **Jonas Savimbi** led 2,000 civilians and military on a 1,864-mile march starting on 14 March 1976 at Gago Coutinho and ending on 28 August 1976 at the UNITA stronghold of Cuelei. Of the original 2,000, only 79 arrived at Cuelei. Some perished, others were deployed for guerrilla activities, and **women** and **children** were sent to secure areas for their safety. UNITA members marched on foot and were able to evade the helicopters, airplanes, and jeep patrols of the Cuban/MPLA forces. The Long March took its place in UNITA lore as the resurrection of the movement after the battlefield losses to Cuban/MPLA troops, and as an inspiration to UNITA supporters and sympathizers as Savimbi walked through the UNITA ethnic/linguistic base rallying support for the cause.

LOURENCO, JOÃO MANUEL GONCALVES (1954–). Born in 1954 and educated in the former **Soviet Union**, Lourenco was a political commissar in the **Forças Armadas Populares de Libertação de Angola** (FAPLA) before becoming governor of **Benguela province** in 1991. In December 1998, Lourenco was elevated to the position of **Movimento Popular de Libertação de Angola** (MPLA) secretary general. Seen as a political moderate, he was willing to negotiate with **União Nacional para a Independência Total de Angola** (UNITA), provided the rebels respected the terms of the **Lusaka Protocol**. Lourenco is very close to President **Eduardo dos Santos** and is seen as perhaps a future presidential contender.

LUANDA. A **province** and its capital city located in north-central Angola. Luanda city is also the site of the national government. It is Angola's largest city, the major port, and the administrative hub of the nation. Once called the "Rio of Africa," Luanda city has a population estimated at 4,100,000, many of them **refugees** from the war. Founded in 1575 by the **Portuguese** as São Paulo de Luanda, the city has a natural harbor with a fine port. From 1550 to 1852, Luanda played a key role in the slave trade to **Brazil**. The climate is tropical-dry. As the smallest of Angola's provinces and containing a burgeoning population, Luanda is in desperate need of access to its major resources: the port, food processing, cotton, **coffee**, **diamonds**, iron, salt, and textiles. In 2003, electric power reached only 102,578 customers, although this was an increase from the 89,727 recorded in 1999. Luanda city faces constant power disruptions, especially in suburban areas, because of network degradation. According to a 1998 **International Monetary Fund** (IMF) study, Luanda was the second most expensive city in the world to live in behind Tokyo. Luanda is the seat of the Roman Catholic archbishop, **Agostinho Neto** University, and the 17th-century fort of São Miguel. In June 2003, the city became a sister city with Houston, Texas, in the **United States**.

LUKAMBA, PAULO "GATO" (1954–). Born in Bailundo, Paulo Lukamba is the son of Zacarias Sanjolomba Paulo and Lussinga Paulo. Paulo Gato was educated in **Huambo** schools. He joined **União Nacional para a Independência Total de Angola** (UNITA) in 1975. Rising through the ranks, he became a general. Gato also held the posts of first director of UNITA's Presidential Office, general secretary of the Juventude Revolucionaria de Angola (JURA) (Revolutionary Youth of Angola), and member of the UNITA delegations to both the Addis Ababa and **Lusaka** peace negotiations. He also served as UNITA representative to Europe, based in Paris. Gato became secretary general of UNITA in 1995. Known as a hard-liner, he agreed to a cease-fire after the death of **Jonas Savimbi**. He became co-coordinator of the UNITA Political Commission in October 2002 and stepped down in February 2003. He also announced at that time that he would not stand for election as UNITA's president. Eventually, he decided to seek the office but lost to **Isaías Samakuva**.

LUKENI, NIMI (Alvaro I). King Alvaro I maintained power in the **Bakongo** kingdom by allying himself with powerful **Portuguese** colonialists based on São Tomé. The Portuguese assisted the king in defeating an invasion of **Jagas** in 1568. King Alvaro, the 14th *manicongo,* was able to maintain Bakongo independence, but with a growing reliance on the Portuguese.

LUNDA NORTE. A **province** located in northeastern Angola. The capital city is Lucapa. The population of Lunda Norte is about 250,000. It is rich in **diamonds**, while **agricultural** products include rice, corn, and palms grown in a tropical-dry climate.

LUNDA SUL. A **province** in the northeastern section of Angola with a population of about 120,000. The capital city is **Saurimo**. The tropical-dry climate allows the growth of rice and corn. Minerals include **diamonds**, iron, and manganese.

LUSAKA CEASE-FIRE AGREEMENT. Agreement reached in Lusaka, **Zambia**, in 1984 that established a Joint Commission of Angola and **South Africa** to monitor the South African withdrawal from Angola by late March 1984, with the **United States** as an observer. The terms included an immediate cease-fire, withdrawal of South African Defense Forces (SADF) from southern Angola, and eventual negotiations over the status of **Namibia**. For its part, Angola pledged to allow no **Cubans** or members of the South West Africa People's Organization (SWAPO) to enter the areas abandoned by South Africa. Angola also agreed to study the possibility of a Cuban withdrawal from Angola. The agreement never worked. South Africa never fully withdrew from Angolan territory, and the **Movimento Popular de Libertação de Angola** (MPLA) had little control over SWAPO guerrilla movements.

LUSAKA PROTOCOL. On 20 November 1994, **Movimento Popular de Libertação de Angola** (MPLA) and **União Nacional para a Independência Total de Angola** (UNITA) signed a third treaty in Lusaka, **Zambia**, attempting to end the 19-year **civil war**. The protocol reflected the weakness of UNITA and the growing military prowess of the national army. In the weeks prior to the ceremony, UNITA had lost **Kuito** and **Huambo**, and other sieges on district capitals or important cities had been broken. The signing ceremony was marred by the absence of the rebel chief **Jonas Savimbi**. Savimbi claimed he could not travel to Lusaka because he feared his plane would be shot down by government aircraft. Instead, General Eugênio Manuvakola signed for UNITA and Angola's foreign minister, Venâncio de Moura, for the government. The protocol called for UNITA to become a junior partner in the government. The rebels were given cabinet positions, ambassadorships, and governorships of three provinces. Savimbi was offered the post of vice president, a job he would later reject. The rebel army would enter cantonment camps to be disbanded, with troops either joining the national army or becoming civilians. Both the MPLA and UNITA would allow freedom of movement for people and goods throughout the nation. The **United Nations** would oversee the implementation of the treaty with a 7,000-member force that would rise to 7,260 by 1996. On 14 December 1996, UN Special Envoy to Angola **Alioune Blondin Beye** announced that UNITA had completed the disarmament of its troops and surrender of weapons and ammunition. Under the protocol's terms, the announcement should have paved the way for a unified army and coalition government. In 1998, the Lusaka Protocol collapsed because of renewed warfare.

LUSO CONFERENCE. A meeting held between **Jonas Savimbi** and **Agostinho Neto** in December 1974. Its purpose was to improve mutual understanding between **União Nacional para a Independência Total de Angola** (UNITA) and the **Movimento Popular de Libertação de Angola** (MPLA) and to work out a common strategy for negotiations with the **Portuguese**.

LUSOTROPICALISM. A theory developed by the **Brazilian** sociologist Gilberto Freyre that claims that when the **Portuguese** arrived in Africa a new type of civilization began. Lusotropicalism was a blending of European values with African ones. The best case of Lusotropicalism was to be found in Cape Verde, where the intermingling of the races had produced "the most perfect Portuguese human being." Freyre's thesis, published by the Portuguese government, became the theoretical justification for the exploitation of Portugal's African and South American colonies and the major political defense of Portugal's colonialist policies. *See also* ESTADO NOVO.

– M –

MAGAZINES. The conclusion of the **civil war** led the government to ease press restrictions. A number of official and private magazines made their ways to vendors' stalls. The *M Magazine,* begun in September 1996, is the official publication of the **Movimento Popular de Libertação de Angola** (MPLA). Although a party magazine, the *M Magazine* accepts advertisements and articles from other political groups. *O Pensador* is the cultural information publication begun by Angola's diplomatic mission to the **United States** in February 2000. *Angoitália* and *Angola Actualidade* are the monthly publications of the Angolan embassies in Italy and France, respectively. *Angola Turistica* is the magazine published by the Angolan Ministry of Hotels and Tourism to lure tourists to Angola. *Economia e Mercado* (Economy and market) is a privately owned quarterly magazine launched in December 1999. It is distributed in Angola, **Portugal**, and southern Africa. *Comercio Externo* (External trade) is a weekly economic news magazine. *Jornal dos Desportos* (Sports journal) is a biweekly publication founded in 1994. In 2003, the magazine also opened a web site. *See also* MEDIA; NEWSPAPERS.

MAGNA CONFERENCE. Meeting held in 1975 in **Bié province** to prepare the **União Nacional para a Independência Total de Angola** (UNITA) members for the electoral process prescribed by the **Alvor Accords**. The meeting was also used to familiarize cadres with the new policies.

MAIOMBE-2003. An operation conducted by the Angolan police in **Cabinda** province to stop the flow of illegal immigrants and goods over the borders between Angola, the Republic of the Congo, and the **Democratic Republic of the Congo**.

MALANGE. A **province** of Angola and the name of its capital city. It is located in the east-central part of the nation and has a tropical-dry climate. The population totals about 700,000. Mineral resources include **diamonds** and copper. **Agricultural** products are rice, corn, beans, and olives.

MALARIA (paludism). A prevalent disease throughout Africa and Angola. It is spread by the female anopheles mosquito. The disease is the cause of 5 out of every 10 deaths among Angolan **children**. Insecticides and netting are effective in stopping transmission of the ailment. Besides death, the disease leads to high rates of absenteeism, strains medical resources, and undermines Angola's economic development. Because the majority of Angola's people live in poverty, they often purchase medicine from street vendors who have diluted the medicine in order to increase profits. The ineffectiveness of this medicine has made malaria more resistant to the most widely used antimalaria drugs, chloroquine and fansidar. *See also* HEALTH CARE.

MANIFESTO PARA PAZ EM ANGOLA (Manifesto for Peace in Angola). A statement by several peace groups in June 1999 that demanded the **Movimento Popular de Libertação de Angola** (MPLA), **União Nacional para a Independência Total de Angola** (UNITA), and **Frente de Libertação do Enclave de Cabinda** (FLEC) observe an immediate cease-fire, resume formal negotiations and accept mediation by civil society, immediately open **humanitarian** corridors to assist people affected by the war, and establish a definitive agenda for peace negotiations, and that UNITA and the government use their war monies in the search for peace. *See also* COALITION FOR RECONCILIATION, TRANSPARENCY AND CITIZENSHIP; COMITÉ INTER-ECLESIAL PARA A PAZ EM ANGOLA; REDE DA PAZ.

MÃOS LIVRES (Free Hands). An Angolan legal aid **nongovernmental organization** (NGO) that provides legal assistance and promotes programs to educate Angolans on how to use the law to protect and exercise legal rights.

MATADI ROYALISTS. Group of **Bakongo** nationalists led by Eduardo Pinnock. In 1955, the group lobbied the **Portuguese** for an educated, independent, and African leader when King Dom Pedro VII died. The Portuguese rejected the nationalist candidate for the throne. After these events, the Matadi Royalists united with other Bakongo nationalists to form the União das Populacões do Norte de Angola (UPNA), the forerunner of the **Frente Nacional de Libertação de Angola** (FNLA).

MATETA, TELA. Angolan sculptor who employs elongated, elliptical bronze figures. Mateta was commissioned by Angolan president **Eduardo dos Santos** to sculpt three Bantu statues for the presidential palace, Futungo de Belas. They were *The Peasant, The Drummer,* and *Motherhood.* Mateta has said, "Many of my figures are about the perpetuation of humanity—that's Bantu custom. It says the family must continue, so **women** and especially mothers—as the origin of the family—always appear."

MAVINGA. A sleepy, dusty town in southeastern Angola. The Portuguese described the area as Terras do Fim Mundo (Land at the End of the World). The city, located near Jamba, has a long airstrip that made it a key battleground in 1985, 1987, and 1990. **União Nacional para a Independência Total de Angola** (UNITA) surrounded Mavinga with 100,000 plastic land mines, many of which are still planted. A lack of consistent rainfall has hampered economic development.

MAYOMBE. A mountain located between **Cabinda** and the **Democratic Republic of the Congo.** One of Cabinda's early liberation movements named itself after the peak.

MAYUKWAYUKWA REFUGEE CAMP. Located in **Zambia,** one of the oldest **refugee** camps in Africa. As of 2003, it was home to 22,000 Angolans living in 53 villages inside of a 101-square-mile area. Built in 1966, the camp was meant to accommodate 4,000 Angolans. With the **civil war** over, many of the refugees are hesitant to leave. They own property and other possessions, their children go to local schools, and for many, Angola is just a memory. Indeed, most of the residents were born in the camp. *See also* ZAMBIA INITIATIVE.

MBANZA CONGO (City of the Congo). Located 100 miles from the mouth of the Congo River, Mbanza Congo was the capital city of the **Bakongo** and the seat of government of the *manicongo*.

MBEMBA, NZINGA (Afonso I). When João II accepted Christianity in 1491, several of his relatives, including his youngest son, Afonso, were also baptized. In 1506, Afonso became the seventh *manicongo*. Afonso had been educated for a decade by **Portuguese** priests. By the time he became *manicongo,* he was in many ways more Portuguese than **Bakongo**. During his reign, he sought to bring the benefits of European civilization to his people, but he was forced to allow the **slave trade** that, in the end, destroyed the Bakongo culture and people. One of Afonso's sons, Henrique, became the first African bishop of the Bakongo in 1520.

MBUNDU GROUP. The second largest ethnic group in Angola is the Mbundu, numbering 2.6 million people, or about 25 percent of the population. They include the Ambundu, Bambeiro, Bangala, Bondo, Cari, Chinje, Dembo, Haco, Holo, Jinga or Ngola, Libolo, Luanda, Luango, Minungo, Ntemo, Puna, Quibala, Quissama, Sende, and Songo. The Mbundu group is found in the present-day **provinces** of **Bengo**, **Luanda**, **Kwanza Norte**, **Kwanza Sul**, and **Malange**. The head of the Mbundu in precolonial times was the Ngola a Kiluanje. By the middle of the 16th century, the kingdom of the Ngola had subjugated all the surrounding neighbors. Early in the 17th century, the Ngola was defeated by a coalition of **Portuguese** and Imbangala. In 1671, the Ngola tried to reassert his independence, which led to another war with the Portuguese. At the Battle of Pungu a Ndongo, the Ngola was slain, many of his subjects were sold into slavery, and the Portuguese constructed a **presídio** on the battle site.

Early Mbundu culture revolved around **agriculture**, **fishing**, trading, hunting, and warfare. With the arrival of Portuguese colonialism, many Mbundu began to learn and practice European trades such as masonry, carpentry, construction, or simple menial labor. Others served as colonial government workers or became active in colonial commerce. Much of the **slave trade** involved Mbundu raiding the interior of Angola for captives to be sold through Luanda to the New World.

The Mbundu had the longest, most sustained interaction with the Portuguese, and although they have their own language, Kimbundu, the Mbundu speak Portuguese more than any other ethnic group. This closeness with the Portuguese led to an erosion of group cohesion, culture, and language. Most of the *mestiço* and *assimilado* population also came from the Mbundu. This assimilation by some Mbundu would later prove difficult as the liberation movements formed in the 1950s. **União Nacional para a Independência Total de Angola** (UNITA) and **Frente Nacional de Libertação de Angola** (FNLA) would be suspicious of **Movimento Popular de Libertação de Angola** (MPLA) mixed-race leadership. *Mestiços* (people of mixed blood), *assimilados* (Africans who adopted Portuguese culture), and Mbundu intellectuals founded the MPLA in 1956. The Mbundu were the first to produce **literature** written by Angolans. Later, many MPLA leaders employed these writing skills in an attempt to garner support for Angolan nationalism. The name Angola comes from a Portuguese derivative of "ngola." *See also* NETO, AGOSTINHO; NZINGA, QUEEN.

MEASLES (sarampo). An airborne, highly contagious viral infection. Measles attacks the immune system, so **children** die of complications such as diarrhea and pneumonia. Signs include fever, a rash, peeling of the skin, and breathing difficulty. Measles can also cause blindness and brain damage. It is a preventable disease that causes havoc for Angola's young. As of 2003, more than 10,000 children were dying each year, with 95 percent of the cases in children under 15. In the developed world, 999 out of 1,000 children will survive measles. In Angola, 100 out of 1,000 will perish. Measles kills more young Angolans than any other preventable disease. During April–May 2003, the **United Nations** Children's Fund (UNICEF) and the Angolan Ministry of Health inoculated 7.1 million children under the age of 15 against the disease. The figure represented 92 percent of all children aged 9 months to 15 years. Nearly 30,000 people were involved representing **nongovernmental organizations** (NGOs), churches, the government, civic groups, and educators. Radio spots in 12 different languages promoted the campaign.

MÉDECINS SANS FRONTIÈRES (MSF) (Doctor's without Borders). One of the most involved **nongovernmental organizations** (NGOs) in Angola. In 2002, MSF had 160 international staff in Angola and employed 2,000 Angolans. Over 14,000 people were being fed at the 44 MSF feeding centers. Although primarily a medical NGO, MSF found malnutrition at such horrendous levels that it fed the most severe cases. Also, in 2002, MSF took the unusual step of criticizing the Angolan government and the **United Nations** for failing to act quickly enough to avert a humanitarian tragedy. *See also* BP-5; HEALTH CARE.

MEDIA. Under **Portuguese** colonial control, the media were entirely state-owned. The print press, television, and radio were nationalized in 1976. Even after independence, the **Movimento Popular de Libertação de Angola** (MPLA)–controlled media propagandized and applied pressure and censorship on independent sources under the guise of national security during the war against **União Nacional para a Independência Total de Angola** (UNITA).

Radio **Nacional de Angola** (RNA) broadcasts in Chokwe, English, Fiote, French, **Kikongo**, **Kimbundu**, Kwanyama, Luvale, Ngangela, **Portuguese**, Songu, Spanish, and **Umbundu**. *Conexão Angola* (Angola Connection) is a popular program of the state-owned radio station. The state-owned *Jornal de Angola*, published in Luanda, has a circulation of approximately 41,000.

The official news agency is the Agência de Notícia de Angola (ANGOP) (Angola News Agency). It was created in 1975 under the name Agência de Notícia Nacional de Angola (ANNA) (Angola National News Agency). On 30 October 1975, following a suggestion by **Agostinho Neto**, the agency assumed its current name. ANGOP sent out its first news story on 2 February 1978. In October 2000, ANGOP celebrated its 25th anniversary. ANGOP's primary mission is to provide news through the World Wide Web, telex, or other channels to local and international subscribers. It gathers, writes, and disseminates news of national and international events. In 2000, Amnesty International (AI) issued a report sharply critical of the Angolan government. AI accused the government of intimidating journalists and using force to quash public opposition to government policies. Also, in 2000, the U.S.-based Committee to Protect Journalists placed Angolan president **Eduardo dos Santos** on the "Ten Enemies of the Press" list. The committee stated that, on 1 June 1999, Minister of Social Communication Hendrick Vaal Neto threatened the independent press with closure if it did not stop reportage of the **União Nacional para a Independência Total de Angola** (UNITA) insurgency. The state-owned television station is Televisão Pública de Angola (TPA). Popular programs include *EM Focus* (In focus), a late-night television program that includes critics of the government, and *Nação Corajoso* (Courageous nation), a weekly public affairs program. One segment of the program called **Ponto da Reunião** (Reunification point) attempts to help reunite families separated by the war. While people wait in line, they can fill out forms for the *Gazeta Cruz Vermelha*. *Reunification Point* is one of the more popular shows on Angolan television. WT Mundovideo is an independent station in Luanda. Angolan journalists are represented by Media Groupo, which attempts to protect their legal rights. *See also* MAGAZINES; NEWSPAPERS.

MELO, DARIO DE. Born in **Benguela province**, Dario de Melo has written 18 children's books and more than 40 articles appearing in magazines, newspapers, and books. In 1998, de Melo won the African Portuguese-Speaking Peoples' (PALOP's) Infant **Literature** prize for the book *As Sete Vidas de Um GATO* (The seven lives of a cat).

MELO, RICARDO DE. The editor of the independent Angolan **newspaper** *Imparcial Fax*, Ricardo de Melo was murdered by an unknown assailant on 18 January 1995. The writer had received many anonymous death threats. His articles angered various military and political figures with his critical reporting and exposés of alleged corruption. Melo was 38 when he was killed. His identification card and money were not taken. No one was ever charged with his murder.

MEMORANDUM OF UNDERSTANDING (MOU). The Memorandum of Understanding was an appendix to the **Lusaka Accords** of 1994. The memorandum, signed on 4 April 2002, formally ended the Angolan civil war. With the deaths of **Jonas Savimbi** and **Antonio Dembo**, the remaining **União Nacional para a Independência Total de Angola** (UNITA) commanders entered into cease-fire discussions with the government military. On 13 March, the government ordered the **Forças Armadas de Angolanas** (FAA) to cease all offensive actions against the rebels. The signing at the parliament building in Luanda was attended by President **Eduardo dos Santos** and **Ibrahim Gambari**, special representative of the **United Nations** to Angola. UNITA chief of staff General Geraldo Abreu Kamorteiro signed for the rebels and General Armando da Cruz Neto signed for the government. The government declared a national holiday to celebrate the event. Under the terms of the memorandum, UNITA members received amnesty from the government. UNITA's armed forces would be demobilized and members would be placed in camps. Some were incorporated into the national police (40) and army (5,000); those soldiers not offered military positions were to receive vocational training. Soldiers' families were to be allowed to join them in the camps. Unlike previous peace agreements in 1975, 1991, and 1994, the Memorandum of Understanding was negotiated and finalized by the two warring parties, not through international mediation. It is believed that the memorandum will stand the test of time because both UNITA and the **Movimento Popular de Libertação de Angola** (MPLA) wanted the war to end. The full title of the memorandum was Memorandum of Understanding as an Addendum to the Lusaka Protocol on the Cessation of Hostilities and the Resolution of Outstanding Military Issues in Accordance with the Lusaka Protocol.

MERCENARIES. At the time of Angolan independence in 1975, all three liberation movements employed mercenaries, including **South Africans**, **Cubans**, **Soviets**, **Portuguese**, and Zairians. Some legendary mercenaries also appeared. Rumors flew of "Mad" Mike Hoare and his "Wild Geese" arriving to fight in Angola. Reports, untrue, that the Central Intelligence Agency (CIA) had recruited one hundred U.S. ex-servicemen to fight in Angola also circulated. As many as 400 "mercs" passed through Great Britain on the way to fight for the **Frente Nacional de Libertação de Angola** (FNLA). One killed several of his own men, while the **Movimento Popular de Libertação de Angola** (MPLA) captured several mercenaries, including three Americans. The men were tried before an international court in Luanda. Daniel Gearhart was sentenced to death, and he was executed on 10 July 1976. Gary Acker and Gustavo Grillo were sentenced to prison terms. In the early stages of the **civil war**, the Soviets, Portuguese, and Cubans fought with the MPLA, although Portuguese mercenaries also fought with **União Nacional para a Independência Total de Angola** (UNITA) and FNLA. President Mobutu Sese Seko "loaned" the FNLA two brigades for its November 1975 assault on **Luanda**. The South Africans fought with UNITA; however, in the 1990s several hundred South Africans working for international security companies fought with Angolan government forces against UNITA. When the civil war ended in April 2002, several dozen Portuguese were still fighting with UNITA. *See also* EXECUTIVE OUTCOMES.

MERCÚRIO VERMELHO (**red mercury**). A mythical substance supposedly found in **unexploded ordinance**. The search for red mercury has led to many injuries and deaths.

MESTIÇO. The shortage of white Portuguese women in the Angolan colony led to numerous relationships between **Portuguese** men and African **women**. The children of these relationships were termed *mestiços*. Later, Lisbon decided to entrench Portuguese domination by building upon the *mestiço* foundation. The colonial authorities allowed *mestiços* to serve as soldiers, work for the colonial government, and achieve class elevation unavailable to the African masses. As nationalism emerged in Angola, the *mestiços* were forced to address the issue of their heritage. Were they African, Portuguese, or a third group? Suffering from an identity crisis, the *mestiços* found solace in journalism and cultural interaction. Discussions about their status led to an attraction to Marxism, which stressed class as opposed to racial conflict. *See also* MOVIMENTO POPULAR DE LIBERTAÇÃO DE ANGOLA.

MINERAL RESOURCES. Angola's mineral resources include **diamonds**, copper, lead, zinc, calcareous, iron ore, phosphate, feldspar, black granite, gypsum, mica, manganese, bauxite, uranium, **petroleum**, and gold. Black granite is mined in **Huíla province**, and the Angolan parastatal Angolstone earned $650,000 from export in 1999. The decorative stone sells well in Europe and southern Africa. Another black granite company is Ango–Rochas Company. Calcareous is a mineral with the characteristics of sodium carbonate, calcium, or limestone.

MINISTÉRIO DA ASSISTÊ NCIA REINSERÇÃO SOCIAL (MINARS) (Ministry of Social Affairs and Reintegration). The Angolan government agency in charge of assisting returning **refugees** and **internally displaced people** (IDPs). Since June 2002, MINARS has changed direction from emergency assistance to resettlement and reintegration.

MISIÓN DE OBSERVADORES DE LAS NACIONES UNIDAS EN ANGOLA (MONUA) (United Nations Observer Mission in Angola). Established 30 June 1997, MONUA was formed to assist in consolidation of the Angolan peace process. It was expected that MONUA would finish its mission by 1 February 1998. **United Nations Security Council** Resolution 1118 creating the mission highlighted the objectives as consolidation of peace and national reconciliation, creation of an environment that would produce long-term stability, and provision of assistance in democratic and economic development. The UN urged both the **Movimento Popular de Libertação de Angola** (MPLA) and **União Nacional para a Independência Total de Angola** (UNITA) to fully cooperate with MONUA. The UN would supply 625 monitors, supported by a staff of 310, at a cost of $64.5 million. In December 1998 and January 1999, two MONUA planes departing **Huambo** were shot down by unknown forces, probably UNITA, killing 29 crew and passengers. On 26 February 1999, as the violence spiraled out of control, the government of Angola and the UN made the decision to end MONUA. From 1995 to 1999, the UN had spent $2 billion and deployed 700 peacekeepers. Nations that staffed MONUA were Bangladesh, **Brazil**, Bulgaria, the Republic of the Congo, Egypt, France, Ghana, Guinea–Bissau, Hungary, India, Jordan, Kenya, Malaysia, Mali, **Namibia**, New Zealand, Nigeria, Norway, Pakistan, Poland, **Portugal**, Romania, the Russian Federation, Senegal, Slovakia, Sweden, the United Republic of Tanzania, Ukraine, Uruguay, **Zambia**, and Zimbabwe.

MITTERRAND, JEAN-CHRISTOPHE. The son of the late French president François Mitterrand, accused in December 2000 of illegally selling arms to Angola. Nicknamed *"Papa m'a dit"* or "Daddy told me," Jean-Christophe Mitterrand was Africa adviser to his father from 1986 to 1992. **Pierre Falcone** and **Arkady Gaydamek**, using

Falcone's company, Brenco International, signed a deal with Angola in 1993 for $47 million worth of Russian military equipment. The next year, a contract was signed for $463 million. Allegedly, Mitterrand received an illegal kickback of $1.9 million for arranging the introduction of Falcone and Gaydamek to Angolan officials. On 24 January 2001, eight members of the Partido de Apoio Democrático e Progreso de Angola (PADPA) (Angolan Party for Democracy and Progress), including party president Carlos Leitão, were arrested and detained for demonstrating to demand that President **Eduardo dos Santos** resign over the scandal. In a show of support, President dos Santos expressed thanks to Falcone and Mitterrand, saying that the weapons had "saved hundreds of thousands of lives." He also hinted that continuance of the case against Falcone, Gaydamek, and Mitterrand could sour Franco–Angolan relations. A French court ruled in June 2001 that the case against Mitterrand be dropped due to a legal technicality regarding the way the charges had been brought by a magistrate. *See also* ANGOLAGATE; LEVIEV, LEV.

MOMBASA AGREEMENT. An agreement between **União Nacional para a Independência Total de Angola** (UNITA), the **Movimento Popular de Libertação de Angola** (MPLA), and **Frente Nacional de Libertação de Angola** (FNLA) on 5 January 1975. At a meeting in Mombasa, Kenya, under the auspices of President Jomo Kenyatta, the three liberation movements pledged to stop fighting and adopted a unified platform from which to negotiate with **Portugal**. The Portuguese–Angolan talks began on 10 January and led to the **Alvor Accords**. *See also* NAKURU AGREEMENT.

MONITORING MECHANISM ON SANCTIONS AGAINST UNITA. Created on 11 July 2000 with Juan Larrain (Chile) as chairman and Christine Gordon (United Kingdom), James Manzou (Zimbabwe), Ismaila Seck (Senegal), and Lena Sundh (Sweden) as members. The mandate for the mechanism was extended on five occasions by the **United Nations**. Wilson Kalumba (Zimbabwe) replaced Manzou on the mechanism in April 2002. The mechanism presented seven reports to the **United Nations Security Council**, including the last, amended, summary report on 13 December 2002. The mechanism studied **União Nacional para a Independência Total de Angola**

(UNITA) violations of UN sanctions in the areas of arms and **diamond** smuggling. By publicly identifying individuals, companies, and nations aiding UNITA, the mechanism was able to stem the flow of diamonds from Angola and weapons into the war-torn nation. The mechanism visited 13 nations and carried out a large volume of correspondence. UNITA General **Paulo Lukumba** reported that the mechanism made it more difficult to secure needed supplies and played a key role in ending the civil war. *See also* FOWLER COMMISSION REPORT; MONITORING MECHANISM'S FINAL REPORT ON SANCTIONS AGAINST UNITA; UNITED NATIONS SECURITY COUNCIL RESOLUTION 1237.

MONITORING MECHANISM'S FINAL REPORT ON SANCTIONS AGAINST UNITA. Issued on 21 December 2000 (with an amended summary report issued on 13 December 2002), the report of the **Monitoring Mechanism on Sanctions against UNITA** documented how **União Nacional para a Independência Total de Angola** (UNITA) broke international sanctions by smuggling large numbers of **diamonds** from Angola and illegally importing large quantities of military equipment into the nation. The Final Report recommended sanctions against **Togo**, Burkina Faso, and Côte d'Ivoire for violating sanctions against the Angolan rebels. The Final Report was also critical of Bulgaria and the Ukraine for selling weapons to the rebels. The mechanism also found that UNITA representatives abroad played a key role in the success of the rebellion. Operating from France, **Portugal**, Italy, Belgium, Ireland, the **United States**, and Switzerland, the representatives were able to advance political and military objectives, market diamonds, and shop for weapons and other needed materiel. The Final Report listed as agents **Isaías Samakuva** in France, **Jardo Muekalia** in the United States, Leon Dias in Ireland, Adalberto da Costa in Italy, Carlos Morgado and others in Portugal, and Azevedo de Oliveira Kanganje in Belgium. It accused **Victor Bout** and his array of air transport companies of breaking sanctions against UNITA. The mechanism estimated that UNITA profited from $3 billion in diamond sales between 1993 and 1998. It suggested a certificate of origin program be initiated to track international diamond sales. *See also* FOWLER COMMISSION REPORT; UNITED NATIONS SECURITY COUNCIL RESOLUTION 1237.

MONTEIRO, MANUEL RUI (1941–). Educated in **Huambo**, Manuel Monteiro writes of everyday life in a satirical and ironic manner. In February 2003, he published *Maninha* (Unfruitful), a collection of chronicles published in the state-owned newspaper *Jornal de Angola.* The text, written from 1992 to 1994, depicts the Angolan peoples' everyday life from a variety of angles. His more famous works are *Regresso Adiado* (The postponed returned), *Memória de Mar* (Memory of the sea), *Quem me Dera ser Onda* (I wish I was a wave), and *Da Palma da Mão* (Of the palm of the hand). In an informal survey in July 2003, Monteiro was one of **Luanda**'s best-selling authors. *See also* LITERATURE.

MORAIS, RAFAEL MARQUES DE. Angolan journalist threatened and jailed by the government in October 1999 after publishing an article titled "The Lipstick of Dictatorship" for *Agora* accusing President **Eduardo dos Santos** of corruption. In January 2000, he received a death threat in a live broadcast session of parliament from a member of the ruling **Movimento Popular de Libertação de Angola** (MPLA), Mendes de Carvalho. Morais was sentenced to six months in prison and ordered to pay a $1,000 fine plus court costs on 31 March 2000. In October 2000, the Supreme Court suspended the sentence for five years. In August 2001, he was briefly arrested for reporting on the forced resettlement program of the **Boa Vista** shantytown by the government. The National Association of Black Journalists awarded him the Percy Qoboza Prize for "work on behalf of freedom of the press." Since 1998, he has been the Angolan representative of the **Abra a Fundação Sociedade** (Open Society Foundation). In July 2003, when Morais was asked to describe the situation in Angola, he replied that a negative peace was in place: "Negative peace is the absence of conflict, yes. But it is a peace without justice, peace without opportunity, peace without democracy. This is not a peace that promises much to the Angolan people." *See also* MEDIA.

MOURA, VENÂNCIO DE (1935–1999). Born in **Uíge province**, Venâncio Moura earned a law degree in **Portugal**. After Angola's independence, he began a long career in the **Movimento Popular de Libertação de Angola** (MPLA) diplomatic corps, highlighted by his service as Angola's foreign minister from 1992 until 1999. In 1994, he signed the **Lusaka Protocol** on behalf of the Angolan government.

MOVIMENTO DAS FORÇAS ARMADAS (MFA) (Armed Forces Movement). The MFA was formed by junior officers in the **Portuguese** military who were disgruntled by the 30-year **António Salazar** dictatorship and the increasing toll of dead and wounded from Portugal's African wars. Inspired by **António de Spinola's** book *Portugal e o Futuro,* the officers led a coup against the rightwing government of **Marcello Caetano** on 25 April 1974. The 30-year dictatorship was overthrown with hardly a shot fired. The military junta made the decision to grant independence to the Portuguese colonies of Guinea, Mozambique, and Angola. *See also* CARNATION REVOLUTION.

MOVIMENTO POPULAR DE LIBERTAÇÃO DE ANGOLA (MPLA) (Popular Movement for the Liberation of Angola). The MPLA was founded in 1956 by a merger between the Movimento para a Independência de Angola (MPIA), the Partido da Luta Unida dos Africanos de Angola (PLUA), and the Partido Comunista de Angola (PCA). In the late 1940s, members of the **Portuguese** Communist Party began to politicize the white and *mestiço* students and intellectuals in **Luanda** and other urban centers. Nationalism was also a force in the community. At first, the MPLA spread its message through cultural publications such as *Mensagem* and *Cultura.* However, the colonial authorities soon put an end to the publications. It was easy for the **Polícia International de Defesa de Estado** (PIDE) to harass and intimidate the MPLA, because it was located in urban areas. In a massive 1960 dragnet, the PIDE arrested the three top MPLA leaders: Illidio Machado, Viriato da Cruz, and **Agostinho Neto**. The remaining leadership decided that steps had to be taken to galvanize the masses. On 4 February 1961, MPLA militants attempted to storm the **prisons** in Luanda. The attempt failed, as did another one on 10 February. In July 1962, Neto reassumed control of the movement and promptly sacked da Cruz. Later, da Cruz would join the **Frente Nacional de Libertação de Angola** (FNLA). The MPLA shifted its base of operations away from Zaire to the Republic of the Congo. However, the only direct point of entrance into Angola was through **Cabinda**. The armed wing of the MPLA, the **Forças Armadas Populares de Libertação de Angola** (FAPLA), launched an offensive in Cabinda. While unsuccessful militarily, it did provide a morale boost and an area to recruit and train. When the government of the Republic of the Congo changed in 1968, the MPLA was forced out. The Republic of the Congo was concerned about the growing number of MPLA fighters with their **Cuban** and **Soviet** advisers. During the early 1970s, the MPLA's weakness showed. It could not supply its fighters throughout Angola, and communications were irregular at best. This, combined with Portuguese military victories, led to a crisis within the MPLA that came to a head in 1974. The Soviet Union stopped supplying the rebels due to their distrust of Neto's leadership. Daniel Chipenda, the MPLA's best commander, complained about a lack of supplies for his fighters. Ultimately, in 1975, Chipenda and most of his soldiers joined the FNLA. Neto also faced a challenge from the party intelligentsia led by **Mario de Andrade**, who resented Neto's secretive ways. However, as independence approached, the breaches were healed, Moscow resumed its support, and the MPLA became the most politically powerful of the three liberation movements. Moscow's resumption of support was based on two events. First, Neto was able to convene a congress inside Angola that was attended by the main MPLA commanders. The congress also adopted a manifesto that was pro-Soviet. Second, the new Portuguese military administrator, Admiral **Rosa Coutinho**, was openly supportive of Neto and the MPLA. As independence neared, the Soviet Union supplied a massive amount of military equipment and Cuba deployed 12,000 soldiers to ensure that the MPLA won the civil war. The MPLA Angolan government signed a 20-year Friendship and Cooperation Treaty with the Soviet Union, and on 10 December 1977 the MPLA transformed itself into the **Movimento Popular de Libertação de Angola, Partido do Trabalho** (MPLA–PT). President Neto explained that the party would be based on "the synthesis of Marxist–Leninist theory with the MPLA's own revolutionary experience." As the **União Nacional para a Independência Total de Angola** (UNITA) insurgency gained strength, the MPLA became more reliant upon Cuba and the Soviet Union. By the 1980s, Cuba had 50,000 troops in Angola and the Soviet Union was supplying $1 billion annually in military equipment, but the events in Eastern Europe and the Soviet Union in the late 1980s convinced the MPLA that socialism was finished. The Third Party Congress, led by President **Eduardo dos Santos**, transformed Angola into a multiparty political system combined with a free-market economy. With Western companies, especially **petroleum** companies, seeking to expand in Angola, the government was able to secure multibillion dollar contracts and loans that were used to pursue a final military victory over UNITA. *See also* JUVENTUDE DO MOVIMENTO POPULAR DE LIBERTAÇÃO DE ANGOLA; ORGANIZAÇÃO DA MULHER ANGOLANA.

MOVIMENTO POPULAR DE LIBERTAÇÃO DE ANGOLA, PARTIDO DO TRABALHO (MPLA–PT) (Popular Movement for the Liberation of Angola, Workers Party). From 1977 until 1990, the MPLA viewed itself as a Marxist–Leninist party. Pictures of Marx, Lenin, and Engels were hung in town squares, and streets were named after key communist figures or events. The MPLA Central Committee referred to 1977 as the "Year of the Founding of the Party and of Production of Socialism." Angola would be a "people's democracy" that could only be achieved if the "whole people were led by clear and scientific political guidance that will necessarily be Marxism–Leninism." The party also launched a rectification campaign reducing its 110,000 card-carrying membership to 31,000, then to 20,000. Events in Eastern Europe and the **Soviet Union** combined with the growing Western business influence in Angola to lead the MPLA to abandon its experiment with socialism.

MOXICO. The largest **province** of Angola. The capital city is Luena and the population is estimated at 230,000. Located in the eastern section of the country, Moxico has a tropical-humid climate. Mineral resources include coal, copper, and iron. **Timber** products are also economically important, as is the poultry industry.

MPLA I PARTY CONGRESS. Prior to the congress, held in **Luanda** in December 1997, the **Movimento Popular de Libertação de Angola** (MPLA) launched the "Year of the Founding of the Party and of Production for Socialism." The MPLA also made extensive efforts to

educate the population about Marxism–Leninism, people's democracy, and scientific political guidance. On 10 December 1977, the MPLA transformed itself into a workers party. National reconstruction would build the **economic** foundations for a Leninist society.

MPLA II PARTY CONGRESS. This second **Movimento Popular de Libertação de Angola** (MPLA) congress, held in **Luanda** in December 1985, strengthened the position of President **Eduardo dos Santos**. Surprising were the demotions of Paulo Jorge and **Iko Carreira**, especially the latter, who had played a key role in recent government successes against **União Nacional para a Independência Total de Angola** (UNITA). Despite events in the **Soviet Union** and Eastern Europe, the speeches and sloganeering showed full socialist unity. The Soviet Union was praised as "the dependable rear guard," while **Cuban** troops had "irrigated our sacred soil with their Angolan brothers."

MPLA III PARTY CONGRESS. Held in **Luanda** in December 1990, the third party congress radically transformed the **Movimento Popular de Libertação de Angola** (MPLA). The ruling party approved the establishment of a multiparty system, discarded its Marxist–Leninist ideology, and gave a vote of confidence to President **Eduardo dos Santos** to continue to negotiate a cease-fire with **União Nacional para a Independência Total de Angola** (UNITA). The congress adopted the ideology of democratic socialism, the direct election of the president, and a measure of private enterprise. The reforms recognized global realities. As President dos Santos said, the "transformation" of international relations, the end of the Cold War, the new U.S.–**Soviet** cooperation, and the democratic revolutions in Eastern Europe made reforms necessary. The 700 delegates also appointed a 90-person Politburo and approved revising the constitution, but only after a military cease-fire.

MPLA IV PARTY CONGRESS. Held in **Luanda** from 5 to 10 December 1998, the fourth party congress of the ruling **Movimento Popular de Libertação de Angola** (MPLA) complained that the **United Nations** had not done enough for peace. President **Eduardo dos Santos** told the 1,275 delegates that **União Nacional para a**

Independência Total de Angola (UNITA) should be isolated, and he called upon the MPLA to mobilize all Angolans to fight the enemies of peace. The delegates voted to enlarge the Central Committee from 179 to 250 members. The congress also broadened the powers of the president and sidelined some party stalwarts, such as General Secretary Lopo do Nascimento, Prime Minister Fernando France Van-Dunem, and former prime minister Marcolino Moco. **Jonas Savimbi** was branded as a war criminal. President dos Santos in his address to the congress said, "The only way to attain definitive peace today is to isolate Dr. Savimbi and his warmongering wing domestically, and internationally, as well as to neutralize him politically and militarily." UNITA viewed the statement as a declaration of war.

MPLA ROUBA, UNITA MATA (The MPLA Steals, UNITA Kills). Graffiti commonly found in towns during the 1992 **elections** that expressed how many Angolans viewed the two parties.

MUEKALIA, DOMINGOS JARDO (1959–). Jardo Muekalia was born to Abias and Belina Pandombela Muekalia on 20 September 1959. He completed his primary **education** in Bela Vista and his secondary studies at the **Huambo** National Secondary School. He joined **União Nacional para a Independência Total de Angola** (UNITA) in 1974 as a member of the Juventude Revolucionaria de Angola (JURA) (Revolutionary Youth of Angola). Muekalia received military training, specializing as a commando. He served as UNITA's representative to Great Britain and later the **United States. United Nations** sanctions prevented him from returning to Angola during the 1990s, and he remains UNITA's chief representative to the United States in the post-**Savimbi** era.

MUSIC. As with **literature**, Angolan music is a blend of European, African, **Brazilian**, *mestiço*, and *assimilado* influences. Angolan artists have attained global honors with this eclectic brand of music. The most prominent musicians include Barcelo de Carvalho **Bonga**, Mario Rui Silva, Teta Lando, Eias dia Kimuezo (the so-called king of Angolan music), As Gingas, Mito Gaspar, Waldemar Bastos, Raul Ouro Negro, Bruna, Patricia Faria, Rei Wabba, and Isidora Campos. *See also* CULTURE; MUSICAL INSTRUMENTS.

MUSICAL INSTRUMENTS. Angola's musical instruments are as varied as its people. The *kisanji* is an instrument consisting of metal sheets attached to a harmonic board and fixed on a trestle. The *kisanji* is held in both hands and played with the thumbs. It is often used when traveling or as background music when an elder is telling a story. The *mbwetete* is like the *kisanji* except it is made with bamboo sheets. The *saxi,* or *katchakatcha,* are more commonly called *maracas;* they are made from maboque, a type of gourd. Once the maboque is dried, a few small holes are drilled and dry seeds are placed inside. More recently, glass beads have replaced the seeds.

The *vandumbu* is a soft wood trumpet coated with matted fibers and used by the Ambwel people of southwest Angola. The *bavugu,* used by the Kung people, is based on the movement of compressed air. Three greased gourds are played by hand on one of two holes, while the other is either open or is closed by pressing it against the thigh. The *mbulumbumba* and the *bavugu* are instruments used by Khoisan people. The *mbulumbumba* is played with a bow that is moved back and forth, away from and toward the stomach. A small stick, held in the right hand, is used to strike the string. Angolan **slaves** took the *mbulumbumba* to **Brazil**, where it was called the *berimbau.* The instrument is used to accompany the aerobatic dance **capoeira** *de Angola.* The *kakocha* is a three-stringed violin, while the *tchihumba* is a violin of five or more strings attached to shafts and a resonance box. It is held in two hands and played using the thumbs.

The *mpungu* is a trumpet that probably originated in the **Bakongo** Kingdom, along with a friction drum called the *mpwita.* Inside the drum is a wooden rod, one end of which is securely attached to the center of the drumhead. The right hand is dampened to give friction, while the left hand presses against the drum skin in accordance with the required rhythm. The *ngoma,* or *bongos* or *tam-tam,* were used to send messages. Shapes and sizes varied by region. The *mjemboerose* is made from an antelope's horn with a resonator greased with beeswax. It is found only among the Himba shepherds of the **Herero** group in southwest Angola. *See also* CULTURE; MUSIC.

MUSSAMO, ANDRE DOMINGOS. A journalist with the independent biweekly **newspaper** *Folha 8* who was arrested in December 1999 for breaking the state security laws. He was jailed in N'Dalatando for over

90 days without charges being filed. Also, the article in question was never printed. The reporter was released from prison on bail on 16 March 2000. At his trial on 2 June 2000, the provincial court found Mussamo innocent of charges he had violated state and military secrets.

MUTILADOS. War veterans who have lost limbs and who panhandle for money in front of **Luanda**'s five-star hotels.

– N –

NAKURU AGREEMENT. Due to the increasing violence in Angola in early 1975, Kenyan president Jomo Kenyatta convened a meeting at Nakuru, Kenya, with **União Nacional para a Independência Total de Angola** (UNITA), the **Movimento Popular de Libertação de Angola** (MPLA), and **Frente Nacional de Libertação de Angola** (FNLA). Meeting from 16 to 21 June 1975, the three groups pledged to free all prisoners, disarm civilian supporters, guarantee the right of free political activity, work toward a new national army, agree on military uniforms, and hold elections in October 1975. The Nakuru Agreement lasted two days. *See also* ALVOR ACCORDS; MOMBASA AGREEMENT.

NAMIBE. Name of an Angolan **province** and its capital city. Namibe has a tropical-dry, arid climate, making **agriculture** difficult. Located on the southern coast, the province looks to the ocean for economic vitality. The port, fish, **fishing industries**, iron ore, and salt mining are important resources for the population of 300,000.

NAMIBIA. A nation located directly to the south of Angola. Once known as South West Africa and controlled by the **Republic of South Africa**, the territory was used by the South African Defense Forces (SADF) as a staging ground for attacks against African National Congress (ANC) bases and camps of the South West Africa People's Organization (SWAPO) in Angola. With the **Brazzaville Protocol**, Namibia became independent in 1989. Initially linked to **União Nacional para a Independência Total de Angola** (UNITA), SWAPO soon accepted aid and bases from the **Movimento Popular de Lib-**

ertação de Angola (MPLA). When Namibia became independent, its foreign policy favored the MPLA, yet it attempted to remain neutral in the face of the continued Angolan civil war. However, in 1999, the government of Namibia allowed Angolan forces to use its soil for attacks on UNITA bases in southern Angola. Later, Namibia introduced its own forces into southern Angola to seek and destroy UNITA units or bases. After the civil war ended, Namibian–Angolan relations revolved around the issues of theft of cattle and cars, guns and drug trafficking, and tax evasion. *See also* BATTLE OF LOMBA RIVER I; BATTLE OF LOMBA RIVER II.

NATALÍCIO, ISIDORO. An Angolan journalist based in N'Dalatando, the capital city of **Kwanza-Norte province**, who reported on the Catholic radio station **Radio Ecclesia** about a public rally where war veterans booed the governor of the province, Manuel Pedro Pacavira, for failing to keep his promise to pay them their pensions in arrears since January 2000. Natalício also taped the crowd booing the provincial chief. Afterward, Pacavira warned Natalício that a crowd unhappy with the report was coming to demonstrate outside the reporter's home. The governor concluded, "I don't know what will happen to you over the next 24 hours." The governor also launched a verbal attack against Radio Ecclesia accusing the station of defaming him and failing to report on positive events in the province. The next day, 8 November 2000, a crowd of approximately 50 teenagers gathered around Natalício's home shouting slogans for 30 minutes. *See also* MEDIA

NATIONAL BIRTH REGISTRATION. From 1998 to May 2003, the Angolan authorities processed 2 million **children** for birth certificates. The government, with **nongovernmental organizations** (NGOs) and churches, hopes to register another 3 million children. Birth certificates are vital because they ensure child medical assistance, **education**, employment, nationality, voting, and **banking** rights.

NATIONAL ELECTORAL COUNCIL. Body established to oversee the September 1992 Angola national **elections**. Critics charged the council did not do enough to register voters from rural areas that were traditional locales of **União Nacional para a Independência Total de Angola** (UNITA) support.

NATIONAL FLAG. The national flag consists of two horizontal bands—the top one red and the bottom one black—with a centered yellow emblem consisting of a five-pointed star within half an industrial gear crossed by a machete. The national flag may change as part of the incorporation of **União Nacional para a Independência Total de Angola** (UNITA) into the government. In October 2003, a new national flag was introduced but was not approved by the **Assembleia Nacional**.

NATIONAL INDEPENDENCE DAY. Celebrated on 11 November in remembrance of Angola's independence from **Portugal**.

NATIONAL RECONSTRUCTION SERVICE. This was begun in 2002 to secure employment for former **União Nacional para a Independência Total de Angola** (UNITA) soldiers.

NATIONAL SOCIETY FOR HUMAN RIGHTS (NSHR). A human rights organization based in Windhoek, **Namibia**. The group was generally hostile toward the government of Angola and favorable toward the **União Nacional para a Independência Total de Angola** (UNITA) rebels.

NEGOCIOS. Or "shady deals" made by **Movimento Popular de Libertação de Angola** (MPLA) politicians and generals.

NEGRITUDE. The philosophy of **União Nacional para a Independência Total de Angola** (UNITA) as enunciated by **Jonas Savimbi**. It is quite different from the philosophy of negritude of late Senegalese president Léopold Senghor. Savimbi defined negritude as follows: "(1) Consensus is the basis of government and all forms of political action; (2) Leadership is characterized by compromise at all stages; (3) Black Africa has its own culture that has been subverted by various colonial powers, resulting in 'rootless African societies without a past.' Yet Africans do have deep roots in Africa that must form the basis of their culture without being exclusive; (4) Inter-state relations in Africa must be based on practical cooperation between free countries, and not on the unrealistic ideals advocated in the concept of 'Pan Africanism'; (5) The basis of any successful form of African government is the recognition of the existence and importance of ethnic [tribal] groupings and systems." Savimbi claimed that negritude was an approach to solving complex problems that confronted multiethnic, ex-colonial societies such as Angola. The philosophy was also a political attack against the ruling **Movimento Popular de Libertação de Angola** (MPLA). UNITA believed that the MPLA did not rule by consensus and would not compromise. The mistrust of Pan-Africanism can be traced to the Organization of African Unity's (OAU) refusal to mediate the Angolan **civil war** and to the OAU Liberation Committee's refusal to fund or arm UNITA. The last point of negritude was a jab at the ***mestiço/assimilado*** leadership of the MPLA. UNITA also described its philosophy as "moderate, democratic, an amalgam of certain features of both capitalism and socialism, Afro-centric, and based on the complimentary principles of compromise and consensus."

NETO, AGOSTINHO (1922–1979). Angola's first president and the son of a teacher and Methodist pastor. Neto was born in a village 40 miles south of **Luanda**. After completing high school, he took a job in the Public Health Department. He attended medical school in **Portugal**, but his studies were interrupted when he was arrested by the **Polícia International de Defesa de Estado** (PIDE) in 1951. During his internment, he was named Amnesty International's "Prisoner of the Year." With a scholarship from the American Methodist Church, he returned and finished medical school in 1958. The same day, he married his Portuguese wife, Maria-Eugenia. He returned to Angola in 1959 to establish a medical practice at a time when many Angolan intellectuals and professionals were fleeing Portuguese repression. In June 1960, the Portuguese arrested Neto at his medical office, prompting a demonstration by friends and supporters. The police opened fire, killing 30 and wounding 200. The incident would be called the "Massacre of Icolo e Bengo." Neto first was exiled to Cape Verde Island and then was sent to jail in Lisbon. Under international pressure, the Portuguese placed Neto under house arrest; a move that allowed him to escape, first to Morocco, then to Zaire. In Zaire, he became president of the **Movimento Popular de Libertação de Angola** (MPLA) and directed the armed struggle against Portuguese colonialism that started in 1961. He visited Moscow in 1964 and received assurances of future **Soviet** military aid. Because of Zaire president Mobutu's support for the **Frente Nacional de Libertação de Angola** (FNLA), Neto was forced to move his base of operations to the Republic of the Congo. From 1961 to 1974, Neto labored to keep the MPLA from factionalism while suffering battlefield defeats from the Portuguese, **FNLA**, and **União Nacional para a Independência Total de Angola** (UNITA). As independence neared in 1975, Neto, a devoted nationalist and Marxist, called upon old friends from **Cuba** and the **Soviet Union** to assist the MPLA. Cuba responded with 12,000 combat troops, while the Soviet Union delivered $200 million in military equipment. Neto's forces won the **civil war** and he became Angola's first African president. However, nationalism proved to be stronger than Marxism. Neto allowed Western companies to develop Angola's **petroleum** resources, sought some type of détente with Washington, and sacked Marxist ideologues in the MPLA, most notably **Nito Alves** and Lopo do Nascimento. Neto was especially angered that the Soviets had not come to his immediate assistance during the 1977 attempted coup by Alves. In September 1979, Neto was scheduled to travel to Havana to attend a Non-Aligned Movement Summit. Instead, on 6 September, he flew to Moscow for what was called a "friendly visit." During an operation on 10 September, Neto died from what was described in various reports as "chronic hepatitis which developed into cirrhosis of the liver" and an obstructed bile duct. The Soviet news agency TASS reported Neto suffered from inoperable cancer of the pancreas. Other reports noted that Neto had leukemia. Neto's death in a Moscow hospital surgery ward led to questions about possible Soviet involvement in his demise. Moscow had invested heavily in the MPLA government. A 20-year friendship treaty had been signed, yet from the Soviet point of view Neto was slipping away from Marxism to non-aligned nationalism. If Moscow didn't support the Alves coup, neither did it seek to stop it. (Cuban forces intervened on behalf of Neto.) The purge of hard-line Marxists from the MPLA also annoyed Moscow. The successor to Neto was **Eduardo dos Santos**, educated in the Soviet Union and wed to a Russian woman. Dos Santos remained loyal to the Soviet Union until the Soviet Union itself collapsed. The truth of Neto's death may emerge as Soviet documents are declassified by the Russian Federation. Neto's birth date of 17 September is a national holiday. Agostinho Neto was also a distinguished poet who wrote several books of verse. A 2003 poll conducted by ANGOP showed that Neto was still one of Angola's most widely read authors.

NETO, GILBERTO. A reporter for *Folha 8,* Gilberto Neto was arrested in July 2001 at the **Malange** airport. The charge was that Neto and a stringer for Reuters News did not receive permission of the **provincial** governor, Flávio Fernandes, to travel to Malange. Police escorted them back to **Luanda**, where the two were detained by officials of the Direção Nacional de Investigação Criminal (DNIC) (National Directorate of Criminal Investigation). The police confiscated passports, press accreditation documents, notebooks, cameras, film, and tape recorders. The two had to return to the DNIC headquarters twice more for further interrogations. In August 2001, Neto was again refused permission to travel abroad, and his passport was confiscated.

NEW PARTNERSHIP FOR AFRICAN DEVELOPMENT (NEPAD) (Nova Parceria de Desenvolvimento do Continte Africano). Joint African–Western program of development focusing on **education**, **health**, energy, potable water, **agriculture**, infrastructure, and **AIDS/HIV**. It is a program designed to promote trade between the 53 nations of Africa, cross-border trade, cultural exchanges, and integration for political stability and sustainable development. Over $6 billion has been donated by Western nations in the hope of encouraging economic development, as well as democracy, good governance, and human rights.

NEW THINKING. A concept initiated by Mikhail Gorbachev reflecting **Soviet** views toward Third World adventurism. For years, the Soviet Union had spent billions of rubles to prop up regimes in Eastern Europe, **Cuba**, Nicaragua, Mozambique, Ethiopia, and Angola. When Gorbachev took power in 1985, he realized that the Soviet economy, in desperate need for U.S. trade and aid, could no longer subsidize its client states. The **Reagan doctrine** provided a mandate for assistance to "freedom fighters" struggling against Moscow-sponsored regimes. The **Movimento Popular de Libertação de Angola** (MPLA) switch from Marxism to capitalism was partially in response to Gorbachev's initiatives. At the signing ceremony for the **Bicesse Accords**, U.S. secretary of state James Baker paid tribute to U.S.–Soviet cooperation in "resolving yet another issue that once deeply divided our countries but that now unites us in common purpose."

NEW TROUSERS. A campaign theme utilized in 1992 by **União Nacional para a Independência Total de Angola** (UNITA) presidential candidate **Jonas Savimbi**. The implication was that UNITA represented new trousers, while the **Movimento Popular de Libertação de Angola** (MPLA) were old trousers that needed to be discarded.

NEWSPAPERS. As with other aspects of the **media**, the end of the **civil war** has seen a dramatic increase in the number and different types of newspapers. *A Capital* is a biweekly newspaper based in **Luanda**. The paper was labeled slanderous by Angola's home minister in August 2003 after it reported on excessive use of police force in a Luanda suburb. *Angolense* is a privately owned newspaper in Luanda that is frequently critical of the government. In 2000, the paper was forced to cease operations for five months because financiers withdrew support and two journalists were accused of defaming senior government officials. However, new monetary sources were found and the paper reopened in August 2000. *Actual* and *Comercio Actualidade* started in 1994, *Tempos Novos* (New times) began in 1995. *O Independente,* and *Agora* (Today) are independent weekly newspapers printed in Luanda. *Correio da Semana* (Weekly post) and *Era Nova* (New era) are weekly newspapers printed in Luanda that have links to the **Movimento Popular de Libertação de Angola** (MPLA). *Jornal do Rangel* is a monthly neighborhood paper in Luanda started in September 1997. *Apostalado* is an independent Catholic monthly newspaper. Other newspapers include the *Palanca News and Business,* a newspaper printed in Luanda under an initiative by Angolans living in **South Africa**. Its target audience is South Africans interested in business opportunities in Angola. Publication began on 31 January 2003. **União Nacional para a Independência Total de Angola** (UNITA) began publication of *Terra Angolana* during the cease-fire of the **Bicesse Accords**. The paper halted publication in Angola after the **Halloween Massacre** of October 1992, but it is occasionally printed in Lisbon, **Portugal**. *See also FOLHA 8; IMPARCIAL FAX;* MAGAZINES.

NGONDA, LUCAS. Lucas Ngonda is one of the two presidents of the **Frente Nacional de Libertação de Angola** (FNLA). Elected in 1999 in a controversial election, Ngonda has feuded with **Holden Roberto** over who should lead the organization. Reconciliation meetings have been unsuccessful.

NHANECA–HUMBE GROUP. Ethnolinguistic group composed of the Cuancas, Donguenas, Gambos, Handas of Quipungo, Hingas, Humbes, Muilas, Quilengues–Humbes, Quilengues–Musos, and Quipungos peoples. They are estimated to be 5 percent of Angola's population. The peoples that make up the group are farmers and cattle herders. Hunting and **fishing** are also an important source of protein. The Nhaneca–Humbe peoples are mostly located in the present-day **provinces** of **Huíla** and **Cunene**. They were formerly governed by a monarch, but the **Portuguese** stripped the crown of any real power. The monarch maintained some influence because the people believed the spirits of dead ancestors resided in him.

NINJA. Name given to the National Police Force, which is also termed the *Antiriot* Police. The term comes from the kung-fu movies popular in **Luanda** in the early 1990s. The Spanish-trained antiriot police played a major role in the **Halloween Massacre**. The Ninjas, along with armed civilians, killed thousands of **União Nacional para a Independência Total de Angola** (UNITA) and **Bakongo** people from October 1992 through January 1993.

NKANGA, VITA (António I). King António was the last ruler, the 25th king, of the centralized **Bakongo** kingdom. He attempted to stop the fragmentation of his kingdom by confronting the Portuguese at the **Battle of Mbwila** in 1665. The king and many of his nobles perished. Thereafter, the Bakongo kingdom began a long decline.

NONGOVERMENTAL ORGANIZATIONS (NGOs). The prolonged civil war in Angola combined with the government's inability, ineffectiveness, or disinterest made the contribution of NGOs invaluable. Their size, organizational structure, and experience allowed them to respond rapidly and appropriately in emergency or rehabilitation situations. The **United Nations** and the NGOs have in effect become the state bureaucracy. The groups are addressing resettlement of **internally displaced people** (IDPs), returning **refugees**, and demobilized soldiers. Other NGOs coordinate **land-mine** removal and institutional and logistical support to rehabilitate Angola's **agricultural**, **health**, and **educational** infrastructure. Prominent NGOs involved in Angola are Christian Aid, **Fatal Transactions**, **Fundação Eduardo dos Santos**, **Global Witness**, Halo Trust, **Mãos Livres**, **Médecins sans Frontières**, Mines Advisory Group, and Norwegian People's Aid. Angolan NGOs are represented by the Foro de ONGs Angolanas (FONGA) (Angolan Forum of Nongovernmental Agencies). *See also* DONOR FATIGUE.

NORMS ON THE RESETTLEMENT AND RETURN OF DISPLACED POPULATIONS. United Nations–written and government-endorsed rules for the return of **refugees** to their home areas. Officially adopted in 2002, the norms call for resettlement areas to be free of **land mines**, state administration to be extended to the site, and **health** and **education** facilities to be made available for the returning populations.

NORWEGIAN MODEL. A **petroleum** plan considered by the Angolan government that would slow down billion-dollar oil projects to protect reserves and place greater emphasis on the indigenous oil industry. Such a policy, if enacted, would lower investment returns and profits for the major oil companies. Angola has observer status, not membership, in the Organization of Petroleum Exporting Countries. Consequently, it is free to choose whether to reduce or increase the flow of petroleum. Independent observers worry that such a policy could bring in smaller companies with no expertise or public accountability, already a problem for Sonangol (**Sociedade Nacional de Combustíveis de Angola**). Angola is pressuring the international oil giants to begin the "Angolanization" of the industry. To help build

Angola's industrial expertise and base, Sonangol is requesting the majors to contract services with Angolan companies. The international giants have preferred to hire contractors on the open market, but may be forced to "Angolanize" rather than lose access to Angolan petroleum.

NOVA HORIZONTE (New Horizon). Government-funded program for the **economic** development of postwar Angola.

NOVA VIDA (New Life). Economic stimulus program begun in 1996 that adopted a gradual approach to economic reform. It stressed a mixed economy and the need to share national revenue with the more vulnerable segments of Angolan society. The program aimed at stabilizing the **kwanza**, improving business confidence, and rooting out public corruption. Steps were taken to halt the circulation of the U.S. dollar on the black market. *See also* PROGRAMA DE AÇÃO GOVERNO; PROGRAMA DE ESTABILIÇÃO E RECUPERÇÃO ECONÔMICA DE MEDIO PRAZO 1998–2000; PROGRAMA ECONÔMICA E SOCIAL PARA 1994; SANEAMENTO ECONÔMICA E FINANCIERO.

NTONI–NZINGA, DANIEL (1946–). One of the founders of Angola's **Grupo Angolano de Reflexao para Paz** (GARP) peace movement. An ordained Baptist minister, Ntoni–Nzinga received a bachelor of social sciences degree from the University of Manchester with a specialization in social anthropology. He holds a doctorate of theology from the University of Leeds. He has served as the executive secretary of the Evangelical Baptist Church in Angola and as secretary general of the Angolan Council of Churches. In April 2000, he became one of the founders of **Comité Inter-Eclesial para a Paz em Angola** (COIEPA), an organization that advocated negotiations and a peaceful resolution to the **civil war**.

NUCLÉO NACIONAL DE RECOLHA E PESQUISA DA LITERATURA ORAL (NNARP) (National Nucleus of Oral Literature Gathering and Research). An organization created in 1998 to strengthen Angolan **culture** by gathering, registering, and retelling oral traditions. NNARP events have featured sacred music of the Esperança de Bethel female choral group and poetry by Feliza Cambango, Ginga Cambango, Moisés Sandombe, and Zuline Bumba. *See also* LITERATURE.

NZINGA, QUEEN (1582–1663). A historical heroine of Angolan nationalism. Queen Nzinga made her first appearance before the **Portuguese** governor in Luanda in 1622. She became a baptized Christian. She also convinced Portuguese officials to recognize the independence of the **Mbundu** despite their having been defeated in battle by Portuguese forces. Further, she extracted a promise of support for assistance in fighting the Imbangala intruding from the east. She assumed the throne after the mysterious death of her brother in 1624. Nzinga allowed Portuguese traders, missionaries, and officials access to the lands of the Mbundu, but relations soured. The Portuguese forced her from the throne. Next, Nzinga allied with the **Dutch** and the Matamba group, which dominated the entire **Mbundu** area. When the Dutch abandoned Angola, she was forced into an alliance with the Portuguese. Through personal, political, and military savvy, the queen was able to dominate Mbundu politics for 40 years by successfully manipulating her enemies to serve Mbundu interests. Shrewd, charismatic, intelligent, and forceful, the queen was able to persuade the Dutch and Portuguese to pursue policies that were inimical to their interests. However, when she died in 1663, the end was near for Mbundu sovereignty. *See also* WOMEN.

– O –

OFENSIVA DO CHRISTMAS (Christmas Offensive). A Forças Armadas de Angolanas (FAA) military operation that resulted in the capture of Bailundo, Andulo, and Catabola in December 1999.

OIL NOMENKLATURA. Term used to describe **Luanda**'s elite, ruling families. *See also* ONE HUNDRED FAMILIES.

OKIMBAKU, GARCIA (Garcia Afonso II) (1641–1661). Under King Garcia, 24th king of the empire, the **Bakongo** reached the height of their power since the arrival of the Portuguese. Garcia negotiated with Rome for more power over the local **Catholic Church**

and allied with the Dutch when they seized **Luanda**. In 1648, the Dutch abandoned Angola, and the Portuguese took revenge against those who had helped the Dutch. Garcia was able to maintain his grip on the kingdom, but when he died in 1661, the **Battle of Mbwila**, which broke the empire, was only four years distant.

OLIVEIRA, DE MURTALA (Dog Murras). Angolan singer who in May 2003 released his third compact disc, which contained 13 songs, two in Zouk and Semba styles and the rest in his traditional Ku-duro style. The compact disc, titled *Bwé Angolano,* deals with the socioeconomic problems facing the Angolan people. Dog Murras's earlier offerings were *Suis Generis,* released in 2000, and *Natural e Diferente,* released in 2001. *See also* MUSIC.

ONDJANGO. An **Umbundu** word for a meeting place. An area for the community to meet, allowing it to maintain itself even if displaced because of warfare. *Ondjango* implies dignity and identity for the villagers.

ONE HUNDRED FAMILIES. Name given to the richest members of Angolan society. The name comes from the belief that Angola's upper social strata is dominated by a few dozen families who have become wealthy through fraud and corruption in the military and the **petroleum** industry. *See also* OIL NOMENKLATURA.

OPERAÇÃO CACIMBO. A **Forças Armadas de Angolanas** (FAA) military operation in 1999 that ended the siege of **Malange** and **Kuito** by **União Nacional para a Independência Total de Angola** (UNITA).

OPERAÇÃO KISSONDE (Operation Violent Ant). Military operation that led to the death of **Jonas Savimbi** in February 2002. *See also* CIVIL WAR.

OPERATION ASKARI. A **South African** Defense Force (SADF) operation against elements of South West Africa People's Organization (SWAPO) and **Forças Armadas Populares de Libertação de Angola** (FAPLA) conducted in December 1983 and January 1984.

South African sources claimed 407 SWAPO dead compared to 32 South Africans killed. The number of FAPLA casualties was unknown, but was believed to be high.

OPERATION CARLOTTA. Name for a **Cuban** operation to transport troops to Angola to support the **Movimento Popular de Libertação de Angola** (MPLA) struggle for power. Carlotta was a black woman who led a slave revolt in Cuba in 1843. *El Vietnam Heroico, El Coral Island,* and *La Plata* were the three transport ships that carried Cuban soldiers to Angola. They arrived on 20 October 1975.

OPERATION MODULAR. South African strike against **Forças Armadas Populares de Libertação de Angola** (FAPLA) and **Cubans** in the **Battle of Lomba River II** in September 1987. The **União Nacional para a Independência Total de Angola** (UNITA) was in danger of losing the **Mavinga/Jamba** complex until South African Defense Forces (SADF) air and ground units intervened.

OPERATION PROTEA. South African military strike in August 1981 against the South West Africa People's Organization (SWAPO) that also included South African units engaging **Forças Armadas Populares de Libertação de Angola** (FAPLA) for the first time since 1976. Soviet personnel were also killed in the raid. The South African Defense Forces (SADF) claimed 1,000 SWAPO/FAPLA casualties, with SADF only losing 10 troops. South Africa's intent seemed to be to disrupt Angola's **economic** and political system, take advantage of a chance to embarrass the Soviet Union, possibly to establish a **União Nacional para a Independência Total de Angola** (UNITA) buffer state on the **Namibian** border, and to apply continuous pressure on SWAPO and the **Movimento Popular de Libertação de Angola** (MPLA) in the event of future negotiations.

OPERATION REINDEER. South African military action against the South West Africa People's Organization (SWAPO) camp at Kassinga in May 1978. SWAPO suffered over 1,000 dead with 200 captured. According to SWAPO, the victims were women and children. Kassinga, located in **Cunene province**, is approximately 100 miles from the **Namibian** border.

OPERATION WALLPAPER. **South African** military strike against Forças Armadas Populares de Libertação de Angola (FAPLA) and **Cuban** units advancing on the **Mavinga/Jamba** area. Launched in September 1985, the strikes helped **União Nacional para a Independência Total de Angola** (UNITA) turn back the government forces in the **Battle of Lomba River I.**

OPERATION ZULU. Military push by **South African** forces with **União Nacional para a Independência Total de Angola** (UNITA), Daniel Chipenda's **Frente Nacional de Libertação de Angola** (FNLA) men, and some **mercenaries.** The operation was launched on 14 October 1975 with the goal of driving up the coast from **Namibia** to **Luanda** before the independence date of 11 November. *See also* FOXBAT COLUMN.

ORGANIZAÇÃO DA MULHER ANGOLANA (OMA) (Organization of Angolan Women). The OMA was founded in 1963 and is the organization that represents women to the **Movimento Popular de Libertação de Angola** (MPLA). Before liberation, the OMA engaged in political work, mobilizing support among **refugees.** Since liberation, the OMA has evolved into a service organization providing classes in literacy, **AIDS/HIV,** and other **health** issues.

ORION. Brazilian public relations firm hired by the **Eduardo dos Santos** team in 1992 to run the president's reelection campaign. Orion initiated the "Hearts and Doves" campaign, which made dos Santos appear as a father figure to Angola, and concocted the "Day of the Doves" campaign trick. Allegedly, both dos Santos and **Jonas Savimbi** were at a campaign function. Both men were handed doves to release as a sign of their commitment to peace. The dos Santos bird flew to freedom, but the Savimbi dove, its wings tightly bound until the moment it was handed to Savimbi, could or would not fly. Thus dos Santos seemed to be a man of peace, while Savimbi did not. *See also* ELECTIONS; MOVIMENTO POPULAR DE LIBERTAÇÃO DE ANGOLA.

OVAHIMBA. A primitive, remote group inhabiting northern **Namibia** and southern Angola. They are fiercely proud of their culture and traditions, and while they want development they are not willing to sacrifice their way of life. Ovahimba women go bare-breasted and wear short skirts made of goatskin and jewelry made from metal and leather. The women coat their bodies with a red paste and animal fat to protect them from the harsh climate. The red paste also coats their long, braided hair. Jobs and **education** require the Ovahimba to leave their home areas. On returning, some bring back **AIDS/HIV**. The Ovahimba believe the virus to be a disease of foreigners, and they are uneducated as to how it is spread. HIV-positive people returning to the bush are ostracized. Attempts by the **United Nations** and Ovahimba teachers to educate the people are usually rejected as interference in the culture and traditions of the group.

OVIMBUNDU GROUP. The largest and most homogeneous of all Angola's ethnolinguistic groups. The Ovimbundu number 3.9 million, or about 37 percent of the population, and are located mainly in the central highland **provinces**, in **Huambo**, **Bié**, **Huíla**, and part of **Kwanza Sul**. They speak the **Umbundu** language, which half of all Angolans understand. For a 50-year period, the Ovimbundu thrived by trading rubber with the **Portuguese**. Other economic activities included beekeeping, hunting, trading crafts, and the occasional conflict. The Ovimbundu were traders throughout central Africa, bringing them into contact with other African peoples and cultures. The Ovimbundu did not come into contact with the Portuguese until the 18th century, and the Portuguese did not fully break the power of the Ovimbundu kings until 1902. Despite their reputations as regional traders, their interior isolation meant the concepts of freedom and nationalism would arrive late. Eventually, however, the **railroads** and missionaries brought the message. **União Nacional para a Independência Total de Angola** (UNITA) draws most of its support from the Ovimbundu people. Politically, the Ovimbundu were organized into several powerful kingdoms—Bié, Andulo, Huambo, and Bailundo—of which Bailundo was dominant. In 1902, under the leadership of Mutu-Ya-Kevela, they rose against Portuguese rule. The **Portuguese**, with Cape Verdeans, coastal Africans, and troops from other parts of the empire, succeeded in ending the rebellion. After the Bailundo War of 1902, the kingdoms became subservient to Portugal. **Jonas Savimbi**'s grandfather, Sakaita, fought in the war. The present king is Ekuikui IV of Bailundo. Important cities of the Ovimbundu include Nhareya, Mungo, Bailundo, and

Andulo, all located in the central highlands. Government forces attempted to capture Andulo in January 1999, but they were ambushed, suffering heavy losses. When government troops entered the city, they encountered no resistance, and the town appeared deserted. As the government soldiers celebrated, UNITA rebels emerged from hidden bunkers to kill over 600 government soldiers and wound 1,000 more. The **Forças Armadas de Angolanas** (FAA) retreated in complete disarray. Andulo and Bailundo were finally captured by government forces in September 1999 after a series of fierce battles.

– P –

PACHECO, CARLOS (1958–). Author of *Repensar Angola* (Rethink Angola), cited in an informal July 2003 report as one of the most widely read books in **Luanda**. *See also* LITERATURE.

PALANCA NEGRA (giant sable antelope or black antelope). Antelope long thought extinct until Professor Wouter van Hoven of the Center for Wildlife Management in **South Africa** visited Angola's **Luanda** Reserve and Cangandala National Park in August 2002. There, he had several sightings of the giant sable antelope, including adults and juveniles. *See also* ARCA DE NOAH DA OPERAÇÃO.

PARA TRÁS À ESCOLA (Back to School). The Angolan government worked in this program with the United Nations Children's Fund (UNICEF) to get **children** back into school. Over 1 million children, or 44 percent, do not attend school. The program began in February 2003 in **Malange** and **Bié** provinces. The numbers in the two provinces totaled 250,000 children returning to 13,000 rebuilt classrooms with thousands of **education** kits for pupils and teachers alike. UNICEF also trained 4,000 people as primary school teachers. The program was so successful that, in June 2003, the government announced plans to hire another 50,000 teachers.

PARTIDO DA ALIANÇA DA JUVENTUDE OPERÁRIOS-CAMPESINOS DE ANGOLA (PAJOCA) (Alliance Party of Angolan Youth, Workers, and Peasants). An opposition party led by its president Alexandre Andre and vice president Joaquim Ferreira de Almeida.

PARTIDO DE APOIO DEMOCRÁTICO E PROGRESSO DE ANGOLA (PADPA) (Angolan Party for Democratic Support and Progress). In January 2001, police used force to disperse a peaceful demonstration led by the president of PADPA, Carlos Alberto de Andrade Leitão, and five other members. The demonstrators were demanding the resignation of President **Eduardo dos Santos** and calling for an investigation into **Angolagate**. The six detainees were tried but acquitted on charges of having failed to obtain the proper authorization for a protest.

PARTIDO DO DESENVOLVIMENTO SOCIAL (PDS) (Social Development Party). Led by Anastácio Finda, the PDS advocates holding national **elections** in 2004. Finda is also executive director of the **Partidos da Oposição Civil** (POC), a coalition of parties founded in 1994.

PARTIDO RENOVAÇÃO DA SOCIAL (PRS) (Social Renewal Party). An opposition party headed by Eduardo Kwangana. The PRS came in third in the 1992 multiparty elections.

PARTIDOS DA OPOSIÇÃO CIVIL (POC) (Civil Opposition Parties). A group of opposition parties founded in 1994. The POC is headed by Paulino Pinto João of the Convenção Nacional Democrática de Angola (National Democratic Party of Angola). Other members include the **Frente Nacional de Libertação de Angola** (FNLA) (National Front for the Liberation of Angola), Frente para a Democracia (Democratic Front of Angola), Movimento Democrático de Angola/Partido da Consciência Nacional (Democratic Movement of Angola/National Conscience Party), Partido Liberal de Angola (Liberal Party of Angola), Partido Nacional de Salvação de Angola (National Salvation Party of Angola), the Partido de Solidariedade e da Consciência de Angola (the Solidarity and Conscience Party of Angola), Partido Social Independente de Angola (Social Independence Party of Angola), Unificação Democrática de Angola (Unified Democratic Party of Angola), and União Nacional para a Democracia (National Democratic Unity Party).

PASTINHA, GRAND MESTRE (1889–1982). In 1941, Pastinha opened the first *capoeira* school in **Brazil**. The school was dedicated to preserving and continuing the long tradition of the African martial art. For Mestre Pastinha, *capoeira* was a path to self-knowledge. Pastinha also wrote the first book on *capoeira*'s practice, history, and philosophy. He made several albums of *capoeira* music. In the 1970s, he traveled to Africa to attend the Festival of African Arts and Culture (FESTAC).

PATRICIO, JOSE GONCALVES MARTINS. Veteran diplomat and journalist who became the vice president of British Petroleum/ Amoco's Angola Business Unit in April 2001. He previously had served as Angola's ambassador to **Portugal** and the **United States**. Patricio served as Angola's permanent representative to the **United Nations** for one year, after replacing Afonso Van Dunem "Mbinda," who returned to Angola to head the **Eduardo dos Santos Foundation** (FESA). From 1974 to 1989, Patricio worked for **Radio Nacional de Angola**, where he was the chief editor, head of the information department, and head of programming. He received advanced degrees from the Belgrade School of Journalism and a postgraduate degree in political marketing from the Independent University of Lisbon. He was a member of the Angolan government negotiating team during the 1990 to 1991 negotiations that led to the **Bicesse Accords**. In 1993, Patricio was named one of the "200 Leaders of the Future" by the World Economic Forum.

PEACE STONE HIROSHIMA. Award established in 1991 by a Japanese **nongovernmental organization** (NGO) to promote world peace. In June 2002, President **Eduardo dos Santos** was awarded the prize for his efforts in Angola's peace process.

PENA, ARLINDO CHENDA ISAAC "BEN BEN" (1955–1998). Born in Caricoque on 17 November 1955 to Isaac Pires Pena and Judite Malheiro Pena, Ben Ben was a nephew of **Jonas Savimbi**. He completed his primary **education** at the Chilesso Mission and his secondary studies at the Industrial and Commercial School and the National High School of **Bié**. Ben Ben joined **União Nacional para a Independência Total de Angola** (UNITA) in 1968 at the age of 13.

His initial involvement included serving as a runner between posts and disseminating UNITA propaganda in cities and towns. After military training in Europe and Morocco, Ben Ben began a steady rise through the UNITA hierarchy. In December 1989, General Ben Ben became chief of staff of **Forças Armadas de Libertação de Angola** (FALA). As part of the unified army called for by the **Bicesse Accords**, he left FALA to join the new national army. When the civil war reignited in 1992, Ben Ben escaped **Luanda** and slowly made his way to **Huambo**, where he rejoined Savimbi and FALA. Again, as part of the 1994 **Lusaka Accord**, Ben Ben was sent as part of the UNITA military delegation to play a role in the **Forças Armadas de Angolanas** (FAA). He was appointed deputy chief of staff. Ben Ben passed away on 19 October 1998 at a clinic in Pretoria, **South Africa**. Rather than seeking help from a military hospital, as stipulated by Angolan military guidelines, he first sought treatment at a private clinic in Luanda. Only after treatment at the clinic failed did he go to a military hospital on 15 October. Noting the seriousness of his illness, the military hospital arranged for a medical evacuation on 16 October to a specialized hospital in South Africa. Unfortunately, the delay in seeking adequate treatment proved fatal. South African hospital authorities determined the cause of death to be cerebral **malaria**. His death remains shrouded in secrecy. No autopsy was performed, nor did his widow allow the traditional military funeral. UNITA claimed Ben Ben was poisoned by the government because he was on the verge of fleeing Luanda to rejoin FALA.

PEREIRA, ANALIA DE VITORIA. Leader of the Partido Liberal Democrático (PLD) (Liberal Democratic Party) who in June 2003 announced her candidacy for the presidency of Angola. In the elections in 2002, Analia Pereira received 11,475 votes, or 0.29 percent of votes cast. The next elections will probably be held some time in 2004–05. Other candidates include **Vicente Pinto de Andrade**, **Feliciano Loa**, **Carlos Contreiras Gouveia**, and **Isaías Samakuva**.

PESTANA, ARTUR "PEPETELA" (1941–). Pepetela over his career has written some renowned books of Angolan **literature**, including *As Aventuras de Ngunga* (Adventures of Ngunga), *Geracao da Utopia* (Utopia generation), *Mayombe*, and *Lueji*. Born in

Benguela, Pepetela saw his *mestiço* origin as a way to bridge the gap between the races. He joined the **Movimento Popular de Libertação de Angola** (MPLA) and was posted in **Cabinda**. After Angola became independent, he served as an undersecretary for education and helped organize the União dos Escritores Angolano (Angolan Writers Union). According to a poll conducted by the Agência De Notícia de Angola (ANGOP) (Angolan News Agency) Pepetela was one of the most widely read authors in Angola in 2003. His newest release, *Jaime Bunda E A Morte Do Americano* (Jaime Bunda and the death of an American), was published in October 2003.

PETROLEUM. Oil companies are attracted to Angola because of the low operating costs, the high probability of a successful strike, and a favorable business climate offered by the Angolan government, even though the **United States** openly supported **União Nacional para a Independência Total de Angola** (UNITA). Major oil companies working in Angola include Exxon/Mobil, Esso Exploration, Agip (Italian), Statoil (Norwegian), British Petroleum, Conoco/Philips, ELF (French), Mobil, Neste (Finnish), Petrobas (Brazilian), Petrogal (Portuguese), Ranger (Canadian), Chevron–Texaco, NorskHydro/Saga (Norwegian), and Den Norske State Oljeselskap (Norwegian). Oil accounts for 90 percent of Angola's gross domestic product (GDP). Its known oil reserves place it third behind Saudi Arabia and Iran. Drilling in the **petroleum blocks** is taking place from 1,670 feet deep to a maximum depth of 8,250 feet. The number of wells has doubled since 1993, reaching 44 in 2002 and 47 in 2003. The only oil refinery in Angola is in **Luanda**. It is run by Fina Petroleos de Angola and has a capacity of 39,000 bpd (barrels per day). In November 2001, Total E and P announced plans to increase capacity to 60,000 bpd by 2004. Sonangol, Angola's national oil company, approved construction of a $5 billion refinery to be constructed in **Lobito**. The refinery was expected to come on line by 2007. By the end of 2002, Angola's oil production had risen to 930,000 bpd and earned almost $7 billion. Nonetheless, in 2002, Angola imported 4 percent of its gasoline needs and 15 percent of its aviation fuel requirements. *See also* INTERNATIONAL MONETARY FUND; NORWEGIAN MODEL; PETROLEUM BLOCKS; SIGNATURE BONUSES.

PETROLEUM BLOCKS. In 1978–79, the Angolan government divided its continental shelf into 13 blocks; they later added another 18, as deep and ultradeep water drilling became feasible. Block 0, located adjacent to **Cabinda**, has produced the Banzala, Kokongo, Lomba, N'Dola, North Nemba, and Numbi wells. Block 1 has only one active field, Safueiro, and its output is small. Block 2, near the mouth of the Congo River, has produced numerous productive wells. Block 3, found near N'Zeto, has also produced numerous productive wells. Block 4 has proven to be a disappointment, despite a significant amount of money spent on drilling. Block 5 had the same result. Block 6 is directly offshore from **Luanda**. Block 7 is located south of Luanda, while block 8 is found between **Bengo** and **Cuanza Sul provinces**. Block 9 is also near Cuanza Sul. Blocks 10–13 are near the coasts of **Namibe** and **Benguela** provinces. Blocks 1–13 have had moderate to scant success. The future of Angola's **petroleum** production will be found in the deep and ultradeep blocks that began production in 2002–03. Petroleum analysts believe that blocks 14, 15, 17, and 18 could produce 10 billion barrels of oil.

PINNOCK, JOHNNY EDUARDO (1943–2000). A member of the Central Committee of the **Movimento Popular de Libertação de Angola** (MPLA), he later served as adviser to President **Eduardo dos Santos**. Pinnock died while posted as Angola's ambassador to Belgium. He was a **Frente Nacional de Libertação de Angola** (FNLA) member years before he switched to the MPLA and was the MPLA's highest-ranking **Bakongo**.

POLÍCIA INTERNATIONAL DE DEFESA DE ESTADO (PIDE) (International Police for Defense of the State). **Portuguese** secret police deployed in the colonies to repress the nationalist movements and other persons, or groups deemed to be threats to Portugal's interests. The PIDE paid informants, tortured and killed prisoners, monitored potential future nationalist leaders, and spread false rumors and propaganda throughout the Portuguese African empire.

POLIO (poliomyelitis). In 1999, Angola suffered Africa's largest outbreak of polio in more than a decade. In 2003, the World Health Organization (WHO) listed Angola as at "high risk for return" of the poliovirus. Many nations employ "immunization days" as a method to vaccinate children. The main tool of a polio campaign is an oral vaccine that contains the weakened strain of the virus. It causes an infection that allows the body's immune system to shield the person from more virulent strains. Polio is difficult to eradicate. Immunization Days have worked in Angola. In 1999, the number of confirmed cases of polio was 1,103; by 2002, the annual number was zero. However, with a great many unvaccinated **internally displaced people** (IDPs) returning to the country, the continuation of immunizations days will remain a priority. *See also* HEALTH CARE.

POLITICAL PARTIES. Under the **Portuguese**, Angolans were forbidden from belonging to political associations of any type. Organizations that hinted at politics were repressed by the **Polícia International de Defesa de Estado** (PIDE). However, Angolans were able to organize literary, self-help, and religious organizations from which the political movements emerged. During 1974–75, a number of **White Settler** parties were formed to try to protect the political and economic rights of the Portuguese Angolans. They felt betrayed by the **Alvor Accords**, which made no mention of the settlers. The parties were outlawed by the colonial authorities, and the settler population for the most part returned to Portugal. Independence, combined with the **civil war** victory by the **Movimento Popular de Libertação de Angola** (MPLA), led to the imposition of a socialist one-party state. The collapse of the **Soviet Union**, the end of the Cold War, the growing military strength of **União Nacional para a Independência Total de Angola** (UNITA), and mounting international pressure obliged the government to sign the **Bicesse Accords**, which guaranteed free, fair elections. The **MPLA III Party Congress** in December 1990 completed the transition. The 1992 **election** saw 11 individuals and 12 parties seek electoral power. Present-day Angolan political parties include UNITA, **Frente Nacional de Libertação de Angola** (FNLA), **Partido Renovação da Social** (PRS), Partido Liberal Democrático (PLD), and a number of smaller ones. Presidential and parliamentary **elections** are scheduled for either 2004 or 2005.

PONTO DE RE-ENCONTRO (Reunification Point). An Angolan group that in June 2003 began attempting to locate over 4,000 people who had disappeared during the **civil war**. The group first sought to locate the missing in **União Nacional para a Independência Total de Angola** (UNITA) quartering areas. *See also* MEDIA.

PORTUGAL. Portugal played a major role in opening the spice trade from India and participated in the scramble for Africa. During the colonial era, Portugal acquired control of Angola, Cape Verde, Guinea–Bissau, Mozambique, and São Tomé and Príncipe. The Portuguese called the colonies **provinces**, but in fact, they encouraged the **slave trade**, destroyed great Angolan kingdoms, and exploited the people and natural resources. By the 1960s, Portugal still ignored the "winds of change" in Africa and sought to maintain control of the colonies in the face of growing nationalist hostility. Very few whites lived in Angola. In 1970, the white population in the five largest Angolan cities was 124,814 in **Luanda**, 14,694 in Nova Lisboa, 14,152 in **Lobito**, 13,429 in Sá da Bandeira, and 10,175 in **Benguela**. Portugal soon found itself fighting wars in Angola, Mozambique, and Guinea–Bissau. By 1974, Portugal's losses in the colonial wars had totaled 12,000 dead with 40,000 wounded. Emigration from Portugal was skyrocketing, and the national debt was growing, as was inflation. A well-respected Portuguese general, **António de Spinola**, wrote the book *Portugal e o Futuro* (Portugal and the future), concluding that Portugal could not win its colonial conflicts. U.S. National Security Study Memorandum 39 (a.k.a. "The Tar Baby Option") concluded that the guerrillas could not defeat the Portuguese, but the Portuguese could not defeat the insurgents. On 25 April 1974, members of the **Movimento das Forças Armadas** (MFA) overthrew the regime of Prime Minister **Marcello Caetano**. The coup signaled the end of Portugal's 500-year African empire. Relations with the **Movimento Popular de Libertação de Angola** (MPLA) government were tepid at best. **União Nacional para a Independência Total de Angola** (UNITA) had many influential friends both inside and outside the Portuguese government. Yet, by the 1990s, Portugal was training Angolan soldiers, and with the death of **Jonas Savimbi**, Lisbon is making a concerted effort to reestablish a strong commercial link with its former colony.

PORTUGUESE ADMINISTRATORS OF ANGOLA. After the final pacification campaigns of the 1930s, **Portuguese** administrators such as Henrique de Paiva Couceiro, Eduardo Ferreira da Costa, and José

Norton de Matos embarked upon measures to decentralize the administration and grant some autonomy. The administrators also sought to increase Portuguese immigration and, where possible, have Portuguese values taught to the native peoples. Norton de Matos argued for a humanistic approach toward the Africans. He criticized the then prevailing contract labor codes and urged his officials to proceed rapidly toward the acculturation process to produce a single, unified state. Norton de Matos's plan of creating a society where no discrimination would occur because of race, creed, or ideology was premature to say the least. Angola would remain a Portuguese state. Thus Norton de Matos repressed African nationalism, foreign missionaries, and political dissent. Later, he would run for president against **António Salazar**, criticizing the government for failing to properly implement the "new state" (**estado novo**) and **Lusotropicalism** in Angola.

PORTUGUESE AFRICA. Term referring to the **Portuguese** African holdings of Angola, Cape Verde, Guinea–Bissau, Mozambique, and São Tomé e Príncipe.

POUCAS PALAVRAS E MAIS TRABALHO (**fewer words and more work**). A government motto for postwar reconstruction. As part of the initiative, the Angolan government drafted legislation for a new investment code to promote foreign investment and a new press law to protect a free, independent **media**.

POWELL, COLIN. The **U.S.** secretary of state who visited **Luanda** in September 2002 and met with President **Eduardo dos Santos** over Angola's **petroleum** production and the lingering strife in the **Democratic Republic of the Congo**. Secretary Powell warned the Angolan president that the **United States** would eventually terminate aid programs to Angola and urged dos Santos to root out corruption in government finances. He met with government, **United Nations**, and **União Nacional para a Independência Total de Angola** (UNITA) officials to hear about implementation of the **Lusaka Protocol**. He also laid the cornerstone for the new U.S. embassy.

PRESÍDIO (fort). The **Portuguese** established a number of forts throughout Angola to protect colonialists from hostile groups and bar access to the interior.

PRISONS (prisãos). Angola's prison system is primarily located in **Luanda** and includes Casa de Reclusão and São Paulo, two of the Luanda prisons stormed by the **Movimento Popular de Libertação de Angola** (MPLA) militants on 4 February 1961. Others are Comercio de Viand, Estrada de Catete—a prison used by government forces during the **Halloween Massacre**—and Labort Rio Prison.

PROGRAMA DE AÇÃO GOVERNO (Government Action Plan). In September 1990, the government replaced the **Saneamento Econômico e Financiero** (SEF) with the Government Action Plan. Measures to be undertaken included cutting unnecessary government expenditures, lifting price controls on most, but not all, items, a significant devaluation of the **kwanza**, an increase of imports to encourage consumption, and replacing the kwanza with the new kwanza in order to reduce the money supply. In addition, the government also agreed to abide by World Bank and **International Monetary Fund** (IMF) agreements. *See also* NOVA VIDA; PROGRAMA DE ESTABILIÇÃO E RECUPERÇÃO ECONÔMICA DE MEDIO PRAZO 1998–2000; PROGRAMA ECONÔMICA E SOCIAL PARA 1994; SANEAMENTO ECONÔMICA E FINANCIERO.

PROGRAMA DE ESTABILIÇÃO E RECUPERÇÃO ECONÔMICA DE MEDIO PRAZO 1998–2000 (Medium-Term Economic Recovery and Stabilization Program for 1998–2000). The Angolan government's attempt to assist in the recovery and stabilization of the **economy**. Measures taken included introduction of a new currency to reduce the total money in circulation, acceptance of the **International Monetary Fund**'s (IMF's) fiscal transparency guidelines (not accomplished as of July 2003), and a staged devaluation of the **kwanza**. *See also* NOVA VIDA; PROGRAMA DE AÇÃO GOVERNO; PROGRAMA ECONÔMICA E SOCIAL PARA 1994; SANEAMENTO ECONÔMICA E FINANCIERO.

PROGRAMA ECONÔMICA E SOCIAL PARA 1994 (PES, Economic and Social Program of 1994). In another attempt to jump-start the Angolan **economy**, **Luanda** announced the Economic and Social Program of 1994. Goals set for the program included instituting a market economy, liberalization of **economic** activity, and privatizing more of the state's business sector. The plan also called for a fluctuating exchange rate system for the new **kwanza**. *See also* NOVA VIDA; PROGRAMA DE AÇÃO GOVERNO; PROGRAMA DE ESTABILIÇÃO E RECUPERÇÃO ECONÔMICA DE MEDIO PRAZO 1998–2000; SANEAMENTO ECONÔMICA E FINANCIERO.

PROVINCES. Angola has 18 provinces: **Bengo, Benguela, Bié, Cabinda, Cuando Cubango, Cuanza Norte, Cuanza Sul, Cunene, Huambo, Huíla, Luanda, Lunda Norte, Lunda Sul, Malange, Moxico, Namibe, Uíge,** and **Zaire**. Each province has a governor appointed by the president. Provincial governments have limited autonomy, with major decisions made in **Luanda**. As of September 2003, the government controlled the provinces in much the same way as the **Portuguese** once did—through strict control from the capital city. The **Movimento Popular de Libertação de Angola** (MPLA) government changed several of the provincial names. Lunda Norte and Lunda Sul were created from Lunda province in the 1980s as a measure to protect the **diamond** resources. Luanda province was split from Bengo in order to better serve the citizens of Luanda.

PUBLIC RELATIONS. With the ups and downs of international opinion and support, both the **Movimento Popular de Libertação de Angola** (MPLA) and **União Nacional para a Independência Total de Angola** (UNITA) hired public relations firms to lobby the U.S. government. UNITA lobbyists successfully prodded Congress into repealing the **Clark Amendment** and beginning a modest program of supplying arms to the rebels. The MPLA firms, during the 1990s, successfully secured diplomatic recognition from the Bill Clinton administration. The government and the rebels spent millions of dollars on the public relations campaigns. Lobbyists for the MPLA included such former high-ranking government officials as Paul Hare, Herman Cohen, James Woods, Robert Cabelly, Stephen Riley, and Elliot Richardson. The firms included America Worldwide, Daniel Edelman, Cohen and Woods International, C/R International, Samuels International Associates, Fleishman–Hillard, Patton Boggs, Laxalt, Washington, Perito and Dubuc, Gray and Company, Fenton Communications, Hill and Knowlton, and Milbank, Tweed, Hadley, and McCoy.

UNITA's major lobbying group was Black, Manafort, Stone, and Kelly, a Washington, D.C., public relations firm with strong links to the **Ronald Reagan** White House. In 1985, UNITA hired the company to help present its cause to the U.S. Congress. The PR firm was helpful in having **Jonas Savimbi** appear as a guest on such programs as *Nightline, 60 Minutes,* and the *MacNeil/Lehrer News Hour.* Also, Savimbi met with Secretary of Defense Caspar Weinberger, Secretary of State George Shultz, and President Ronald Reagan. The initial contract was for $600,000, although total billing ended at over $1 million.

PUNA, MIGUEL NZAU. Former **União Nacional para a Independência Total de Angola** (UNITA) secretary-general who defected in 1992. A **Cabindan** by birth, Puna is the grandson of Manuel José Puna, the chief whose 1885 Treaty of Simulambuco with **Portugal** is the legal basis for Cabinda's claim to independence. As of September 2003, Puna was Angola's ambassador to Canada.

– Q –

QUARTERING CAMPS. With the cease-fire in April 2002, **União Nacional para a Independência Total de Angola** (UNITA) soldiers and their families were to report to one of 38 quartering camps around the country. Eventually, a total of 400,000 moved to the camps, and they were immediately faced with shortages of food, medicine, tents, and blankets. Some camps reported UNITA members dying of starvation. According to the **United Nations**, between 10 and 12 people were dying every day. After disarmament, the soldiers were to be reintegrated into society through vocational training or by receiving enough **agricultural** implements to return to their farms. However, by October 2002, only $22 million had been spent on programs, while another $23 million had been allocated by the government. Concern was expressed that if the former combatants were not properly treated some might leave the camps and resort to banditry to survive. By June 2003, the Angolan government had closed the camps, yet over 200,000 soldiers and family members remained. Meanwhile, 200,000 UNITA members and families had returned home. The Angolan government claimed to have spent over $130 million on the quartering camps.

QUICAMA NATIONAL PARK. A wildlife reserve located 43 miles south of **Luanda**. Established as a game reserve in 1938, Quicama was proclaimed a national park on 11 January 1957. Before the **civil war**, the park teemed with rhino, elephants, the giant black sable antelope, bushbuck, waterbuck, and roan antelope, to name but a few. The conflict decimated Angola's wildlife, as animals were hunted for food or profit. The park was forced to seek regional assistance in restocking. **South Africa** and Botswana agreed to provide a variety of animals as the Angolan government prepared Quicama to be a tourist showcase. Surveys are being completed to determine what and how many animals still reside in Quicama. *See also* ARCA DE NOAH DA OPERAÇÃO.

QUILOMBOS. Places of refuge and resistance for Angolans opposed to the **slave trade**.

QUINTALÕES (slave enclosures). Enclosures used at Angolan port cities to control enslaved Africans. *See also* SLAVE TRADE.

– R –

RÁDIO ECCLÉSIA. Catholic Church–owned FM station based in **Luanda** that began operation in January 1955. It was temporarily shut down in August 1999 for airing an interview with **Jonas Savimbi**. Three employees of the station were repeatedly interrogated by the police. In July 2001, the station temporarily suspended programs in favor of religious broadcasts after the state-run newspaper *Jornal de Angola* accused the radio station of being an "instrument of subversion." Later, in 2003, Minister of Social Communication Hendrick Vaal Neto labeled the station a "vehicle of offenses, defamation, and false propaganda against Angolan institutions and individuals." *See also* MEDIA.

RADIO NACIONAL DE ANGOLA (RNA) (National Radio of Angola). The official government-operated radio station. One of the more popular programs on RNA is *Radio 5,* the sports channel. Another is *Manhã Informative* (Morning information). Other, private stations in Angola include Ràdio **Cabinda** Comercial; Ràdio Morena

Comercial, an FM station that broadcasts from Lubango; Luanda Antena Comercial (Luanda Commercial Radio), an independent station broadcasting from **Luanda**; and Ràdio 2000, which also airs from Lubango. *See also* RÀDIO ECCLÉSIA; VORGAN.

RAILROADS. Angola has 1,925 miles of track on the four major lines in the country: **Benguela**, Caminho de Ferro de Amboim, **Namibe**, and **Luanda**. The lines were built by the **Portuguese** and run east to west rather than **north** to south. Portugal built the railways in order to bring goods from the interior to the coast and ship goods from Portugal into the interior. The railways were to benefit Portugal, not the people of Angola. The **civil war**, combined with neglect and lack of funds, has led to a serious decline in rail services. The cost of rehabilitating track, rebuilding bridges, purchasing locomotives and freight cars, locating experienced workers, and emplacing telecommunications equipment is estimated at nearly $1 billion. Rehabilitation of the railways would benefit Angola's economy. The **Democratic Republic of the Congo** and **Zambia** could also resume use of the Benguela Railroad to ship their copper and zinc for export, which could earn as much as $100 million per year. Angola's ports would increase revenues and Angola could use the lines to export its own goods and services or move **agricultural** products, **livestock**, or **timber** throughout Angola.

RAPID ASSESSMENT OF CRITICAL NEEDS (RACN). United **Nations** humanitarian agencies do an RACN when they enter areas of social, **economic**, cultural, or political distress. Between April and September 2002, the UN conducted 358 assessments in 16 Angolan **provinces**. The RACN allows aid agencies to immediately provide the most needed assistance. Such assistance should include food supplies, seeds and **agricultural** equipment, security, **transportation**, **health**, **education**, and **land-mine** removal.

REAGAN DOCTRINE. Policy enunciated by former American president **Ronald Reagan** (1981–89) that advocated backing anti-Marxist insurgencies in the Third World, especially in Angola, Afghanistan, and Nicaragua. In March 1986, the **United States** covertly began to provide **União Nacional para a Independência Total de Angola**

(UNITA) with lethal weaponry, including the shoulder-fired **Stinger missile**. *See also* CLARK AMENDMENT.

REAGAN, RONALD WILSON (1911–). The 40th president of the **United States**. During the 1980 presidential campaign, the *Wall Street Journal* asked candidate Reagan about Angola: "How about aid to the Angolan rebels, who are fighting the **Soviet** regime and the **Cuban mercenaries**?" Reagan replied, "Well, frankly, I would provide them with weapons. It doesn't take American manpower: **Savimbi** , the leader, controls more than half of Angola. Apparently he's got quite a force there, and he's never asked for any kind of help, except weapons, and I don't see anything wrong with someone who wants to free themselves from the rule of an outside power, which is **Cubans** and East Germans—I don't see why we shouldn't provide them with the weapons to do it."

REDE DA PAZ (Peace Network). A group working with the **Comité Inter-Eclesial Para a Paz em Angola** (COIEPA) to establish a method to disarm the thousands of civilians throughout Angola. *See also* GRUPO ANGOLANO DE REFLEXAO PARA PAZ.

REFUGEES. By 2003, over 450,000 Angolan refugees were scattered across southern Africa. The **United Nations** High Commissioner for Refugees (UNHCR) planned to repatriate Angolans beginning May–September 2003, with a completion date scheduled for some time in 2005. Angolan refugees number 211,000 in **Zambia**, where they are housed in Maheba (founded in 1971), Nangweshi, Ukwimi, Kala, and **Mayukwayukwa** refugee camps; 193,000 in the **Democratic Republic of the Congo**; 18,000 in **Namibia**, at the Osire and Kassava camps; 16,000 in the Republic of the Congo; and 10,000 in **South Africa**. Between February and December 2002, over 70,000 refugees spontaneously returned to Angola from surrounding nations. In June 2003, the first group of 543 refugees arrived from the **Democratic Republic of the Congo**. Also, in June 2003, Angola and Botswana signed an agreement to repatriate 2,400 Angolans. However, plans to begin the repatriation of Angolans from Zambia were delayed until mid-July, after a tank mine was found on the main highway linking Angola to Zambia. Over 25,000 people had signed the voluntary repatriation form in the Maheba Camp. However, refugees deemed to be vulnerable because of disability or ill health were not allowed to leave because of United Nations guidelines. Zambian officials hoped to repatriate 20,000 Angolans in 2003 and another 40,000 in 2004. Angolan refugees living in Namibia began repatriation in June 2003. Once the refugees returned to Angola, they were given medical exams and received **land-mine** awareness training and **AIDS/HIV** information. The families were supplied with food rations, a building kit to assist in home construction, soap, blankets, buckets, and kitchen items. A **health** kit was also supplied that included a toothbrush, toothpaste, soap, washcloth, wash towel, comb, fingernail clippers, and bandages. Food assistance should last until April 2004, when the families will be given seed and **agricultural** tools for the planting season.

RELIGION. Traditionally and up to the present, in many parts of Angola there is a belief that life does not end at death, but that the spirit continues and plays an important role in the lives of the living, providing protection and advice and assuring communal harmony and continuity. The physical body decays, but the spirit transcends. Most Angolans believe that magical power resides in many objects. The power can be neutral or used for evil by witches. A person encountering problems may seek a diviner for spiritual assistance. The diviner, known as a *kimbanda*, can communicate with the spirit world. The better diviners commanded higher prices. **Portugal** imposed Christianity on the Angolans. **Catholicism**, the state religion of Portugal, was the official religion of Angola. According to church sources, by 1973 some 40–45 percent of Angolans were Catholic. Protestant missionaries were active in the **Bakongo** areas until 1961, when the Portuguese banned further missionary activity. The other religions faced bureaucratic obstacles in attempting to proselytize the native population. Other Christian denominations involved in colonial Angola included the Methodist Episcopal Church, the United Church of Canada, the United Church of Christ Congregational, the Plymouth Brethren, the Phil African Mission, and the Seventh-day Adventists. There is also a rapidly growing community of Muslims. *See also* ISLAM; TOCOISTS.

REPÙBLICA DE PESSOA DEMOCRÀTICA DE ANGOLA (DPRA) (Democratic People's Republic of Angola). The nation formed on 11 November 1975 at **Huambo** with a temporary merger of **Frente Nacional de Libertação de Angola** (FNLA) and **União Nacional para a Independência Total de Angola** (UNITA). The DPRA lasted until 27 January 1976, when **Movimento Popular de Libertação de Angola** (MPLA)/**Cuban** forces captured the city.

RESTAURAR DA OPERAÇÃO (Operation Restore). Launched in the fall of 1999, the operation successfully captured the **União Nacional para a Independência Total de Angola** (UNITA) strongholds of Andulo and Bailundo. By December 1999, Angolan Army chief of staff General João de Matos claimed that 80 percent of UNITA's conventional military capability had been destroyed. The **Forças Armadas de Angolanas** (FAA) asserted the capture of 15,000 tons of military materiel, including tanks, self-propelled cannon, missiles, and other vehicles. *See also* CIVIL WAR.

RETORNADOS. **Portuguese** term for those who returned to Portugal from the African colonies. *See also* SAUDADE.

ROBERTO, HOLDEN (1923–). The founder of the **Frente Nacional de Libertação de Angola** (FNLA), Roberto was born in São Salvador province in **Zaire** on 12 January 1923, the son of Garci'a Diasiwa Roberto and Joana Lala Nekaka. Roberto was baptized by the Baptist Missionary Church and completed his primary and secondary studies in Léopoldville in the then Belgian Congo. He worked in the Finance Department of the Belgian administration in Léopoldville, Bukavu, and Stanleyville. Making several trips to Angola inspired him along with several others to found the União das Populações do Norte de Angola (UPNA) (Union of People of North Angola) on 14 July 1956. Later, in order to broaden the organization's nationalist base, he renamed it the União das Populacões de Angola (UPA) (Union of People of Angola). Roberto traveled throughout Europe and Africa and appeared in Accra, Ghana, in December 1958 as the representative of UPA and as the leading Angolan nationalist. On 15 March 1961, UPA activists launched military operations against **Portuguese** settlers in northern Angola. Portuguese retribution was swift.

Tens of thousands of Africans were killed in retaliation. Roberto merged the UPA with the smaller Partido Democrático Angola (PDA) (Democratic Party of Angola) in March 1962 to form the FNLA. The FNLA fought inconclusively against Portugal from 1961 to 1974. However, when the **Movimento das Forças Armadas** overthrew the Portuguese government, it announced plans to free Angola and the other colonies. The FNLA was militarily the strongest and largest of the liberation movements. However, the **Battle of Death Road** effectively crippled the FNLA's military capabilities, and Roberto drifted back to Mobutu Sese Seko in Zaire, to whom he was related by marriage.

Under the **Bicesse Accords**, Roberto returned to Angola to campaign for president and as a parliamentarian. In the presidential contest, Roberto received 2.1 percent of the vote. FNLA won five seats in the parliamentary elections, but refused to accept a role in the **Governo da Unidade e da Reconciliação Nacional** (GURN). FNLA has been split since 1999, when **Lucas Ngonda** and younger members voted out Roberto as president. Reconciliation meetings have been held, but with little success. Roberto, now an elder statesman of Angolan politics, is working on his memoirs.

ROQUE, FÁTIMA (1951–). Former **União Nacional para a Independência Total de Angola** (UNITA) member who fled **Luanda** in February 1993 for the Universidade Lusofónia in Lisbon, where she became a professor of economics. Dr. Roque was a member of the UNITA central committee and of the political commission responsible for finance and economics. She was also a member of the UNITA delegation to the Negotiations to Restore Peace in Angola. As an elected member of parliament and a negotiator, Roque was in Luanda when the **Halloween Massacre** occurred. Her dual Portuguese/Angolan citizenship probably saved her life during that period. She later wrote a book about her experiences titled *Em Nome da Esperança* (In the name of hope). Roque was expelled from UNITA in 1997 after a disagreement with **Jonas Savimbi**. As of October 2003, Roque remained at the university in Lisbon. She is chairwoman of the Building the Future foundation, which is dedicated to building schools, hospitals, libraries, homes, and other needed facilities.

ROQUE SANTEIRO. The huge black market outside of **Luanda**. Named for a popular **Brazilian** soap opera, it is often cited as one of the biggest markets in Africa. It is estimated that $8 to $12 million changes hands weekly in the market. Anything can be purchased, from stereos to automobiles. *See also* INFORMAL MARKETS.

RUSGAS (conscription). A **Forças Armadas de Angolanas** (FAA) conscription effort that usually occurred at night in outlying urban regions. The aim was to secure recruits, underage or not.

– S –

SAKAITA, ANACLETO KAJITA ULULI. A son of **Jonas Savimbi** who departed Abidjan, Côte d'Ivoire, for **Luanda** in September 2000. **União Nacional para a Independência Total de Angola** (UNITA) claimed he was kidnapped, while the government said Sakaita contacted it.

SAKAITA, ARAUJO DOMINGOS. A son of **Jonas Savimbi** who departed from his school in Lomé, **Togo**, in November 1999 to return to **Luanda** to surrender to authorities. Sakaita, reportedly one of Savimbi's 28, gave the government an important propaganda boost. **União Nacional para a Independência Total de Angola** (UNITA) claimed Sakaita had been kidnapped.

SALAZAR, ANTÓNIO DE OLIVEIRA (1889–1970). Portuguese dictator. António Salazar received his **education** at the University of Coimbra. Later, he became a professor of political economy. After the military coup of 1926, Salazar was made minister of finance. He stabilized **Portugal's** finances for the first time in the 20th century. He became prime minister in 1932 and eventually became a dictator. Determined to maintain Portugal's empire in Africa, Salazar spent considerable monies and manpower. He suffered a stroke in 1968 and was replaced as prime minister by **Marcello Caetano**.

SAMAKUVA, ISAÍAS HENRIQUE NGOLA (1946–). Born on 8 July 1946 at the Cunje Outpost, Isaías Samakuva is the son of Henrique

Ngola Samakuva and Rosilia Ani Ulondo. He finished his primary **education** at Chissamba Evangelical Mission and his secondary studies at Dondi's Currie Institute, **Bié** Industrial and Commercial School, and **Huambo** Industrial School. He joined **União Nacional para a Independência Total de Angola** (UNITA) in 1974. In 1984, at the **First Extraordinary Congress** of UNITA, he was elected an alternate member of the Political Bureau. During the **UNITA VI Party Congress**, he was appointed permanent secretary. Samakuva served as UNITA's representative to Great Britain and during the latter stages of the **civil war** was stationed in Paris. In 2002, he returned to **Luanda** to participate in the scheduled UNITA Congress to elect a new president. In June 2003, Samakuva was chosen by the party to replace **Jonas Savimbi**.

SANEAMENTO ECONÔMICO E FINANCIERO (SEF) (Economic and Financial Rehabilitation). A government **economic** plan that would encourage profit and investment by private companies. The SEF would devalue the **kwanza**, reform banks and monetary institutions, allow more freedom for state-owned firms, and restrict imports while encouraging exports. The stabilization measures included reducing the state budget, seeking new methods of financing state debt, reforming domestic credit policies, and maintaining stricter control of monetary and fiscal policies. The plan was instituted in 1990, but quickly suffered from bureaucratic incompetence, official mismanagement, and governmental indifference. *See also* NOVA VIDA; PROGRAMA DE AÇÃO GOVERNO; PROGRAMA DE ESTABILIÇÃO E RECUPERÇÃO ECONÔMICA DE MEDIO PRAZO 1998–2000; PROGRAMA ECONÔMICA E SOCIAL PARA 1994.

SANTOS, AGUIAR DOS. Publisher of **Agora** who was tried for defaming President **Eduardo dos Santos** (no relation) in an editorial entitled "Loneliness, Power, and Succession." In the article, Aguiar dos Santos described the Angolan president as a manipulator with a Machiavellian approach to government. The Angolan Supreme Court reduced his sentence to two months in jail, suspended for three years, plus a fine of $2,000. In addition, he was ordered to pay court expenses for the case. *See also* MEDIA.

SANTOS, ARNALDO (1935–). Born and educated in **Luanda**, Arnaldo Santos helped found the Grupo da Cultura and several other literary organizations. His works include *Prosas* (You chat), *A Boneca de Quilengues* (The doll of Quilengues), and *A Casa Velha das Margens* (The old house of the edge). *See also* LITERATURE.

SANTOS, EDUARDO DOS (1942–). Born 28 August 1942 in the Sambizanga district of **Luanda**, Eduardo dos Santos joined the **Movimento Popular de Libertação de Angola** (MPLA) at 19, participating in the youth organization. He also became the MPLA's representative to the Republic of the Congo. In 1963, he was awarded a scholarship to study at the Institute of **Petroleum** and Gas in the **Soviet Union**, where he received a degree in petroleum engineering. After graduating in 1969, he continued his studies in telecommunications. Prior to independence, he served as coordinator of foreign affairs for the MPLA. The post allowed him to travel throughout Africa seeking support for the MPLA efforts. He was appointed minister of foreign affairs following independence in November 1975 and minister of planning in 1978. Dos Santos became president after the death of Angola's first president, **Agostinho Neto**. As president, he actively pursued the war against **União Nacional para a Independência Total de Angola** (UNITA) while building African and international support against the guerrilla movement. Either because of UNITA's gains or due to a sincere desire to achieve peace, dos Santos was instrumental through treaty in gaining the withdrawal of **South African** forces from **Namibia**, independence for the territory, and the repatriation of **Cuban** troops from Angola. In the early 1990s, he steered the MPLA away from a Soviet-style, centrally planned **economy** to a Western-oriented market economy. In 1991, he signed the **Bicesse Accords**, which guaranteed free, fair elections in Angola. The MPLA won the parliamentary contest, but dos Santos did not receive a majority vote in the presidential contest. He has been able to maintain his political longevity by preserving his popularity among the MPLA's traditional base of support, outmaneuvering rivals within the MPLA, managing to avoid urban protests against the lowered standard of living, and making the military a tool of the party, not an independent power base from which generals could launch coups. After the elections of 1992, the **civil war** reignited until 1994, when UNITA, due to military pressure, and the

MPLA, under duress from Western nations, signed the **Lusaka Agreement**. Dos Santos assumed extraordinary powers in 1998 in order to achieve a military victory over UNITA. Employing tactics that were criticized by **nongovernmental organizations** (NGOs), the government army successfully emptied the countryside of people, forcing UNITA troops to be constantly on the move and depriving them of traditional sources of food and support. With the death of rebel leader **Jonas Savimbi** in February 2002, the civil war ended. Dos Santos now leads a country in desperate need of infrastructure, reconciliation, and nation-building. In August 2001, dos Santos announced he would not run for reelection in the next presidential contest. However, the date for the next election could be as late as 2005, making the announcement not as important as first believed. The president, previously married to a Russian woman with whom he had a daughter, **Isabel**, is presently married to Ana Paula dos Santos. The couple has three children.

SANTOS, EDUARDO MACEDO DOS (1925–2001). One of the founders of the **Movimento Popular de Libertação de Angola** (MPLA), Eduardo dos Santos was the son of a **Portuguese** military officer and an Angolan woman. In 1960, Dos Santos was in the first MPLA group to travel to the People's Republic of China. The next year, he established the MPLA's first foreign delegation, to Brazzaville, Congo. He lobbied African and European capitals on behalf of the MPLA. Educated as a physician, he became the personal doctor of **President Agostinho Neto**. Later, he became president of the Angolan Football Federation.

SANTOS, FERNANDO DA PIEDADE DIAS DOS "NANDO" (1952–). Born in **Luanda**, dos Santos joined the **Portuguese** colonial army, but defected in 1974 to join the **Movimento Popular de Libertação de Angola** (MPLA) guerrilla forces. Rising through the ranks, he eventually became a major general in the **Forças Armadas Populares de Libertação de Angola** (FAPLA). He was elected to the MPLA Central Committee in 1985 and the ruling Politburo in 1998. From 1996 until his appointment as prime minister, dos Santos was interior minister. Holding a law degree from **Agostinho Neto** University, he was appointed prime minister in December 2002. The appointment was seen as a move toward political normality and stability. Dos Santos will be very important in the future. He is viewed as a political moderate with a willingness to work with other political parties. More technocrat than ideologue, he can be persuaded to attempt new administrative ideas and techniques.

SANTOS, ISABEL DOS. Isabel is **Eduardo dos Santos**'s daughter by his first wife. She is an executive in the Luanda Conoco Oil company, and it is rumored that she is a shareholder in several offshore oil-drilling and **diamond**-selling ventures. She also owns the popular nightspot Miami Beach.

SAPALALO, ALTINO BANGO "BOCK" (1954–2002?). Altino Bock was born at Andulo in **Bié province** on 5 November 1954. He was the son of Nunes Sapalalo and Catarina Salumbo. After graduation from **Huambo** National High School, Bock enrolled in the School of Veterinary Medicine at the University of **Luanda**. In 1974, he left school to join **União Nacional para a Independência Total de Angola** (UNITA). He took part in the **Long March**, rising to the rank of captain. At the battle of Menongue in June 1978, Bock lost his left hand in combat. By 1986, he was appointed to the rank of general. Throughout the 1990s, Bock held different positions within the UNITA military hierarchy. According to some sources, Bock either was executed on orders of **Jonas Savimbi** for his failure to capture **Kuito** in 1998 or was killed in combat in 2001 or 2002.

SAUDADE. **Portuguese** for wistful nostalgia or bittersweet taste. Portuguese who fled Angola in 1975 use the word to describe their feelings about being away from "home." *See also* RETORNADOS.

SAURIMO. The capital city of **Lunda Sul province**. Normally, the city has a population of 200,000, but during the **civil war**, refugees increased the number to 300,000. The city was significant militarily because of its airport and economically as the gateway to Angola's **diamond**-producing regions.

SAVIMBI, JONAS MALHEIRO (1934–2002). Longtime head of **União Nacional para a Independência Total de Angola** (UNITA) (National Union for the Total Independence of Angola). Born in

Munhango on 3 August 1934, Savimbi was the son of Loth Malheiro Savimbi and Helena Mbundu Savimbi. He attended Lutamo Primary School in Bela Vista, Atende Evangelical Centre, and Chilesso Mission School in Andulo. For his secondary schooling, Savimbi attended the Currie Institute of Dondi in Bela Vista, the Marist Brothers College in **Bié**, and Diogo Cão School in Lubango. In 1958, Savimbi left for **Portugal** to finish his high school **education** and begin courses in medicine. Becoming active in Angolan exile politics, he was harassed by the **Polícia International de Defesa de Estado** (PIDE). He fled Portugal for Switzerland, where he studied medicine for two years at Fribourg University, then studied at Lausanne University, where he graduated with honors in political and juridical sciences. Later, he traveled to the People's Republic of China, where he studied Maoist guerrilla tactics at the Nanking Military Academy. Savimbi contacted both the **Movimento Popular de Libertação de Angola** (MPLA) and **União das Populações de Angola** (UPA), but was dissatisfied with their organizational structures. While in Kenya, he met Jomo Kenyatta, who advised him to join the UPA.

On 1 February 1961, Savimbi traveled to Léopoldville (now Kinshasa) to follow Kenyatta's advice. He was made foreign minister of the Govêrno Revolucionário de Angola no Exílio (GRAE) (Angola's Revolutionary Government-in-Exile) but he chafed under the domineering **Holden Roberto**. On 6 July 1964, appearing before the Organization of African Unity's (OAU's) conference in Cairo, he announced his resignation from the **Frente Nacional de Libertação de Angola** (FNLA)/GRAE. Savimbi, convinced that the MPLA and FNLA had failed, began to construct his own organization. He was able to draw from three distinct constituencies: **Ovimbundu** in the Congo who issued the Amigos do Manifesto Angolano (Amangola) calling for all exiled Angolans to return home to prepare the masses for guerrilla war; a core of politically active students within the União Nacional dos Estudantes Angolanos (UNEA); and leaders of the Chokwe, Lwena, and Luchazi self-help organizations based in Zambia. Seeking support for his new movement, Savimbi traveled to Algeria, Tanzania, Egypt, Czechoslovakia, East Germany, Hungary, and the **Soviet Union**. His only positive response came from China. Savimbi and 10 others traveled to China in January 1965 to receive military training. Savimbi believed that a war of national liberation could not be fought outside of Angola. A political–military force had to work with and indoctrinate the masses. Toward that goal, Savimbi formed the Comitê Preparatória de Accão Directa (CPAD). He persuaded the president of **Zambia**, **Kenneth Kaunda**, to invite Roberto and **Agostinho Neto** to Lusaka for discussions toward forming a unified liberation movement. They refused. Six months later, on 13 March 1966, UNITA was founded by Savimbi and his followers at Muangai in eastern **Moxico province**.

UNITA forces began to attack the **Benguela Railroad**, a lifeline for Zambia and Zaire. In July 1967, he was arrested in Zambia because of continued UNITA attacks on the rail line. Finally, in July 1968, Savimbi secretly crossed the Zambian border into Angola. He concentrated his efforts on indoctrinating the masses in preparation for a political struggle. With the **Movimento das Forças Armadas** (MFA) revolution in 1974, the door seemed open for UNITA to do well in the promised elections of the **Alvor Accords**. The **civil war** aborted the planned elections. Rather than be destroyed by the MPLA/**Cuban** juggernaut, Savimbi returned to the bush to fight the new colonialists, the **Soviet Union** and **Cuba**. In the legendary **Long March**, Savimbi walked throughout central Angola, reviving hopes and recruiting an army to fight a Maoist struggle.

By 1976, UNITA forces were again militarily active. Realizing the need for South African assistance to counter the Cubans and Soviet weaponry, Savimbi established himself in **Jamba** in the southeastern corner of Angola, near the **Namibian** border. The Portuguese had called this area the "Land at the End of the Earth." Jamba, located near **Mavinga**, was termed the capital of the Free Land of Angola. Throughout the 1980s, UNITA forces grew in strength, eventually operating in 17 of Angola's 18 provinces. The **Bicesse Accords** of 1991 called for presidential and legislative **elections** for September 1992. After UNITA lost the controversial and disputed elections, the civil war resumed. The government, with **petroleum** dollars, could hire **mercenaries** and purchase modern military equipment, and it thus forced UNITA to sign the 1994 **Lusaka Protocol**. Savimbi, always distrustful of the MPLA leadership, never fully implemented the terms of the agreement. Finally, in 1998, the government began efforts to militarily resolve the civil war. The **Assembleia Nacional** (National Assembly) voted on 27 January 1999 to declare Savimbi "a war criminal and an international terrorist." On 23 July, the National Police issued an arrest warrant for the rebel leader. Knowing that Savimbi was in Moxico province, special forces of the Angolan army slowly tightened the noose around the UNITA leader. On 22 February 2002, the **Forças Armadas de Angolanas** (FAA) soldiers caught Savimbi in an ambush, killing him. Finally, after claiming Savimbi's death for years, the government showed his body on state-run television, dispelling any rumors that Savimbi had somehow survived.

Savimbi has been criticized for his autocratic rule and alleged human rights abuses, yet at the end, over 100,000 soldiers remained loyal to his cause. Charismatic, intense, and driven, Savimbi could rally support in six different languages. To his people, Savimbi was known as *Molowini* (Son of the People), *O Mais Velho* (the Wise One), or *Jaguar Negro das Jagas* (Black Jaguar of the Hunters). He gained support from **South Africa** and the **United States**. The **United Nations** invoked sanctions against his movement that eventually proved to be successful. Savimbi could have accepted safe haven in a third country or retired from politics to live in **Huambo**, but he believed in the righteousness of his movement. He died at 67 years of age with a rifle in his hand. His personal physician added to the legend by claiming Savimbi took his own life after realizing he was surrounded by government troops. He did not fight for liberation from a five-star hotel as so many "liberation" leaders did. Instead, he fought, and ultimately died, with his soldiers. In February 2003, the remaining leadership called on the government to allow for a reburial of their fallen leader. Originally buried at Lucusse, the corpse was exhumed and reburied at Luena after locals complained. UNITA requested to move the coffin to Lopitango, a village near Andulo. The government never responded to the request for fear of canonizing the rebel leader. *See also* FORÇAS ARMADAS DE LIBERTAÇÃO DE ANGOLA; NEGRITUDE.

SCORCHED-EARTH POLICY. Many **nongovernmental organizations**(NGOs) sharply criticized the government and, to a lesser extent, **União Nacional para a Independência Total de Angola** (UNITA) for the scorched-earth policy of the Angolan military from 1998 to 2002. In order to isolate UNITA troops, the **Forças Armadas**

de Angolanas (FAA) forced residents away from the rural areas to the **provincial** capitals. The remaining forces were thus UNITA members. However, the government made no provisions to receive the tens of thousands of **refugees** who flocked to the cities with nothing but the clothes on their backs. Once in the cities, the refugees placed a strain on an already overloaded socioeconomic system. The FAA, especially in **Moxico** province, succeeded in isolating **Jonas Savimbi**. Satellite photos helped the FAA track down Savimbi and UNITA forces. The **humanitarian** crisis that followed continues in the present. *See also* VICTORY BY SOCIAL EXPLOSION.

SIGNATURE BONUSES. As the **civil war** went against the government in 1999, Angola took the unusual step of demanding up-front advance payments from oil companies to explore for **petroleum** offshore of Angola. The down payments, known as "signature bonuses" and totaling over $900 million, gave the government access to enormous sums of money in order to purchase military equipment. The tactic was successful, as the government army slowly gained the upper hand against the **União Nacional para a Independência Total de Angola** (UNITA) rebels by 2002.

SLAVE TRADE. Angola, like many other parts of Africa, was devastated by one of the cruelest crimes imaginable: slavery. Islamic societies benefited from the slave trade from as early as the ninth century, taking both Africans and Arabs as slaves. The European/Atlantic slave trade, which lasted from the 16th to the 19th centuries, dealt only in Africans. The African slave trade weakened the continent economically, spiritually, and culturally. The best labor was removed and local industries and products withered, to be replaced by European ones. The slave trade set brother against brother. It so weakened societies that Africa became an easy prey for European colonialists.

The market began with the need for laborers on the sugar plantations on São Tome. Some 50 years later, the demand for slaves increased as sugar production was introduced in **Brazil** and the Caribbean. In Angola, occasional slave raids gradually turned into full-time commerce. Various African societies were lured into participating by deriving benefit for themselves. **Nzinga Bemba** (Afonso I), a ruler of the **Kongo** Kingdom, was baptized a Roman Catholic in

1491. When he became king in 1506, he asked his **Portuguese** "brothers" why they were taking his subjects as slaves. Afonso grew to accept the slave trade after the Portuguese offered rifles and ammunition. Only kingdoms that were equipped with modern weapons could protect themselves or engage in expansionist policies. The Europeans became involved in African wars with the assistance of Africans and mixed bloods. The Portuguese were known as *lançados* (those who dared enter the Angolan interior). By employing coastal groups to exploit the human resources of interior clans, the Portuguese created a cultural chasm between the coastal and interior peoples. **Jonas Savimbi**'s political philosophy, **negritude**, outlines the hostility of the Ovimbundu toward the groups he perceived had exploited his people.

In the 16th century, **Luanda** became the center of Portuguese slaving efforts. One of the most prominent slavers of the 19th century was D. Ana Joaquina, herself of mixed race. Slave caravans would emerge from the interior and return there with many goods to be traded or sold. The payment for a slave included rifles, gunpowder, whiskey, cloth, glassware, ironware, and trinkets. Before the voyage, slaves were branded on either the left or right hand or on the side. No one knows how many Africans were sold into slavery. Various studies estimate that 3 to 4 million slaves, mostly destined for Brazil, left from Angola. The **Catholic Church**, needing Portuguese protection, was forced to support the slave trade. In the name of religion, however, the church insisted that slaves be baptized before they were loaded onto ships as cargo. The Industrial Revolution in Europe and America, the American civil war, and a growing international distaste for the trade led to a number of nations banning slavery. By the 1840s, most nations had laws abolishing slavery. The practice ended in Angola in 1865, but not through the efforts of Portugal; instead, it was imposed by the British Royal Navy. Slavery inside Angola continued until 1878, but the institution was transformed as slavery was replaced by forced labor, which continued until the 1960s. *See also QUILOMBOS; QUINTALÕES.*

SOB OS POVOS DAS ÁRVORES (under the trees people). A term used to describe **refugees** who return to Angola too ill or lacking materials to build homes. *See also* HUMANITARIAN SITUATION.

SOCIEDADE NACIONAL DE COMBUSTÍVEIS DE ANGOLA (Sonangol) (National Fuel Company of Angola). Angola's state-owned oil company, which oversees offshore and onshore **petroleum** operations in Angola. Sonangol has been criticized for maintaining its own **bank** accounts instead of depositing profits in the national bank of Angola. The **International Monetary Fund** (IMF) has made transparency of the oil sector a prerequisite for IMF and World Bank loans to the government of Angola. In October 2001, the state-owned company decided to remake itself into an integrated company with the capacity to explore, produce, refine, and transport petroleum and petroleum products. *See also* SIGNATURE BONUSES.

SONAREF. The name of the new **petroleum** refinery to be constructed in **Lobito** and expected to go on line in 2007. Work on the 200,000-barrels-a-day refinery, which had an expected cost of $3.6 billion, began in early 2003. Angola planned to market the production of Sonaref to the U.S., European, and **Brazilian** markets. The refinery will be 50 percent owned by Sonangol (**Sociedade Nacional de Combustíveis de Angola**), 20 percent owned by a foreign financial backer, 20 percent owned by a foreign technical backer, and 10 percent owned by members of the **Southern African Development Community** (SADC).

SOUTH AFRICA. The Republic of South Africa initially did little more than offer vocal encouragement to the **Portuguese** in Angola. However, with the **Movimento das Forças Armadas** (MFA) coup in 1974, South Africa decided to take steps to protect its economic and political stakes. South Africa had a large investment in the **Cunene River** Hydroelectric Complex along the Angola–**Namibia** border and private investments in the **Benguela Railroad, diamond** mines, and mineral extraction firms. Politically, South Africa feared a Marxist **Movimento Popular de Libertação de Angola** (MPLA) would assist the African National Congress (ANC) and the South West Africa People's Organization (SWAPO) with military support and "safe bases" in Angola. In August 1975, South African forces entered Angola to assist **União Nacional para a Independência Total de Angola** (UNITA) against the MPLA. MPLA's allies, **Cuba** and the **Soviet Union**, entered as well. South Africa claimed it was acting on behalf of the North Atlantic Treaty Organization (NATO) and the **United States**. Bitter disappointment was expressed when Europe and the United States criticized South African involvement. The revival of UNITA, coupled with the MPLA's promise to assist the ANC and SWAPO, led South Africa to intervene numerous times in the late 1970s and the 1980s. Military raids were launched against ANC, SWAPO, and **Forças Armadas Populares de Libertação de Angola** (FAPLA) and also to assist UNITA. With major change on the South African horizon, politicians sought to withdraw from Namibia and Angola. The battle of **Cuito Cuanavale** provided the SADF an honorable exit. *See also* BATTLE OF LOMBA RIVER I; BATTLE OF LOMBA RIVER II; FORÇAS ARMADAS DE LIBERTAÇÃO DE ANGOLA.

SOUTH AFRICA–ANGOLA CHAMBER OF COMMERCE (SA–ACC). Organization begun in March 2003 as a way to boost and smooth investment opportunities between **South Africa** and Angola. South African companies involved in Angola include the supermarket chain Shoprite, the construction firm Grinaker–LTA, the telecom companies Vodacom and MTN, Investec Bank, and South African Breweries.

SOUTHERN AFRICAN DEVELOPMENT COMMUNITY (SADC). Originally conceived as an antiapartheid organization, the Southern Africa Development Coordination Conference (SADCC) was founded in 1979–80 as an antiapartheid group of Front Line States. In 1992, it was transformed into the SADC. The members include Angola, Botswana, the **Democratic Republic of the Congo**, Lesotho, Malawi, Mauritius, Mozambique, **Namibia**, the Seychelles, **South Africa**, Swaziland, Tanzania, **Zambia**, and Zimbabwe. The SADC headquarters is located in Gaborone, Botswana. Peace seems to be returning to the region; consequently, the SADC will focus on reconstruction, economic development and integration through trade, joint projects, and tourism. The organization will also attempt to tackle more serious problems, such as endemic diseases, poverty, and illiteracy.

SOVIET UNION. The Soviet Union, or Union of Soviet Socialist Republics (USSR), was the closest ally to the **Movimento Popular de**

Libertação de Angola (MPLA) during the struggle for independence and into the postindependence period. The Soviets first made contact with the MPLA through the Portuguese Communist Party. By the late 1960s, Moscow was providing limited weaponry to the MPLA. However, Moscow was unsure about the leadership of **Agostinho Neto**. The Kremlin concluded he was too secretive for their liking. When the **Movimento das Forças Armadas** (MFA) in Portugal declared the independence of Angola, the USSR made certain its client would prevail in the quest for power in the new nation. Arms shipments were sharply increased. Soviet military advisers went to **Luanda** after the MPLA successfully evicted **União Nacional para a Independência Total de Angola** (UNITA) and **Frente Nacional de Libertação de Angola** (FNLA) from the city in August 1975. **Cuba**, with or without Moscow's permission, sent 12,000 combat troops to Angola. Armed with $200 million in Soviet weaponry, the MPLA/Cuban forces were often victorious. In October 1976, the Soviet Union and Angola signed a 20-year Treaty of Friendship and Cooperation.

As the civil war with UNITA intensified, the Soviet Union increased its military contribution to the MPLA government. From 1981 to 1987, this averaged $1 billion per year. In the **Battles of Lomba River**, the **Forças Armadas Populares de Libertação de Angola** (FAPLA) and Cuban forces were commanded by Soviet generals. However, when Mikhail Gorbachev became general secretary of the Soviet Union in 1985, he advocated *glasnost* and *perestroika*. He also realized that Moscow's foreign commitments were too costly and harmed attempts to woo the **United States**. Gorbachev launched the **"new thinking"** policy, which encouraged a negotiated solution to the civil war. Washington pressured UNITA, while Moscow did the same to the MPLA. The result was the **Bicesse Accords** of 1991. The collapse of the Soviet Union gave rise to the Russian Federation. The Russian Federation has maintained some commercial relations with Angola and is negotiating repayment of the $9 billion debt, mostly for weapons, owed to the former Soviet Union by Angola.

SOVIET UNION BATTLE TACTICS IN ANGOLA. The **Soviet Union**'s strategy in the Angolan **civil war** was to provide it's ally, the **Movimento Popular de Libertação de Angola** (MPLA), with tremendous firepower and apply conventional military strategy. However, in a guerrilla bush war, speed of movement and knowledge of the terrain are more important. In extremely rough terrain, the Soviets, **Cubans**, and **Forças Armadas Populares de Libertação de Angola** (FAPLA) employed very heavy, sophisticated weaponry, including, "Stalin's Organ," the derogatory term for the Soviet-built 122-mm launcher so effectively employed against **Frente Nacional de Libertação de Angola** (FNLA) forces during the **Battle of Death Road**. The cost of maintenance and transport was prohibitive. Yet the Soviets continued to flood Angola with equally bulky, difficult to maintain equipment. The **União Nacional para a Independência Total de Angola** (UNITA) and **South African** troops traveled light and moved swiftly. South African heavy vehicles, unlike the Soviets, had been adapted to the rugged southern African terrain. It is believed that at the height of the civil war the Soviet Union had deployed 900 military personnel and 250 civilians, mostly KGB agents in Angola. *See also* BATTLE OF LOMBA RIVER I; BATTLE OF LOMBA RIVER II.

SPINOLA, ANTÓNIO SEBASTIÃO RIBEIRO DE (1910–1996). Born at Estremoz in southern **Portugal** on 11 April, António Spinola attended military school and graduated as a second lieutenant. By 1968, he was a brigadier general in Portuguese Guinea fighting the Communist-backed guerrillas of the Partido Africano da Independência de Guiné e Cabo Verde (African Party of Independence of Guinea and Cape Verde). There, he often led his troops into battle and became a popular commander, despite his no-nonsense reputation. Eventually, he was appointed governor of Guinea. Spinola realized military victory was unlikely, and therefore he secretly negotiated with the rebels. He also had Portuguese troops construct hospitals and schools. Spinola even supported a referendum in the colonies to decide their future. Returning home to Portugal as a hero in 1973, Spinola wrote a book titled *Portugal e o Futuro* (Portugal and the future). He admitted that the Portuguese colonies were more of a burden than a prize. Portugal, one of Europe's weakest economies, was spending 40 percent of its budget pursuing wars in Angola, Guinea, and Mozambique. The book became a best-seller and sparked more radical officers to launch the **Movimento das Forças Armadas**

(MFA). The revolution occurred on 25 April 1974. By mid-May, Spinola was head of a seven-man junta and the provisional president. But the Socialist leader, Mario Soares, and Communist head, Alvaro Cunhal, returned from exile determined to radicalize the MFA revolution. Spinola was forced to flee Portugal in March 1975, after he was accused of attempting to launch a countercoup to restore order. Allowed to return in 1976, he avoided politics. *See also* CARNATION REVOLUTION.

STINGER MISSILE. A shoulder-fired, ground-to-air missile produced by General Dynamics Corporation. It weighs 34 pounds, is five feet long, and has a range of six miles. The **Ronald Reagan** administration supplied the weapon to **União Nacional para a Independência Total de Angola** (UNITA) to use against Angolan government air power. The Stinger is fired from a disposable tube and requires no testing or maintenance. The missile uses infrared seekers to zero in on aircraft and is equipped with a six-pound penetrating warhead. *See also* REAGAN DOCTRINE.

STOCKWELL, JOHN. Former Central Intelligence Agency (CIA) operative who wrote the book *In Search of Enemies,* in which he charges that CIA advisers were in Angola without the knowledge of the White House, Congress, or the U.S. State Department. *See also* CIVIL WAR.

STREET GANGS. Over the course of the **civil war**, Luanda was overwhelmed by a massive influx of **refugees**, including many abandoned, homeless, or orphaned **children**. The large number caused the economic/cultural infrastructure to collapse. Except for **nongovernmental organizations** (NGOs), social services were nonexistent. Many children earned a living by hawking goods, washing or protecting automobiles, or engaging in crime. A number of street gangs emerged, as youngsters often found comfort, companionship, and a livelihood in the gangs. Some of the more notorious gangs include the Adaozinho, Betox, Groupo Band, Mauro, Michel, Nirvana, Toy, and Stringers. In September 2002, several Mauro members were arrested after a series of carjackings and homicides.

– T –

TARALLO, ANDRE. Former director of the Africa Division of the French state-owned oil company TotalElfFina Group (ELF). Tarallo revealed in 2000 that he had, over the span of 20 years, paid $40 million to leading African personalities, including President **Eduardo dos Santos**. ELF, the world's fourth largest oil producer, denied the accusation, as did the office of the Angolan president. *See also* PETROLEUM.

TEACHERS STRIKE. Teachers in **Huíla**, **Bié**, **Malange**, and **Kwanza Sul provinces** began a strike in 2000 protesting the lack of teacher training and low or no salaries. They returned to work in September 2000 after extracting some concessions from the government. Angola's **education** system is one of the worst in Africa, and the treatment of teachers is poor. Salaries, when delivered, can be as low as $7 per month. Teachers are supposed to have an eighth-grade education in order to qualify for the profession, but few do.

TELESERVICES. Protection-service company partly owned by Joaquim David, former director of the state oil company **Sociedade Nacional de Combustveis de Angola** (Sonangol). Teleservices was a partnership between Angolan security personnel and **South Africa**'s Gray Security Services. Gray Security Services had former members of **Executive Outcomes** on its payroll. At first, Teleservices concentrated on the **petroleum** sector, but later it moved into mineral extraction protection as well. *See also* ALPHA 5.

31ST BATTALION. Unit formed by the South African Defense Forces (SADF) in the late 1970s that used **Khoisan** soldiers as trackers against the South West Africa People's Organization (SWAPO), the African National Congress (ANC), and **Forças Armadas Populares de Libertação de Angola** (FAPLA). In July 1998, members of the !Xu community asked the **South African** Truth and Reconciliation Commission to investigate charges of abuse against the Khoisan soldiers by the SADF.

32ND BATTALION (Buffalo Soldiers). Unit formed on 27 March 1976 by **South African** colonel Jan Breytenbach. It was composed of members from Daniel Chipenda's **Frente Nacional de Libertação de Angola** (FNLA) unit, which had been sent south to fight the **Movimento Popular de Libertação de Angola** (MPLA). As the **civil war** wound down, Chipenda's unit, having no place to go, crossed into **Namibia** to surrender to South African forces. The troops were retrained and incorporated into the South African Defense Forces (SADF). The 32nd was used extensively against South West Africa People's Organization (SWAPO) guerrillas and to support **União Nacional para a Independência Total de Angola** (UNITA) forces. The battalion was proficient in conventional, counterinsurgency, and guerrilla tactics. In September 2002, many of the 10,000 former Buffalo Soldiers met with Angolan government officials seeking permission to return to Angola. The former 32nd Battalion troops cited poor living conditions and discrimination in South Africa as reasons for seeking to return. *See also* BATTLE OF LOMBA RIVER I; BATTLE OF LOMBA RIVER II.

TIMBER. Many valuable tree species are found in Angola. Because of the civil war and the loss of **Portuguese** expertise in 1975, Angola's timber industry is now run down. The Maiombe rainforest in **Cabinda** has such species as rosewood, ebony, and sandalwood. The Dembos forest in northwestern Angola has mahogany, mulberry, and tola trees. Other exportable trees include cypress, pine, girassonde, mussibi, and eucalyptus. Cabinda has the best chance to quickly begin a profitable export of timber products. The wood is of the highest quality and is located near ports.

TOCOISTS. Religion founded by Simão Toco in 1949. The Tocoist movement is also known as the Church of Jesus Christ in the World. Toco was the prophet of the church. His philosophy called for a puritanical lifestyle, self-reliance, and separation from white society. The Angolan government was suspicious of the Tocoists because of their following in **Ovimbundu** areas. Concern was also voiced that the Tocoists were allied with the **União Nacional para a Independência Total de Angola** (UNITA). After numerous confrontations with the government, the Tocoists were banned in 1986. However, in March 1988, the government reversed itself when it declared the Tocoists a legal religion. Simão Toco died in 1984, but his religious philosophy has maintained its appeal to many Angolans.

TOGO. African nation headed by President **Gnassingbé Eyadéma** from 1967 to the present day. The **United Nations** accused Togo and its president of aiding **União Nacional para a Independência Total de Angola** (UNITA) in violation of UN sanctions. On 19 May 2000, Togo expelled 56 members of UNITA, including some who had lived in Togo for over 20 years. Eighteen of those expelled were direct relatives of **Jonas Savimbi**. *See also* FOWLER COMMISSION REPORT.

TONET, WILLIAM. The director of the **Luanda**-based weekly **newspaper** *Folha 8*. He was arrested and convicted several times for printing articles deemed dangerous to the sovereignty of Angola, crimes against state security, and attempting to demoralize the military. Nevertheless, Tonet continued to question government decisions and policies. He was interrogated on 3 April 1999, supposedly for inciting young men to avoid the draft. *See also* MEDIA.

TOURISM. In May 2003, Luanda hosted the 39th Conference of the World Tourism Organization Commission for Africa. Angola believes it can compete for tourists in the burgeoning southern Africa tourist trade. However, it must be able to provide tourists with basic sanitation, regular and potable water, reliable energy sources, and advanced **health** facilities. Moreover, Angola needs to revitalize its hotel and restaurant industry. In September 2002, the Tropicana Cip Service announced plans to build a 15-story, four-star hotel in Lubango. Angola boasts over a thousand miles of ocean front. The country possesses mountains such as Moco Hill and Meco. The basins of the Zaire, **Cunene**, Cubango, and Queve Rivers form in Angola. Operation Noah's Ark (**Arca de Noah Operação**) is restocking the national parks. *See also* IONA NATIONAL PARK; QUICAMA NATIONAL PARK.

TRANSPORTATION. The transportation network will take the longest time to restore and be the most expensive project in the **economic** recovery of Angola. Roadways, bridges, and the **rail** network were severely damaged during the civil war. Angola has approximately 45,000 miles of roads. However, only 5,200 miles, most of them in or near the major cities, are paved. Angola's roadways are in a state of severe disrepair. The rainy season, **land mines**, and lack of maintenance or any modernization mean that enormous outlays of money, manpower, and time will be needed to repair and rebuild the system. Until the internal transportation network is operable, the whole economic recovery will be sluggish. The government of Angola estimates that the repair time could be 10 to 15 years. Most Angolans do not own motor vehicles, so roads have been used mainly by aid agencies, the **United Nations**, and the military. However, a free-flowing transportation system is vital if goods and services, economic expansion, travel, employment, or even a sense of nationhood are to be attained. *See also* RAILROADS; TRANSPORTES AÉREOS DE ANGOLA.

TRANSPORTES AÉREOS DE ANGOLA (TAAG) (Air Transportation of Angola). State-owned airline system. The company started in 1938 and became TAAG in 1973. On 3 March 1976, the first Boeing 737, and the first jetliner in the fleet, was delivered to the company. One million passengers were flown in 1986, in part because of the war, and also due to the low cost of jet fuel. The airline has been upgraded in recent years and flies domestically and abroad.

The first Boeing 747 was acquired in 1997, allowing transoceanic flights. The 747 was named *Cidade do Cuito* to pay homage to the citizens of the devastated city. In June 1997, TAAG inaugurated direct flights between Houston, Texas, and Luanda. By late 2003, TAAG operated routes to Brazzaville, Harare, Havana, Houston, Johannesburg, Kinshasa, Lisbon, Lusaka, Paris, Pointe Noire, Rio de Janeiro, Sal, São Tomé, and Windhoek.

TROCA DA OPERAÇÃO (Operation Exchange). Program that forced citizens to turn in their old **kwanzas** for new ones. However, for every 100 kwanzas turned in, only 5 new kwanzas were returned. For the remainder, the government issued an IOU. The rationale behind the October 1990 program was to restore some fiscal responsibility by absorbing 90 billion out of the 150 billion kwanzas in circulation. Initially successful, the program suffered as many businesses refused to accept the new kwanza as a method of payment.

TROIKA. Comprising **Portugal**, the **Soviet Union** (Russia), and the **United States**, the troika was intended to monitor implementation of the **Bicesse Accords**. On 24 August 1998, the **União Nacional para a Independência Total de Angola** (UNITA) cut its ties with the troika, accusing its members of siding with the **Movimento Popular de Libertação de Angola** (MPLA) government.

TRYPANOSOMIASIS. The medical term for sleeping sickness, caused by the bite of a tsetse fly. The full term is human African trypanosomiasis. In 1965, the disease was believed to have been eradicated. However, population displacement, warfare, political instability, and the collapse of **health** systems has led to a resurgence of the disease. Clinically, there are two types. The first, caused by the parasite *Trypanosoma brucei gambiense,* is responsible for the current outbreak. It is a chronic disease that takes several years to reach the advanced stage. The second, caused by *T. b. rhodesiense,* is an acute ailment that is fatal within weeks. The disease is found in 14 of Angola's 18 provinces. In 2000, over 6,000 cases were reported nationwide. Between 1992 and 2002, the incidence of sleeping sickness rose from 0.06 percent to 10 percent. A number of **nongovernmental organizations** (NGOs) working throughout Africa have formed a Programme against Africa Trypanosomiasis, designed to place all interested agencies under one umbrella. In Angola, during the colonial era, the **Portuguese** sprayed pesticides over forests. The **civil war** made such efforts impossible. The major way to combat the tsetse fly is by setting traps. In 2000, in **Uíge province**, 111,025 tsetse flies were caught in 1,250 traps in 58 villages. Symptoms include rash, fever, aching muscles, headaches, and extreme fatigue. In the latter stages, the disease manifests itself in seizures, sleepiness, personality changes, confusion, and, if left untreated, death. The most commonly prescribed drug is Eflornithine. In May 2001, **Médecins sans Frontières** (Doctor's without Borders), the World Health Organization (WHO), and the pharmaceutical company Aventis agreed to resume production of Eflornithine and Pentamidine.

TYPHOON BATTALION. During the **civil war**, the **Movimento Popular de Libertação de Angola** (MPLA) allowed the African National Congress (ANC) and the South West Africa People's Organization (SWAPO) to establish training bases in Angola. As part of the price for this hospitality, the ANC and SWAPO forces had to fight against **União Nacional para a Independência Total de Angola** (UNITA). The Typhoon Battalion, regarded as the elite unit of the People's Liberation Army of Namibia, was "loaned" to the Angolan government to fight UNITA. Some ANC forces were also sent to fight. Several mutinied, but the rebellion was crushed and led to a widespread purge of ANC cadres in Angola.

– U –

UÍGE. A **province** and the name of its capital city. Located in northeastern Angola, Uíge has a tropical-dry climate. The population numbers about 500,000. Silver and cobalt are important mineral resources. **Agriculturally**, the province grows **coffee**, cocoa, and fruits.

ULTIMO ASSALTA DA OPERAÇÃO (Operation Final Assault). The code name for the 1989–90 attempt by the **Forças Armadas Populares de Libertação de Angola** (FAPLA) to capture the **Mavinga/Jamba** area. As with the **Battles of Lomba River**, FAPLA did succeed in capturing a portion of Mavinga, but not the airstrip. FAPLA became bogged down trying to defend its 100-mile defensive position. Supplies could not be flown into the area, so convoys were deployed that suffered massive losses from the **União Nacional para a Independência Total de Angola** (UNITA) guerrilla attacks. UNITA also launched preemptive actions throughout Angola, making reinforcements for the Mavinga area impossible. By 15 May 1990, the units fleeing the Mavinga area had arrived safely at **Cuito Cuanavale** but suffered severe losses.

UMBUNDU. Language spoken by the **Ovimbundu** people.

UNEXPLODED ORDNANCE. A serious problem for the future stability of Angola is the millions of rounds of unexploded ordnance littering the countryside. **Children**, the curious, and money seekers may attempt to handle the munitions that might detonate and kill or maim. *See also* MERCÚRIO VERMELHO.

UNIÃO NACIONAL DOS TRABALHADORES DE ANGOLA, CONFEDERÃO SINDICAL (UNTA–CS) (National Workers Union of Angola, Trade Union Confederation). Labor union that launched strikes for higher wages in December 2000 and January 2001. The government and the union eventually agreed to a minimum wage of U.S. $50, after the union had initially demanded $300 per month.

UNIÃO NACIONAL PARA A INDEPENDÊNCIA TOTAL DE ANGOLA (UNITA) (National Union for the Total Independence of Angola). Organization founded by **Jonas Savimbi** on 13 August 1966. Although UNITA was primarily an **Ovimbundu** group, Savimbi drew upon three distinct factions. First, a number of Ovimbundu withdrew from **Frente Nacional de Libertação de Angola** (FNLA) after Savimbi's departure. In December 1964, 24 defectors issued the Amigos do Manifesto Angolano (Amangola), which called for all Angolan exiles to return home to prepare the masses for guerrilla warfare against the Portuguese. Second, politically active students in the União Nacional dos Estudantes Angolanos (UNEA) grew disenchanted with the revolutionary leaders conducting the war from outside of Angola. Third, the Chokwe, Lwena, and Luchazi self-help organizations based in Lusaka, Zambia, provided support. In order to consolidate and prepare the revolution within Angola, Savimbi created the Comitê Preparatória da Accão Directa (CPAD). **Zambian** President **Kenneth Kaunda** was persuaded to invite the leadership of the **Movimento Popular de Libertação de Angola** (MPLA) and FNLA to Lusaka to discuss the creation of a single liberation movement for Angola. But **Holden Roberto** and **Agostinho Neto** refused. Six months later, UNITA was formed inside Angola.

Based on his Maoist training, Savimbi believed that politically educated peasants were the key to success. UNITA cadres were ordered to respect tribal customs and leaders. He wanted the movement to be totally self-reliant. He also developed the concept of **negritude** to explain UNITA's political philosophy. When the **Movimento das Forças Armadas** (MFA) coup occurred in **Portugal** in 1974, some observers commented that UNITA was the best prepared to take advantage of the promised elections in Angola. However, when the elections did not occur, UNITA was ill suited to fight a **civil war**. **South African** support was not enough, either, and UNITA retreated to the bush to fight what it saw as **Soviet/Cuban** imperialism.

The corruption of the government, South African aid, and Savimbi's charismatic personality led UNITA to the verge of victory by 1990. The **Bicesse Accords** called for elections, which were held in September 1992. While UNITA and 12 other parties declared the elections to be fraudulent, they agreed to participate in the scheduled second-round presidential contest.

When the civil war resumed, UNITA's **Forças Armadas de Libertação de Angola** (FALA) was well positioned to take advantage, and they seized several **provincial** capitals by mid-1994. However, after that point, government firepower forced UNITA to accept the **Lusaka Protocol**. Even then, the enmity between UNITA and the MPLA could not be resolved, leading to a resumption of hostilities in 1998. With the death of Savimbi in February 2002 and the subsequent peace agreement, UNITA moved to the capital to become the largest political party in opposition. **Paulo Lukamba Gato** was appointed to head the 40-member Political Committee of UNITA in August 2002. **Isaías Samakuva** was elected to succeed Jonas Savimbi at the **UNITA IX Party Congress** in June 2003.

UNIÃO NACIONAL PARA A INDEPENDÊNCIA TOTAL DE ANGOLA, RENOVADA (UNITA–R). Founded in 1998 by UNITA defector Jorge Valentim and former UNITA secretary general Eugenio Manuvakola, UNITA–R was never able to establish itself as a viable alternative to the **Jonas Savimbi**-led UNITA. In most quarters, UNITA–R was seen as being on the payroll of the government. Rumors circulating through **Luanda** at the time claimed the top UNITA–R leadership had been paid $3 million each to abandon Savimbi. More respected figures such as Jaka Jamba and **Abel Chivukuvuku** distanced themselves from the breakaway organization. The government of Angola recognized UNITA–R as the "only valid interlocutors" for the Lusaka peace process. UNITA under Savimbi was no longer recognized as a leading faction of the movement. In July 2002, Manuvakola resigned from UNITA–R, claiming his action would pave the way for reunification of the party. As UNITA demobilized to become a legitimate political party, the veterans returning from the bush offered little support for those they regarded as being in the pocket of the government. Consequently, General **Lukamba Gato** was able to effectively sideline UNITA–R.

UNION OF SOVIET SOCIALIST REPUBLICS. *See* SOVIET UNION.

UNITA MANAGEMENT COMMISSION. Formed after the February 2002 death of **Jonas Savimbi**, the **União Nacional para a Independência Total de Angola** (UNITA) Management Commission, headed by **Paulo Lukamba Gato**, was to reunite the party until a national congress could be held. The Management Commission was accepted by the military wing, officials abroad, and most parliamentarians. However, **União Nacional para a Independência Total de Angola–Renovada** (UNITA–R) did not accept the leadership of Gato. The Management Commission expired with the opening of the **UNITA IX Party Congress** in June 2003.

UNITA MILITARY BASES. A full accounting of UNITA military bases may be impossible to obtain. Some of the more important bases were at **Jamba**, **Mavinga**, Bailundo, Andulo, and for a time, **Huambo**. Others included Epongoloko, located in **Benguela province** and described as the command center for the province. It was captured and destroyed by government forces in October 2001. Mufumbo Base served as a UNITA regional operations headquarters in the central province of **Cuanza Sul**. The base was also captured and destroyed in October 2001. Located in Zaire (now the **Democratic Republic of the Congo**), the Kamina Airbase became an important staging area for Central Intelligence Agency (CIA) flights carrying lethal weaponry for the rebels in UNITA-held territory. C-130 and Boeing 707 cargo jets bearing the markings of "Santa Lucia Airways" made nightly runs into Angola. Massavi base, located in **Moxico** province, was a facility employed for political and military training. It opened soon after the 1974 cease-fire with the **Portuguese**. The Kwame N'Krumah base in southeast Angola played an undetermined role in the **Forças Armadas de Libertação de Angola** (FALA) military structure.

UNITA I EXTRAORDINARY CONGRESS. Held at **Jamba** in September 1984, the UNITA I Extraordinary Congress listed the **Movimento Popular de Libertação de Angola** (MPLA) casualty figures for the year. The party expressed hope that American president **Ronald**

Reagan would win reelection. UNITA also noted that any negotiations involving the **Soviet Union**, **Cuba**, **South Africa**, the **United States**, and the MPLA would also have to include the rebels. UNITA described itself as ready to take the war nationwide in order to achieve its political objectives. Prophetically, the final communiqué stated that the MPLA would attempt to capture **Mavinga/Jamba** in 1985.

UNITA II EXTRAORDINARY CONGRESS. UNITA held its second extraordinary congress from 26 to 29 September 1989. Over 3,000 delegates voted for direct negotiations between UNITA and the **Movimento Popular de Libertação de Angola** (MPLA), implementation of a cease-fire with a release of all prisoners, support of a transitional government, revision of the constitution, and support of free and fair elections.

UNITA III EXTRAORDINARY CONGRESS. UNITA party meeting held in August 1996 in Bailundo. At this congress, **Jonas Savimbi** rejected appointment to the vice presidency. In his speech to the delegates, Savimbi criticized the delays in implementing the **Lusaka Protocol**. He blamed the government's use of **mercenaries** for the slow pace of military integration and for security concerns prompting his refusal to return to **Luanda**. The congress did vote to send five UNITA generals to take up posts in the new unified army. One of the generals was **Arlindo Chenda Pena** (Ben-Ben).

UNITA I PARTY CONGRESS. Held in Lusaka, **Zambia**, on 18 September 1966, the congress established a permanent Central Committee. The 47 delegates heard reports on aspects of the political–military struggle and on UNITA's efforts to strengthen its political organs and military capability.

UNITA II PARTY CONGRESS. The second congress met inside eastern Angola during August 1969. A 25-member Central Committee was elected, and the top 12 members formed the Political Bureau. The congress established policies that would dominate UNITA's strategy over the next four years. Efforts were taken to recruit the best students, expand military-political areas, and incorporate UNITA's influence and ideology in all sectors of the peasants' lives.

UNITA III PARTY CONGRESS. Held from 13 to 19 August 1973 in the interior of Angola. The Central Committee was reduced in size and People's Assemblies were formed in UNITA-controlled areas. Reports on progress since the second congress were heard. **Agriculture** was discussed, as was **women**'s place in the liberation struggle. Foreign guests also attended.

UNITA IV PARTY CONGRESS. Convening at a location 40 miles from **Huambo**, the 530 members met for five days in March 1977.

UNITA V PARTY CONGRESS. The fifth party congress met at **Mavinga** from 26 to 31 July 1982. The delegates numbered 1,553 and included Central Committee members, the Juventude Revolucionaria de Angola (JURA), the Liga da Mulher Angolana (LIMA), the **Forças Armadas de Libertação de Angola** (FALA), and local committees. The congress agreed to "reaffirm UNITA's readiness to negotiate the ending of the armed conflict."

UNITA VI PARTY CONGRESS. Meeting from 27 to 31 August 1986, the 2,154 delegates came from every **province** of Angola. Seventeen foreign guests also attended. The congress authorized the leadership "to launch an immediate effort for peace and national reconciliation."

UNITA VII PARTY CONGRESS. Held at the Kwame N'Krumah military base in southeast Angola, the party congress met from 11 to 17 March 1991. The 3,200 delegates (100 foreign observers also attended) voted to convert UNITA from a military organization to a political one, ratified the principle of a national army, liberalized UNITA's **economic** program, voted confidence in **Portugal**'s mediation, accepted the April 1991 cease-fire with elections in 1992, defined Angolan citizenship and who could vote in national elections, thanked the **Catholic Church** for support of free elections, and affirmed the leadership of **Jonas Savimbi**.

UNITA VIII PARTY CONGRESS. The eighth party congress was held at Bailundo from 7 to 11 February 1995. It was attended by 1,200 delegates from all 18 **provinces** and from abroad. The congress approved all peace plans for Angola, supported all necessary steps for national reconciliation, encouraged a meeting between **Jonas Savimbi** and President **Eduardo dos Santos** as soon as possible, thanked the **United Nations** for its efforts toward peace, demanded the expulsion of all **mercenaries** from Angola, and urged that all civilian elements be disarmed, especially in **Luanda**.

UNITA IX PARTY CONGRESS. The first party congress held after the death of UNITA founder **Jonas Savimbi**. It convened in Viana, near **Luanda**, from 24 to 27 June 2003. Some 1,500 delegates from the 18 Angolan provinces participated. Three men stood for the presidency of UNITA: **Isaías Samakuva**, **Paulo Lukamba Gato**, and Eduardo Jonatão "Dinho" Chingunji. Samakuva was overwhelmingly elected as UNITA's president, receiving 1,067 votes to Gato's 277 and Chingunji's 20. Ernest Mulato was elected vice president, Mario Miguel Vatuva secretary general, Tiago Kandanda secretary for international affairs, and **Abel Chivukuvuku** head of the office of constitutional and electoral affairs. The congress also dealt with the upcoming elections, rewrote party statutes and regulations to conform with the new political situation, adopted a party platform, and discussed strategies to expand the party's presence throughout Angola.

UNITA–R FIRST PARTY CONGRESS. Seven hundred UNITA–R members attended the Congress held from 11 to 14 January 1999 in **Luanda**. Eugenio Manuvakola was elected president, Jorgé Valentim secretary of foreign affairs, and Silvestre Gabriel Samy secretary general of the party. The party vowed to uphold and support the **Lusaka Protocol** and to seek peace and national reconciliation. The three main priorities for the party were the complete demilitarization of **Forças Armadas de Libertação de Angola** (FALA), encouraging **economic** development and providing jobs for all Angolans, and removal of the **land mines** scattered throughout Angola. UNITA–R placed the blame for the renewed civil war on **Jonas Savimbi**. However, UNITA–R did not remove Savimbi's name from the membership roster, only from the presidency.

UNITA'S AIR FORCE. In 1999, intelligence reports indicated that UNITA had acquired three Russian-built Hind 25 helicopters (and had seven more being delivered), six Russian-built Mig-23s, and 20

Russian-built ground-to-ground mini-Scud missiles known as FROGS. Reportedly, the armaments were purchased from Ukraine and would be operated by Ukrainians. Other analysts cited the high maintenance requirements of the weapons systems and the incongruity of a guerrilla force employing high-tech weapons. Ultimately, it was discovered that UNITA's air force was nothing more than rebel propaganda trying to mislead government forces as to UNITA's military strength.

UNITA'S *ECONOMIC DEMOCRACY IN ANGOLA*. Written in 1991, before Angola's national **elections**, this document outlined UNITA's vision for the **economy** of Angola. The Angolan government, presumably a UNITA-led one, would enact emergency programs in the fields of **health**, nutrition, **education**, housing construction, and repair of the damaged economic infrastructure. Troops must be either incorporated into the new national army or given retraining for civilian employment. UNITA placed heavy emphasis on rural development corresponding to the rebel belief that **Luanda** ruled only while making war on the rest of Angola. The emphasis needed to be placed on rural markets, financial institutions, and better communication between local governments and Luanda. Finally, UNITA advocated implementation of programs to assist small and medium-sized businesses, restructuring of public investment, and adoption of investment codes to protect small and medium-sized business concerns.

UNITA'S TWELVE POINT PEACE PLAN. On 30 October 2000, UNITA issued a set of 12 peace proposals. They included forming a national unity government, depoliticizing the army and police, depoliticizing the government bureaucracy, establishing a national commission to oversee disbursal and expenditure of public funds, establishing true separation of powers within the Angolan government, guaranteeing freedom of the **media**, using impartial mediators, discussing the **cultural**, political, historical, and social causes of the **civil war**, establishing a genuine national identity, guaranteeing the right to life and equal opportunities for all Angolans, negotiating the future of Angola's social and **economic** development, and discussing the **Cabinda** Enclave. UNITA rejected **Portugal**, the **United States**, and Russia as mediators, asking instead that the **Catholic Church**, the independent press, and genuine opposition parties mediate. The next day, Angola's foreign minister, speaking in Helsinki, Finland, dismissed UNITA's plan.

UNITED NATIONS. The United Nations has been actively involved in Angola since 1988. It oversaw the **Cuban** withdrawal from Angola, monitored and oversaw the implementation of the **Bicesse Accords**, attempted to force all parties, especially **União Nacional para a Independência Total de Angola** (UNITA), to obey the terms of the **Lusaka Protocol**, and is assisting in the postwar reconstruction of Angola. UN secretary-general Kofi Annan, in a speech in Luanda in August 2002, pledged support in alleviating the humanitarian crisis, removing **land mines**, demobilizing ex-combatants, and rebuilding an Angolan society devastated by years of **civil war**. UN organizations in Angola include the United Nations Children's Fund (UNICEF), an organization that has been very active in Angola, working to assist **children** through nutrition packages, **education**, and **health** care; the Office of the United Nations High Commissioner for Refugees (UNHCR), which is responsible for coordination of relief assistance to Angola's **refugees** and protecting their rights; and the World Food Programme, the main agency concerned with food aid. The World Health Organization (WHO) is playing a more prominent role in the country since the end of hostilities in April 2002.

The UN has always played an important role in peacekeeping. The United Nations Verification Missions (UNAVEM) I, II, and III and the Misión de Observadores de las Naciones Unidas en Angola (MONUA) (United Nations Observer Mission in Angola) attempted to mediate and implement the cease-fires and peace agreements between UNITA and the government. The UN also exerted pressure on the rebels through sanctions adopted by the Security Council. However, the UN could not assist a process the principals had no intention of honoring. In January 1999, UN secretary-general Kofi Annan said, "In light of the expressed determination of the parties to test their fortunes on the battlefield, the steadily worsening security situation and the inability of MONUA to carry out its mandate, it has become increasingly clear that, for the time being, the conditions for a meaningful United Nations peacekeeping role in Angola ceased to exist."

UNITED NATIONS ANGOLA VERIFICATION MISSION I (UN-AVEM I). Lasting from January 1989 to June 1991, UNAVEM I was to monitor the **Cuban** withdrawal from Angola, the **South African** withdrawal from **Namibia**, and the elections in Namibia. The United Nations also used its influence to advocate a peace treaty between **União Nacional para a Independência Total de Angola** (UNITA) and the **Movimento Popular de Libertação de Angola** (MPLA). *See also* UNITED NATIONS ANGOLA VERIFICATION MISSION II and III; UNITED NATIONS MISSION TO ANGOLA.

UNITED NATIONS ANGOLA VERIFICATION MISSION II (UNAVEM II). A United Nations mission to oversee implementation of the **Bicesse Accords**. Later, the mission evolved into an attempt to halt the reignited **civil war**. The mission lasted from June 1991 until February 1995. The UN was harshly criticized for the UNAVEM II operation. Critics complained that it was underfunded and under-staffed and had no clear mission objective. In **Namibia**, with a population of 1.5 million, the UN had 7,900 civilian and military monitors at a cost of $373 million. In Angola, with a population of 10 million, the UN provided only 800 monitors, while spending approximately $200 million. *See also* ANSTEE, MARGARET; UNITED NATIONS ANGOLA VERIFICATION MISSION I and III; UNITED NATIONS MISSION TO ANGOLA.

UNITED NATIONS ANGOLA VERIFICATION MISSION III (UN-AVEM III). Created to oversee the implementation of the **Lusaka Protocol**, this United Nations mission lasted from February 1995 until June 1997. The UN was charged with demobilizing and disarming **União Nacional para a Independência Total de Angola** (UNITA) troops, encouraging UNITA to participate in the national government, and attempting to restore basic travel rights, **economic** stability, **land-mine** removal, and trust between UNITA and the **Movimento Popular de Libertação de Angola** (MPLA). The mission was highly criti-cized for claiming to have verified the demobilization of UNITA troops despite evidence to the contrary. During the term of UNAVEM III, UNITA rearmed, regrouped, and violated UN sanctions with impunity. *See also* UNITED NATIONS ANGOLA VERIFICATION MISSION I and II; UNITED NATIONS MISSION TO ANGOLA.

UNITED NATIONS MISSION TO ANGOLA (UNMA). In August 2002, the United Nations Security Council and the government of Angola agreed to establish a new mission with a six-month mandate, from 15 August to 15 February 2003. UNMA was entrusted with **humanitarian** assistance, human rights issues, and helping conclude the peace process. After UNMA closed, the UN announced it would not have a "mission" in Angola, only a "presence."

UNITED NATIONS OBSERVER MISSION TO ANGOLA. See MISIÓN DE OBSERVADORES DE LAS NACIONES UNIDAS EN ANGOLA (MONUA).

UNITED NATIONS OFFICE IN ANGOLA (UNOA). Established on 15 October 1999, the United Nations Office was staffed by 30 professional personnel and would "liaise with the political, military, police and other civilian authorities, with a view to exploring effective measures for restoring peace, assisting the Angolan people in the area of capacity-building, **humanitarian** assistance, the promotion of human rights and coordinating other activities."

UNITED NATIONS SANCTIONS. The first set of United Nations sanctions against **União Nacional para a Independência Total de Angola** (UNITA) were adopted on 15 September 1993. The Security Council, by a 15-0 vote, imposed a **petroleum** and arms embargo on UNITA military forces. The embargo required that all weapons, ammunition, oil, and oil by-products destined for Angola be sent to points designated by the Angolan government. On 30 October 1997, the Security Council, by a vote of 15-0, instituted further sanctions against UNITA for "failing to comply with the peace process." UNITA members were prohibited from traveling abroad, all UNITA overseas offices were to be closed, and UNITA was banned from purchasing airplanes or aviation components. The sanctions were in response to UNITA's refusal to demobilize its troops and its failure to return Bailundo and Andulo to government control. The Security Council did request that **Jonas Savimbi** and President **Eduardo dos Santos** meet to discuss the peace process. Another set of sanctions was implemented on 1 July 1998. The sanctions froze UNITA bank accounts, banned its **diamond**

exports, and prohibited all air and water transport into and out of territories controlled by the rebel movement. The Security Council voted unanimously in October 2002 to lift the travel ban imposed on UNITA leaders and their families. The remaining sanctions were lifted by the Security Council in December 2002. President George W. Bush lifted U.S. sanctions against UNITA in May 2003. UN sanctions were first imposed in 1993, and they gradually grew more restrictive as UNITA refused to obey peace treaties or fulfill promises to the government. The UN Security Council passed the following resolutions: No. 864, establishing an arms and petroleum embargo against UNITA, in 1993; No. 1127, placing a travel ban on senior members of UNITA, in 1997; No. 1173, freezing UNITA funds in all nations except for Angola, in 1998; No. 1237, establishing a panel of experts to trace violations regarding arms, petroleum, representation, travel, and diamonds, in 1999; No. 1295, creating the **Monitoring Mechanism on Sanctions against UNITA** to collect additional relevant information about violations of sanctions, in 2000; No. 1336, extending the Monitoring Mechanism for three months, in 2001; Nos.1348, 1374, and 1404, each extending the Monitoring Mechanism for six months, in 2001–02; No.1412, suspending the travel ban on UNITA officials for 90 days, in 2002; No.1432, suspending the travel ban on UNITA officials for a further 90 days, in 2002; No.1439, extending the Monitoring Mechanism for two months, in 2002; and No.1448, terminating all sanctions against UNITA, in 2002.

UNITED NATIONS SECURITY COUNCIL. In September 2002, Angola was elected to a two-year term on the United Nations Security Council to replace Mauritius as Africa's representative on the body. While not allowed to veto Security Council resolutions, Angola would be able to introduce resolutions, chair committees, hold the rotating council presidency, and vote on resolutions. During the 2003 debate on the war in Iraq, Angola's vote was actively courted by France and the **United States**.

UNITED NATIONS SECURITY COUNCIL RESOLUTION 1237. In May 1999, the **United Nations Security Council** decided to establish a panel of experts to explore how **União Nacional para a In-**

dependência Total de Angola (UNITA) was successfully violating sanctions and what countries were assisting UNITA in the process. The panel was to visit various nations, identify individuals or states violating UN sanctions, and recommend measures to improve implementation of existing sanctions. Robert Fowler of Canada was named chairman of the Security Council Sanctions Committee for Angola. *See also* FOWLER COMMISSION REPORT.

UNITED STATES–ANGOLA CHAMBER OF COMMERCE. The chamber was founded in 1990 with a membership of over 75 corporations, associations, and interested individuals. To promote trade and investment in Angola, the chamber helps members identify and respond to business opportunities, sponsors trade missions to Angola, represents private interests to the governments of Angola and the **United States**, hosts officials from both nations, and keeps members informed of **economic**, social, and political developments. Some of the U.S. members of the chamber are Amoco Overseas Exploration Company, Chevron Overseas Petroleum Company, Citizens Energy Corporation, Cohen and Woods International, Exxon Exploration Company, Fleishman–Hillard Incorporated, Mobil Corporation, Samuels International Associates, and Texaco.

UNITED STATES OF AMERICA. After years of supporting government opposition groups, most notably the **União Nacional para a Independência Total de Angola** (UNITA), Washington granted diplomatic recognition to Angola on 19 May 1993. In the 1980s, while it was openly supporting UNITA, the United States nonetheless became Angola's largest trading partner, while Angola was the United States' third leading trading partner in Africa, behind Nigeria and **South Africa**. Between 1982 and 1984, U.S.–Angola trade rose from $856 million to $1.1 billion. Yet, during this period, the United States and Angola had no diplomatic relations. Throughout the 1980s, UNITA received a substantial amount of money and weaponry to fight the **Movimento Popular de Libertação de Angola** (MPLA) government. When the MPLA dropped its Marxist ideology, asked the **Cuban** soldiers to depart, and conducted **elections**, the Cold War mentality seemed pointless. The administration of Bill Clinton was also concerned about UNITA's resumption of the war and refusal to engage in serious negotiations. In 1993, President Clinton, in an executive order, denounced "the unusual and extraordinary threat to the foreign policy of the United States by the actions and policies of UNITA." The order banned any governmental agency or U.S. citizen from actively assisting UNITA. It remained in effect until the death of **Jonas Savimbi**. There is some evidence that the Clinton and George W. Bush administrations provided satellite photos and telephone intercepts to the government of Angola in the hunt for the rebel leader.

UNIVERSIDADE CATHOLICA DE ANGOLA (UCAN) (Catholic University of Angola). Founded in 1999 and located in **Luanda**, the Catholic University of Angola initially had two faculties, **economics** and law, but added a third in theology as mandated by the Vatican. Angola's other institutions of higher learning are the state-owned **Agostinho Neto** University and the **Universidade Independente de Angola** (UNIANG). Much of the money to fund UCAN was provided by the U.S. Citizens Energy Corporation Fund. *See also* EDUCATION.

UNIVERSIDADE INDEPENDENTE DE ANGOLA (UNIANG) (Independent University of Angola). A new university started in August 2003, located at Sumbe in **Kwanza-Sul province**, and dedicated to agronomy, forestry, and veterinary science. UNIANG is part of the government's effort to locate institutions of higher learning throughout Angola. *See also* EDUCATION.

– V –

VAN-DUNEM, PEDRO DE CASTRO "LOY" (1941–1996). Born in **Bengo province**, Van-Dunem served for the **Movimento Popular de Libertação de Angola** (MPLA) government as the third vice prime minister in 1976, the minister of energy and oil in 1980, the minister of foreign affairs in 1989, the chairman of the Board of Directors of the Central **Bank** of Angola, and at the time of his death, the minister of public works and construction. He died of a heart attack in September 1996.

VICTORY BY SOCIAL EXPLOSION. Reportedly a **União Nacional para a Independência Total de Angola** (UNITA) political and military tactic used in 1999. UNITA would not capture the **provincial** capitals; instead the rebels would shell the cities almost continuously, while at the same time forcing farmers away from the fields into the cities, which were already seriously overcrowded. The resulting social explosion would force the **Movimento Popular de Libertação de Angola** (MPLA) to negotiate with UNITA. *See also* SCORCHED-EARTH POLICY.

VIEIRA, LUANDINO. One of Angola's most widely read authors, according to an informal poll taken in July 2003. His recent work, *O Nosso Musseque* (Our suburb) was favored by **Luanda**'s book buyers. *See also* LITERATURE.

VINDO COM MIM (Come with Me). A government program to reintegrate former **União Nacional para a Independência Total de Angola** (UNITA) soldiers into civil society.

A VOZ DA RESISTÊNCIA DO GALO NEGRO (VORGAN) (Voice of the Resistance of the Black Cockerel). On 4 January 1979, Vorgan first signed on the air with the sounds of a crowing rooster. Vorgan was the propaganda mouthpiece for **União Nacional para a Independência Total de Angola** (UNITA). The programs were designed to report UNITA battlefield successes and damage the morale of government troops. Initially, Vorgan broadcast from either **Namibia** or **South Africa**, using South African transmitters. Later, broadcasts came from UNITA-held territory, employing 10-kw shortwave transmitters supplied by the **United States**. The Angolan government repeatedly tried to destroy the Vorgan facilities or jam the signals by creating a bogus radio station supplying loyal UNITA listeners with anti-UNITA propaganda. Under the **Lusaka Protocol**, Vorgan was to cease broadcasts. UNITA delayed until 1 April 1998, when the station signed off the air. UNITA forces destroyed the equipment rather than hand it over to the government. Vorgan was to be replaced by Radio Despertar (Wake-Up Radio), a nonpartisan station on an FM band. Radio Despertar never signed on the air. Some of the former staff of Vorgan went to work for **Rádio Nacional de Angola**. *See also* MEDIA.

– W –

WAR POWERS. As the security situation worsened throughout Angola, on 30 January 1999, President **Eduardo dos Santos** reshuffled the cabinet, combining the presidency with the post of prime minister. The move placed the government and military under dos Santos's direct authority. The strategy paid dividends as the **civil war** turned against **União Nacional para a Independência Total de Angola** (UNITA), culminating in **Jonas Savimbi**'s death in February 2002. The post of prime minister was reinstated in December 2002.

WHITE SETTLER PARTIES. As the **Portuguese** colonialists realized the **Alvor Accords** included no provisions for them, several settler parties formed, including the Amigos para a Resistência de Angola (ARA) (Friends of the Resistance of Angola), the Exército Angolan Nacional da Intervenção e do Salvation (ESINA) (National Angolan Army of Intervention and Salvation), and the Resistência Unida de Angolana (RUA) (United Resistance of Angola), all of which were founded in 1974 to protect white settler rights either politically or militarily. The Partido Democrático Christian de Angola (PDCA) (Christian Democratic Party of Angola) was a white settler group that attempted a coup in October 1974. Although easily dispersed by security forces, it reinforced fears of a white settler unilateral declaration of independence, as Ian Smith had done in Rhodesia.

The Frente de Unidade Angolana (FUA) (United Front for Angola) was a white settler group that served as a political outlet for Portuguese living in Angola. It emerged after the **Movimento das Forças Armadas** (MFA) coup in 1974, with permission from Lisbon. Led by Fernando Falção, the FUA demanded inclusion in the tripartite government outlined in the Alvor Accords. It was also known as the "Fourth Force," to indicate violence was also an option.

Eventually, the white settler population would forgo any plan. Over 300,000 settlers fled Angola in the months before independence. The RUA, ESINA, FUA, Christian Democratic Party, and ARA were outlawed by colonial authorities.

WILD WEST. A term applied to **Lunda Norte** and **Lunda Sul provinces** in 1991, when 100,000 to 200,000 *garimpeiros* began to seek illegal fortune in **diamonds**. The term "Wild West" was applied because of the lawlessness and violence that emerged in the region.

WOMEN. It could be argued that women have been the backbone of Angolan society since 1961 and long before. The traditional role of the female in Angola was to cook, clean, take care of the children, the old, and the sick, and take charge of visitors. Women were also expected to work in the fields planting and harvesting crops and fetch water from distant streams or rivers. Illiterate and experiencing high levels of infant mortality, the Angolan woman was considered the property of her husband. With the onset of the **civil war** in 1961, women were in charge of landholdings, **children**, and homes as the men left to fight. As the conflict grew in intensity, women were left to struggle to find safe haven, food, and medicine for their children, while maintaining some personal dignity in the face of soldiers and rebels bent upon violating the norms of civil society. Traditionally, women were shortchanged in **educational** opportunities, political participation, employment, and **health** services. Women had to battle poverty, food insecurity, unequal legal and political rights, and the male expectation that they would bear children and do little more. The end of the civil war along with new attitudes toward the role of the female in society should allow women and their families better access to health care, housing, education, food security, and a peaceful environment. Angolan women's groups have a broader agenda. Noting that the **Assembleia Nacional** has 20 female members, that a woman is vice president on the Supreme Court, that Albina Assis is oil minister, and that Fátima Jarden is fisheries minister, the groups seek fuller participation in the political process, support for the legislative process of providing equal rights for women, and the guarantee that young women receive proper education and training to succeed in present-day Angola. The Liga da Mulher Angolana (LIMA) (League of Angolan Women) of the **União Nacional para a Independência Total de Angola (UNITA)** is monitoring the economic and political rights of the demobilized soldiers and their families. See also BEATRICE, DOÑA; DIAKITE, JOSEFINA PITRA; NZINGA, QUEEN; ORGANIZAÇÃO DA MULHER ANGOLANA; PEREIRA, ANALIA; ROQUE, FÁTIMA.

– Y –

YETWENE MINE. Diamond mine located in **Lunda Norte province**. Operated by Diamond Works Ltd., the mine was attacked in November 1998 by **União Nacional para a Independência Total de Angola** (UNITA) forces, which killed five and took four hostages. The mine was then producing 5,000–6,000 carats per month. The mine resumed operation in April 1999.

– Z –

ZAIRE. A **province** located in the eastern part of the nation. The capital city is M'Banza Congo. The climate is regarded as tropical-dry and allows the harvesting of cocoa, cashews, bananas, and **fish**. Crude oil is found offshore.

ZAIRE (country). See DEMOCRATIC REPUBLIC OF THE CONGO.

ZAIRENSES. Derogatory term used to describe **Bakongo** living in **Luanda**.

ZAIRIAN CIVIL WAR. When **Laurent Kabila** launched his war against Zaire's president Mobutu Sese Seko in 1996, it became part of Angola's civil strife as well. The **União Nacional para a Independência Total de Angola** (UNITA) supported its longtime patron Mobutu, while the Angolan government supported Kabila. Mobutu had long supported UNITA with weapons, safe haven, use of the Kamina Airbase, and a diplomatic and economic base to market illegal **diamonds**. The Angolan government supported Kabila simply because he was not Mobutu. UNITA supplied Zaire with approximately 2,000 fighters, while Angola's government provided Kabila with 3,500 soldiers equipped with heavy tanks and armor. The Zairian army was unwilling to fight to save the regime of Mobutu, and UNITA did not deploy enough troops to make a difference, nor did it possess tanks or artillery. On 7 May 1997, President Mobutu left Kinshasa for a summit in Gabon, but he would never return. Laurent Kabila's rebels, backed by Angola, Rwanda, Uganda, and **Zambia**, seized power on 20 May. The loss of support from President Mobutu was a serious blow to UNITA over the succeeding years. *See also* DEMOCRATIC REPUBLIC OF THE CONGO; ZAIRIAN DIAMOND INVOLVEMENT WITH UNITA.

ZAIRIAN DIAMOND INVOLVEMENT WITH UNITA. Until May 1997, the main channel for **União Nacional para a Independência Total de Angola** (UNITA) illegal **diamond** trading was Zaire. The trafficking had the full support of President Mobutu Sese Seko, his son General Mobutu Kongulo (head of the Presidential Guard), General Nzimbi Wale Kongo (head of the Special Presidential Division), and General Kapama Baramoto (head of the Special Council on Security Matters). According to the **Fowler Commission Report**, Ali Said Ahmad, with two Antwerp-based diamond companies called Triple A Diamonds and Sierra Gem Diamonds, purchased diamonds from UNITA. Hassan Nassour also purchased diamonds from UNITA. The individuals and companies named may have had close links to Amal and Hizbullah in Lebanon and even Al-Qaida. Another Lebanese with ties to UNITA and Hizbullah was Imad Bakri. He reportedly purchased arms for UNITA from 1995 to 1999. UNITA General Jacinto Bandua, head of UNITA's Strategic Procurement, traveled to Kinshasa, where he met with the commander of the Special Presidential Division, Nzimbi Wale Kongo, and Imad Bakri. The death of **Jonas Savimbi**, with the accompanying end of the **civil war**, combined with implementation of the **Kimberley Process** to inhibit the illegal trading of Angola's diamonds. It is doubtful that UNITA realized the connection of Nassour, Bakri, and Ahmad to terrorist groups.

ZAMBIA. A country located to the southeast of Angola. Because of a long common border, the **União Nacional para a Independência Total de Angola** (UNITA) used Zambia as an area of rest and resupply. After overthrowing the governments of Zaire and the Republic of the Congo because of their alleged support for UNITA, Angola began to threaten Zambia. In February 1999, the Angolan government announced details of Zambia's involvement with UNITA. Angola blamed Vice President Christian Tembo, former defense minister

Benjamin Mwila, former commerce and industry minister Enock Kavindele, and the Zambian intelligence services for supplying UNITA with needed war materials. The allegations were denied by Zambia. To heighten the tension, a bomb exploded at the Angolan embassy in Lusaka on 28 February, killing one Angolan guard and wounding another. The government of Angola was angered that Zambia responded to the blast by deploying only a single policeman to protect Angolan property and personnel. The bomb blast occurred days after Angolan president **Eduardo dos Santos** was quoted as saying he would not meet with Zambian president **Frederick Chiluba** as long as Zambia continued to destabilize Angola. *See also* INDENI PETROLEUM REFINERY.

ZAMBIA INITIATIVE. Program begun in 2002 to incorporate Angolan **refugees** into **Zambian** society. A flood of refugees destabilizes a nation. The refugees wish to return home, but meanwhile are a burden to the host nation. The Zambian Initiative would integrate those refugees who, having been born in Zambia, speaking the local language, and having learned the cultural habits, might wish to become productive citizens of Zambia. *See also* HUMANITARIAN SITUATION; MAYUKWAYUKWA REFUGEE CAMP.

Appendix 1
Selected Place-Name Changes

Former Name	New Name
Ambrizete	Nzeto
Carmona	Uige
Cassinga	Kassinga
Henrique de Carvalho	Saurimo
João de Almeida	Chibia
Luso	Luena
Malanje	Malange
Nova Lisboa	Huambo
Novo Redondo	Ngunza
Vila Pereira d'Éca	Ngiva
Portugalia	Luachimo
Sá da Bandeira	Lubango
São Salvador do Congo	Mbanza Kongo
Serpa Pinto	Menongue
Silva Porto	Bíe
Teixeira de Silva	Bailundo
Teixeira de Sousa	Luau

Appendix 2
Government of Unity and National Reconciliation, September 2003

Title	Name
Head of State	José Eduardo dos Santos
Prime Minister	Fernando Da Piedade Dias dos Santos
Central Bank Governor	Amadeu Maurício
Minister of Defense	Kundi Paihama
Minister of Interior	Osvaldo de Jesus Serra Van-Dúnem
Minister of Foreign Relations	João Bernardo de Miranda
Minister of Justice	Paulo Tjipilica
Minister of Planning	Ana Afonso Dias Lourenco
Minister of Finance	José Pedro de Morais
Minister of Public Administration, Employment, and Social Security	António Domingos Pitra de Costa Neto
Minister of Territorial Administration	Fernando Faustino Muteka
Minister of Industry	Joaquim Duarte da Costa David
Minister of Agriculture and Rural Development	Gilberto Buta Lutukuta
Minister of Transportation	André Luís Brandão
Minister of Geology and Mines	Manuel António Africano
Minister of Energy and Water	José Maria Botelho de Vasconcelos
Minister of Posts and Telecommunications	Licínio Tavares Ribiero
Minister of Petroleum	Desidério da Graca Veríssimo da Costa
Minister of Health	Albertina Júlia Henrique Hamukuya

Title	Name
Minister of Commerce	Vitorino Domingos Hossi
Minister of Hotels and Tourism	Jorge Aliceres Valentim
Minister of Youth and Sports	José Marcos Barrica
Minister of Former Combatants and War Veterans	Pedro José Van-Dúnem
Minister of Social Assistance and Reintegration	João Baptista Kussumua
Minister of Social Communication	Pedro Hendrik Vaal-Neto
Minister of Science and Technology	João Baptista Ngandagina
Ministry of Education	António Burity Da Silva
Ministry of Fisheries	Salomão Luheto Xirimbimbi
Ministry of Public Works and Housing	Francisco Higino Carneiro
Ministry of Family and the Promotion of Women	Celestial Cândida Da Silva
Ministry of Urban Affairs and Environment	Vergílio Ferreira Fontes Pereira
Ministry of Culture	Boaventura Cardoso

Appendix 3
Angola's Oil Production

Year	Barrels per Day
1992	526,000
1993	509,000
1994	536,000
1995	646,000
1996	709,000
1997	714,000
1998	735,000
1999	745,000
2000	746,000
2001	742,000
2002	930,000
2003	990,000 (est.)

Bibliography

CONTENTS

Introduction 190
  I. Bibliographies, General Works, and Dictionaries 191
  II. The Colonial Power: Portugal 192
  III. International Actors and Influences 194
    A. Communism 194
    B. Cuba 194
    C. People's Republic of China 195
    D. South Africa 196
    E. Soviet Union/Russian Federation 196
    F. United States 197
    G. Other International Actors 198
    H. Regional Actors 198
  IV. History 200
    A. Ancient 200
    B. Colonial 201
  V. Struggle for Independence 202
  VI. The Angolan Civil War: 1975–2002 206
  VII. General 213
    A. Agriculture and Fisheries 213
    B. Anthropology and Sociology 214
    C. Arts and Literature 215
    D. Congressional Hearings and Reports 216
    E. Disaster Assistance Programs 218
    F. Economy 219
    G. Energy and Minerals 221
    H. Human Rights and Politics 222
    I. Public Health and Safety 225
    J. Religion 225
    K. Wildlife 226
    L. Women and Women's Issues 226
    M. Websites, Newspapers, and Journals 227

INTRODUCTION

To adequately study Angola, a good working knowledge of Portuguese is required. However, since the Historical Dictionary Series is primarily meant for English-speakers, only major works in Portuguese or other languages have been included. Also, the reader should consult the previous editions of the *Historical Dictionary of Angola,* by Phyllis Martin and by Susan Herlin Broadhead, which include strong bibliography sections. This bibliography includes newer works, especially ones written after 1990.

The World Wide Web has changed the nature of research. Private sources, newspapers, journals, organizations, individuals, and more can all be found on the web. Most of the web content is valuable to a researcher, though some bogus information can also be encountered. Typing "Angola" into one search engine retrieved 5,490,000 entries. The sites for the Hoover Institute and the African Studies Center at the University of Pennsylvania contain excellent information. The last section of this bibliography includes some of the more prominent Angolan web sites with addresses.

Libraries will include the searchable databases of *ABI/Informal Global, Books in Print with Reviews, Digital Library Search, Ebsco Host, Factsdotcom, First Search, Lexis–Nexis, ProquestDirect,* and *Databases on CD-ROM.*

Still, hard-copy research must be done. The archives of the *Washington Post, New York Times, Los Angeles Times, Wall Street Journal,* and *Boston Globe* can be found in major libraries or on the web. Nationally known newspapers and journals on Africa will include articles about Angola. African journals are archived, and the diligent researcher can locate information.

Writings on the early history of Angola were by Portuguese or other non-Angolan writers. The Portuguese wrote mainly from their perspective, paying scant attention to ethnic groups or local historical events. Angolans have relied upon oral history passed from generation to generation. Consequently, very little of Angola's past has been written by Angolans. With the end of the civil war, Angolan scholars will begin to explore all eras of their history.

Angola's civil war played a major role in the Cold War. There are innumerable works on various aspects of the conflict penned from every perspective. Many of the books and articles of the past 30 years focus exclusively on the war. With the war over, there is a flood of nongovernmental organization (NGO) reports on the devastation caused by the 27-year conflict.

The Angolan government has moved from socialism to democracy. There has been a gradual easing of the stringent rules governing the press. It is fair to assume that, once basic services such as housing, electricity, sanitation, food, health care, and, especially, education are restored, Angola will experience an increase in literacy and research dealing with all aspects of its heritage.

I. BIBLIOGRAPHIES, GENERAL WORKS, AND DICTIONARIES

American University. *Angola: A Country Study.* Washington, D.C.: American University Press, 1979.

Birmingham, David. "Themes and Resources of Angolan History." *African Affairs* 73, no. 291 (April 1974): 188–203.

Broadhead, Susan H. *Historical Dictionary of Angola.* Lanham, Md.: Scarecrow, 1992.

Capello, Guilherme Augusto de Brito. *Aspects of Angolan History.* Lisbon: Imprensa Nacional, 1889.

Carter, Gwendolyn. *Independence for Africa.* New York: Praeger, 1960.

Cartey, Wilfred, and Martin Kilson. *The Africa Reader: Colonial Africa.* New York: Vintage, 1970.

——. *The Africa Reader: Independent Africa.* New York: Vintage, 1970.

Davidson, Basil. *The African Awakening.* London: Macmillan, 1955.

Deutschmann, David. *Changing the History of Africa: Angola and Namibia.* North Melbourne, Australia: Ocean, 1991.

Gavin, R. J., and J. A. Betley, eds. *The Scramble for Africa: Documents on the Berlin West Africa Conference and Related Subjects 1884/1885.* Ibadan, Nigeria: Ibadan University Press, 1973.

Gibson, Richard. *African Liberation Movements: Contemporary Struggles against White Minority Rule.* London: Oxford University Press, 1972.

Hallett, Robin. *Africa to 1875.* Ann Arbor: University of Michigan Press, 1970.

Hargreaves, J. D. *Decolonization of Africa.* New York: Longman, 1988.

Harris, Joseph E. *Africans and Their History.* New York: New American Library Press, 1987.

Herrick, Allison Butler. *Area Handbook for Angola.* Washington, D.C.: U.S. Government Printing Office, 1967.

Hodgkin, Thomas, *Nationalism in Colonial Africa.* London: Muller, 1956.

July, Robert W. *A History of the African People.* New York: Scribner's Sons, 1970.

Kaplan, I. Angola: *A Country Study.* Washington, D.C.: American University Press, 1979.

Legum, Colin. "'National Liberation' in Southern Africa." *Problems of Communism* 24, no.1 (January–February 1975): 1–20.

Mao Zedong. *On Guerrilla Warfare.* Trans. Samuel T. Griffith. New York: Praeger, 1961.

Martin, Phyllis. *Historical Dictionary of Angola.* Metuchen, N.J.: Scarecrow, 1980.

Memmi, Albert. *The Colonizer and the Colonized.* Boston: Beacon, 1975.

Nevinson, Henry. A *Modern Slavery.* London: Harpers, 1906.

Oliver, Roland, and Brian M. Fagan. *Africa in the Iron Age, c. 500 B.C. to A.D. 1400.* Cambridge: Cambridge University Press, 1975.
Rodney, Walter. *How Europe Underdeveloped Africa.* Washington, D.C.: Howard University Press, 1982.
Rodrigues, Jose Honorio. *Brazil and Africa.* Berkeley: University of California Press, 1965.
Turner, John W. *Continent Ablaze: The Insurgency Wars in Africa: 1960 to the Present.* London: Arms and Armour, 1998.
Venter, Al. *The Terror Fighters: A Profile of Guerrilla Warfare in Southern Africa.* Cape Town: Purnell, 1969.
Young, Crawford. *Ideology and Development in Africa.* New Haven, Conn.: Yale University Press, 1982.

II. THE COLONIAL POWER: PORTUGAL

Axelson, Eric. *Portugal and the Scramble for Africa, 1875–1891.* Johannesburg: Witwatersrand University Press, 1967.
Birmingham, David. *Portugal and Africa.* London: Macmillan, 1999.
Boxer, C. R. *Salvador de Saa and the Struggle for Brazil and Angola, 1602–1686.* London: University of London Press, 1952.
——. *Race Relations in the Portuguese Colonial Empire, 1415–1825.* Oxford: Clarendon, 1963.
——. *Four Centuries of Portuguese Expansion: 1415–1825.* Berkeley: University of California Press, 1969.
Boyd, Herb. *Former Portuguese Colonies: Angola, Mozambique, Guinea–Bissau, Cape Verde, and São Tomé e Príncipe.* London: Watts, 1981.
Bruce, Neil. *Portugal: The Last Empire.* New York: Wiley and Sons, 1975.
Cadbury, William A. *Labour in Portuguese West Africa.* Westport, Conn.: Negro Universities Press, 1969.
Chilcote, Ronald H. *Emerging Nationalism in Portuguese Africa.* Stanford, Calif.: Hoover Institution Press, 1969.
Emerging Nationalism in Portuguese Africa: Documents. Stanford, Calif.: Hoover Institution Press, 1972.
——. *Protest and Resistance in Angola and Brazil.* Berkeley: University of California Press, 1972.
Clarence–Smith, William G. *The Third Portuguese Empire.* Manchester, England: Manchester University Press, 1985.
Collins, Robert O. *Europeans in Africa.* New York: Knopf, 1971.
Daponte, B. *The Last to Leave: Portuguese Colonialism in Africa.* London: International Defence and Aid Fund, 1974.

Duffy, James. *Portugal in Africa.* Cambridge: Harvard University Press, 1962.

Ehnmark, Anders, and Per Wastberg. *Angola and Mozambique: The Case against Portugal.* London: Pall Mall, 1963.

The Fate of Portuguese Africa. London: Atlantic Education Trust, 1975.

Ferreira, Eduardo de Sousa. *Portuguese Colonialism in Africa: The End of an Era.* Paris: UNESCO, 1974.

Fields, Rona M. *The Portuguese Revolution and the Armed Forces Movement.* New York: Praeger, 1975.

Galvao, Henrique. *Santa Maria: My Crusade for Portugal.* Trans. William Longfellow. Cleveland: World, 1961.

Gann, L. H., and Peter Duignan. *White Settlers in Tropical Africa.* Baltimore: Penguin, 1962.

Hammond, R. J. *Portugal and Africa, 1815–1910: A Study in Uneconomic Imperialism.* Stanford, Calif.: Stanford University Press, 1966.

Humbaraci, Arslan, and Nicole Muchnik. *Portugal's African Wars.* New York: Joseph Okpaku, 1974.

Intelligence International. *Portuguese Africa.* Cheltenham, England: Intelligence International, 1974.

Kay, Hugh. *Salazar and Modern Portugal.* New York: Hawthorn, 1970.

MacQueen, Norrie. *The Decolonization of Portuguese Africa: Metropolitan Revolution and the Dissolution of Empire.* London: Longman, 1997.

Marques, A. H. de Oliveira. *History of Portugal.* 2 Vols. New York: Columbia University Press, 1972.

Miller, Joseph. "The Politics of Decolonization in Portuguese Africa." *African Affairs* 74, no. 295 (April 1975): 135–47.

Minter, William. *Portuguese Africa and the West.* New York: Monthly Review, 1972.

Newitt, Malyn. *Portugal in Africa: The Last Hundred Years.* London: Hurst, 1981.

Nogueira, Franco. *The United Nations and Portugal: A Study in Anti-Colonialism.* London: Sidgwick and Jackson, 1963.

Nowell, Charles E. *Portugal.* Englewood Cliffs, N.J.: Prentice Hall, 1973.

Porch, Douglas. *The Portuguese Armed Forces and the Revolution.* London: Croom Helm, 1977.

Smith, Alan K. "Antonio Salazar and the Reversal of Portuguese Colonial Policy." *Journal of African History* 15, no. 4 (1974): 653–67.

Spínola, António de. *Portugal e o Futuro* (Portugal and the future). Lisbon: Arcádia, 1974.

Sykes, John. *Portugal and Africa.* London: Hutchison, 1971.

Van Der Waals, Willem. *Portugal's War in Angola: 1961–1974.* Rivonia, South Africa: Ashanti, 1993.

Wohlgemuth, Patricia. *The Portuguese Territories and the United Nations.* New York: Carnegie Endowment for International Peace, 1963.
Zeiger, Henry A. *The Seizing of the Santa Maria.* New York: Popular Library, 1961.

III. INTERNATIONAL ACTORS AND INFLUENCES

A. Communism

African Countries Foreign Policy. Moscow: Progress, 1981.
Albright, David E., ed. *Communism in Africa.* Bloomington: Indiana University Press, 1980.
Brutents, Karen. *The Newly Free Countries in the Seventies.* Moscow: Progress, 1983.
Fighters for National Liberation. Moscow: Progress, 1983.
Greig, Ian. *The Communist Challenge to Africa.* London: Foreign Affairs, 1977.
Gromyko, Anatoly. *Africa: Progress, Problems, Prospects.* Moscow: Progress, 1981.
Horowitz, Gus. *Revolutionists and the Fight against Imperialist Intervention in Angola: A Reply to Nahuel Moreno.* New York: Pathfinder, 1978.
Ignatyev, Oleg. *Secret Weapon in Africa.* Moscow: Progress, 1977.
Labuschagne, Gerhardus S. *Moscow, Havana, and the MPLA Takeover of Angola.* Pretoria: Foreign Affairs Association, 1976.
Legum, Colin. "The Soviet Union, China, and the West in Southern Africa." *Foreign Affairs* 54 no. 4 (July 1976): 745–62.
Leighton, Marian. *The Moscow–Havana Axis.* New York: Radio Liberty Research, 1978.
Luce, Phillip Abbott. *The New Imperialism: Cuba and the Soviets in Africa.* Washington, D.C.: Council for InterAmerican Security, 1979.
Maxwell, Kenneth. "The Communists and the Portuguese Revolution." *Dissent* (Spring 1980): 194–201.
U.S. Information Agency. "Communist Propaganda Activities in Sub-Saharan Africa and the Implications of Angola." *USIA Office of Research* (November 1976): 1–26.
Valenta, Jiri. "The Soviet–Cuban Intervention in Angola." *Studies in Comparative Communism* 9, nos. 1 and 2 (Spring–Summer 1978): 3–33.

B. Cuba

Adams, Gordon, and Michael Locker. "Cuba and Africa: The Politics of the Liberation Struggle." *Cuba Review* 8, no. 1 (October 1978): 3–9.

Adams, Tom. "Cuba in Angola: A Balance Sheet." *Military Intelligence* 8 (January–March 1982): 32–36.

Brooke, James. "Cuba's Strange Mission in Angola." *New York Times Magazine* (February 1, 1987): 24, 28, 45, 47–48.

Castro, Fidel. *Angola–Africa Giron.* Havana: Editorial de Ciencias Sociales, 1976.

———. "Cuba's Internationalist Volunteers in Angola." *New Internationalists* 5 (Autumn 1985): 119–35.

Dominguez, Jorge I. "The Cuban Operation in Angola: Costs and Benefits for the Armed Forces." *Cuban Studies* 8, no. 1 (January 1978): 10–20.

Durch, William J. "The Cuban Military in Africa and Middle East: From Algeria to Angola." *Studies in Comparative Communism,* nos. 1 and 2 (Spring–Summer 1978): 34–74.

Falk, Pamela S. "Cuba in Africa." *Foreign Affairs* 65, no. 5 (Summer 1987): 1077–1096.

Garcia Marquez, Gabriel. *Fidel Castro Speeches: Cuba's Internationalist Foreign Policy.* New York: Pathfinder Press, 1981.

George, Edward. *Moscow's Gurkhas or the Tail Wagging the Dog? Cuban Internationalism in Angola, 1965–1991.* Bristol, England: University of Bristol Press, Department of Hispanic, Portuguese and Latin American Studies, 1999.

LeoGrande, William M. "Cuban–Soviet Relations and Cuban Policy in Africa." *Cuban Studies* 10, no. 1 (January 1980): 1–48.

———. *Cuba's Policy in Africa, 1959–1980.* Berkeley: University of California Press, 1980.

Schechter, Danny. "The Havana–Luanda Connection." *Cuba Review* 6 (March 1976): 5–13.

C. People's Republic of China

"Africa Will Not Submit to the Soviet Baton." *Peking Review* 18, no.18 (August 1975): 6–7.

Hutchison, Alan. *China's African Revolution.* Boulder, Colo.: Westview Press, 1976.

Kaur, Harmala. "China and the Angolan National Liberation Movement." *China Report* 13, no. 4 (July–August 1977): 19–33.

Kun, Joseph. "Peking Censures Moscow's Involvement in Angola." *Radio Liberty Research* 26/76 (February 1976): 1–5.

"Soviet Interference in Angola Condemned." *Peking Review,* no. 50 (December 1975): 7–8.

Ya-Chun, Chang. *Chinese Communist Activities in Africa: Policies and Challenges.* Taipei: World Anti-Communist League, 1981.

D. South Africa

Cawthra, Gavin. *Brutal Force: The Apartheid War Machine.* London: IDAFSA, 1986.

Frankel, P. H. *Pretoria's Praetorians.* Cambridge: Cambridge University Press, 1984.

Grundy, Kenneth. *The Militarization of South Africa Politics.* London: I. B. Tauris, 1986.

Hallett, Robin. "The South African Intervention in Angola, 1975–76." *African Affairs* 77, no. 7 (July 1978): 347–86.

Hanlon, J. *Beggar Your Neighbors: Apartheid Power in Southern African.* London: Catholic Institute for International Relations Press, 1984.

Heitman, Helmoed–Römer. *South African War Machine.* Novato, Calif.: Presidio, 1985.

Holness, M. *Apartheid's War against Angola.* New York: United Nations Center against Apartheid; World Campaign against Military and Nuclear Collaboration with South Africa, 1983.

Leonard, Richard. *South Africa at War.* Westport, Conn.: Lawrence Hill, 1983.

Lord, R. S. "Operation Askari: A Sub-Commander's Retrospective View of the Operation." *Militaria* 22, no. 4 (1992): 1–13.

Minter, William. *Apartheid's Contras: An Inquiry into the Roots of War in Angola and Mozambique.* London: Zed, 1994.

Stiff, Peter. *Nine Days of War and South Africa's Final Days in Namibia.* Alberton, South Africa: Lemur, 1991.

E. Soviet Union/Russian Federation

Butlitskii, A. "Angola: The Intrigues of Imperialist Reaction Are Frustrated." *International Journal of Politics* 6, no. 6 (Winter 1976–1977): 50–66.

Chernyavsky, Vitaly. "CIA Subversion in Angola." *New Times* (Moscow), no. 3 (March 1976): 10–11.

Fyodorov, V. "USSR–Angola: Friendship and Solidarity." *International Affairs* 12 (December 1976): 75–78.

Gorbachev, Mikhail. *Perestroika: New Thinking for Our Country and the World.* New York: Harper and Row, 1987.

Hahn, Walter F., and Alvin J. Cottrell. *Soviet Shadow over Africa.* Coral Gables, Fla.: Center for Advanced International Studies, 1976.

Janke, Peter. "Angola as a Springboard for Moscow." *Soviet Analyst* 7, no. 16 (August 1978): 1–3.

Kappi, R. C., and M. K. Kappi. *The Soviet Impact in Africa.* Lexington, Mass.: Heath, 1984.

Klinghoffer, Arthur J. *The Angolan War: A Study of Soviet Policy in the Third World.* Boulder, Colo.: Westview, 1980.

Larrabee, Stephen. "Moscow, Angola and Dialectics of Détente." *World Today* 32 (May 1976): 173–82.

———. "Angola Signs Friendship Treaty with Moscow." *Radio Liberty Research* 436/76. (October 1976): 1–3.

Pilyatskin, Boris. "Conspiracy against Angola." *New Times* 52 (December 1975): 14–15.

Porter, Bruce, *The USSR in Third World Conflicts: Soviet Arms and Diplomacy in Local Wars, 1945–1980.* Cambridge: Cambridge University Press, 1984.

Shubin, Vladimir, and Andrei Tokarev. "War in Angola: A Soviet Dimension." *Review of African Political Economy* 28, no. 90 (December 2001): 607–18.

Stevens, Christopher. "The Soviet Union and Angola." *African Affairs* 75, no. 299 (April 1976): 137–52.

Vanneman, Peter, and W. Martin James. The Soviet Intervention in Angola: Intentions and Implications." *Strategic Review* (Summer 1976): 92–103.

Westad, Odd Arne. "Moscow and the Angolan Crisis, 1974–1976: A New Pattern of Intervention." *Woodrow Wilson International Center for Scholars/Cold War International History Project Electronic Bulletin Homepage* (Winter 1976–1977): 1–21.

F. United States

Bloomfield, Richard J., ed. *Regional Conflict and U.S. Policy: Angola and Mozambique.* Algonac, Mich.: Reference, 1988.

Butterfield, Ian. "U.S. Policy toward Angola: Past Failures and Present Opportunities." *Heritage Foundation Backgrounder,* no. 149 (August 1981): 1–18.

Congressional Digest. "U.S. Policy toward Angola: Pro and Con." *Congressional Digest* 65 (April 1986): 99–128.

Cooper, Mary H. "Angola and the Reagan Doctrine." *Congressional Quarterly Editorial Research Reports* 1, no. 2 (January 1976): 23–40.

El-Kwahas, Mohamed A., and Barry Cohen, eds. *The Kissinger Study of Southern Africa: National Security Memorandum 39.* Westport, Conn.: Lawrence Hill, 1976.

Harsch, Ernest, and Tony Thomas. *Angola: The Hidden History of Washington's War.* New York: Pathfinder, 1976.

Holness, M. *Memorandum on the Clark Amendment: The United States Threat to Destabilizing Angola.* London: Mozambique, Angola, and Guinea Center, 1981.

James, W. Martin. "Profit Motive Spins Revolving-Door Policymaking at State." *Insight,* no. 7 (February 1998): 30.

Kitchen, Helen, ed. *Angola, Mozambique, and the West.* Washington Papers, no. 130. New York: Praeger, 1987.

Legum, Colin, "A Letter on Angola to American Liberals." *New Republic* 174, (January 31, 1976): 15–19.

Lin, Yung-Lo. "Angola: Congressional Role and U.S. Policy." *Issues and Studies* 25 (October 1989): 111–30.

Livingstone, Neil C., and Manfred von Nordheim. "The U.S. Congress and the Angola Crisis." *Strategic Review* 5, no. 2 (Spring 1977): 34–45.

McFaul, Michael. "Rethinking the 'Reagan Doctrine' in Angola." *International Security* 14, no. 3 (Winter 1989–1990): 99–135.

Moekenna, K., ed. *United States and Angola.* Washington, D.C.: National Security Archives, 1992.

Peterzell, Jay. "Angola: Reagan's Covert Action Policy VI." *Center for National Security Studies* 2, no. 3 (January–February 1986): 1–10.

Potts, James. "Angola and the U.S.: The Shape of a Prudent Compromise." *Heritage Foundation Backgrounder,* no. 347 (May 1984): 1–10.

Solarz, Stephen J. "Next Stop, Angola: Six Questions for the Reagan Doctrine." *New Republic* 193 (December 2, 1985): 18–21.

Stockwell, John. *In Search of Enemies.* New York: Norton, 1978.

Walters, Ronald W. "The Clark Amendment: Analysis of U.S. Policy Choices in Angola." *Black Scholar* 12 (July–August 1981): 2–12.

Weissman, Stephen M. "CIA Covert Action in Zaire and Angola: Patterns and Consequences." *Political Science Quarterly* 94 (Summer 1979): 263–86.

Weitz, Richard. "The Reagan Doctrine Defeated Moscow in Angola." *Orbis* 36, no. 1 (Winter 1992): 57–69.

Winchester, Joan. "The Vietnam Syndrome: Implications for U.S. Policy in Angola and El Salvador." *World Outlook,* no. 13 (Summer 1991): 1–30.

G. Other International Actors

Coker, Christopher. *NATO, the Warsaw Pact and Africa.* London: Macmillan, 1985.

McCauley, Martin. "East Germany on Safari." *Soviet Analyst* 9 (September 1990): 3–6.

North London Haslemere Group. *Coffee for Britain Means Blood for Angola.* London: Third World, 1970.

H. Regional Actors

Akinyemi, A. Bolaji. *Angola and Nigeria: A Study in the National Interest.* Geneva: Graduate Institute of International Studies, 1978.

Birmingham, David. *Frontline Nationalism in Angola and Mozambique.* Trenton, N.J.: Africa World, 1992.

Bradshaw, York. *The Uncertain Promise of Southern Africa.* Bloomington: University of Indiana Press, 2000.

Burchett, Wilfred. *Southern Africa Stands Up.* New York: Urizen, 1978.

Cowell, Alan. *Killing the Wizards: Wars of Power and Freedom from Zaire to South Africa.* New York: Simon and Schuster, 1992.

Gavshon, Arthur. *Crisis in Africa: Battleground of East and West.* New York: Penguin, 1981.

Glickman, Harvey, ed. *Toward Peace and Security in Southern Africa.* New York: Gordon and Breach Science Publications, 1990.

Grundy, Kenneth. *Confrontation and Accommodation in Southern Africa.* Berkeley: University of California Press, 1973.

Hooper, Jim. *Koevoet! The Inside Story.* Johannesburg: Southern Book, 1988.

———. *Beneath the Visiting Moon: Images of Combat in Southern Africa.* Lexington, Mass.: Lexington, 1990.

———. *Bloodsong!* New York: HarperCollins Press, 2002.

Jaster, Robert S. *Southern Africa Regional Security Problems and Prospects.* Aldershot, England: International Institute for Strategic Studies, 1985.

———. *The 1988 Peace Accords and the Future of Southwestern Africa.* London: International Institute of Strategic Studies, 1989.

Khadiagala, G. M. *Allies in Adversity: The Frontline States in Southern African Security, 1975–1993.* Athens: Ohio University Press, 1994.

Legum, Colin. *The Battlefronts of Southern Africa.* New York: Africana Library, 1988.

Martin, Phyllis, and David Martin. *Destructive Engagement: Southern Africa at War.* Harare: Zimbabwe Publishing House, 1986.

Martin, Roger. "Regional Security in Southern Africa: More Angolas, Mozambiques or Neutrals?" *Survival* 29, no. 5 (September–October 1987): 387–402.

Ohlson, T., S. J. Stedman, and R. Davies. *The New Is Not Yet Born: Conflict Resolution in Southern Africa.* Washington, D.C.: Brookings Institution Press, 1994.

Rich, Paul, ed. *The Dynamics of Change in Southern Africa.* New York: St. Martin's, 1994.

Saul, John. *Recolonization and Resistance in Southern Africa in the 1990s.* Trenton, N.J.: Africa World, 1993.

Seidman, Ann. *The Roots of Crisis in Southern Africa.* Trenton, N.J.: Africa World, 1985.

Seiler, John, ed. *Southern Africa since the Portuguese Coup.* Boulder, Colo.: Westview, 1980.

Sotumbi, Abiodun Olufemi. *Nigeria's Recognition of the MPLA Government of Angola: A Case Study in Decision-Making and Implementation.* Lagos: Nigerian Institute of International Affairs, 1981.

SWAPO. *Massacre at Kassinga: Climax of Pretoria's All-Out Campaign against Namibian Resistance.* Luanda: Special Bulletin of the South West Africa People's Organization, 1978.

———. *To Be Born a Nation.* London: Zed, 1981.

IV. HISTORY

A. Ancient

Balandier, George. *Daily Life in the Kingdom of the Kongo from the Sixteenth to the Eighteenth Century.* New York: World, 1969.

Birmingham, David. "The Date and Significance of the Imbangala Invasion of Angola." *Journal of African History* 6, no. 2 (1965): 143–52.

Bowdich, T. Edward. *Account of Discoveries of the Portuguese in the Interior of Angola and Mozambique.* New York: AMS, 1980.

Davidson, Basil. *The African Slave Trade: Pre-colonial History, 1450–1850.* Boston: Little Brown, Atlantic Monthly, 1961.

Fraser, Antonia. *The Warrior Queens.* New York: Vintage, 1990.

Gibson, A. *Between Cape Town and Loanda: A Record of Two Journeys in Southwest Africa.* London: Wells, Gardner, Darton, 1905.

Graham, R. H. Carson. *Under Seven Congo Kings.* London: Carey, 1930.

Hilton, Ann. *The Kingdom of the Kongo.* Oxford: Oxford University Press, 1985.

La Fleur, James D. *Pieter Van Den Broecke's Journal of Voyages to Cape Verde, Guinea and Angola (1605–1612).* Hakluyt Society Works. Iola, Wisc..: Kraus International, 2001.

Miller, Joseph C. *Kings and Kinsmen: Early Mbundu States in Angola.* Oxford: Clarendon, 1976.

Monteiro, Joachim John. *Angola and the River Congo.* 2 Vols. London: Macmillan, 1875.

Morliere, Jacques-Rochette de la. *Angola: An Eastern Tale.* London: Chapman and Hall, 1926.

Pelissier, Rene. *Explorer Voyages in Angola.* Paris: Editions Pelissier, 1993.

Ravenstein, E. G., ed. *Strange Adventures of Andrew Battell in Angola and the Adjoining Regions.* Hakluyt Society Works. Iola, Wisc..: Kraus International, 1988.

Thornton, John. "Demography and History in the Kingdom of the Kongo, 1550–1750." *Journal of African History* 18, no. 4 (1977): 507–30.

———. *The Kingdom of the Kongo.* Madison: University of Wisconsin Press, 1983.

———. "Legitimacy and Political Power: Queen Njinga, 1624–1663." *Journal of African History* 32, no. 1 (January 1991): 25–41.

———. *The Kongolese Saint Anthony: Dona Beatriz Kimpa Vita and the Antonian Movement, 1684–1706.* Cambridge: Cambridge University Press, 1998.

Tucker, John T. *Angola: Land of the Blacksmith Prince.* London: World Dominion, 1933.

Vansina, Jan. *Kingdoms of the Savanna.* Madison: University of Wisconsin Press, 1966.

———. "More on the Invasions of Kongo and Angola by the Jaga and the Lunda." *Journal of African History* 7, no. 3 (1966): 421–29.

B. Colonial

Abshire, David M., and Michael A. Samuels, eds. *Portuguese Africa: A Handbook.* New York: Praeger, 1969.

Addicott, Len. *Cry Angola!* London: SCM, 1962.

Amandio, Cesar. *Angola 1961.* Lisbon: Verbo, 1962.

Barnes, T. Alexander. *Angolan Sketches.* London: Metheun, 1928.

Bender, Gerald J. *Angola under the Portuguese.* London: Heinemann Educational, 1978.

Bender, Gerald J., and P. Stanley Yoder. "Whites in Angola on the Eve of Independence: The Politics of Numbers." *Africa Today* 21, no. 4 (Fall 1974): 23–37.

Birmingham, David. *The Portuguese Conquest of Angola.* London: Oxford University Press, 1965.

———. *Trade and Conflict in Angola: The Mbundu and Their Neighbors under the Influence of the Portuguese, 1483–1790.* Oxford: Clarendon, 1966.

Boa, Vida A. *Angola: Five Centuries of Portuguese Exploitation.* Richmond, B.C.: Liberation Support Movement, 1972.

Chapman, Michael. *Angola on the Road to Progress.* Luanda: Angola Consultantes, 1971.

Clarence-Smith, W. G. *Slaves, Peasants and Capitalists in Southern Angola, 1840–1926.* New York: Cambridge University Press, 1979.

Davidson, Basil. *Angola, 1961: The Factual Record.* London: Union of Democratic Control, 1962.

Dias, Jill R. "Black Chiefs, White Traders, and Colonial Policy Near Kwanza: Kabuku, Kambilo and the Portuguese, 1873–1896." *Journal of African History* 17, no. 2 (1976): 245–65.

Edgerton, F. Clement. *Angola without Prejudice.* Lisbon: Agencia Geral do Ultramar, 1955.

———. *Angola in Perspective: Endeavor and Achievement in Portuguese West Africa.* London: Routledge and Kegan Paul, 1957.

Fish, Bruce, and Becky Durost Fish. *Angola: 1880 to the Present: Slavery, Exploitation, and Revolt.* Broomall, Penn.: Chelsea House, 2001.

Henderson, Lawrence W. *Angola: Five Centuries of Conflict.* Ithaca, N.Y.: Cornell University Press, 1979.

Huibregtse, P. K. *Angola: The Real Story.* Amsterdam: orum, 1970.

Irvine, Keith. "Angola: A Non–Self-Governing Territory." *Current History* 45, no. 268 (December 1963): 321–29.

Marjay, Frederic. *Angola.* Lisbon: Livraria Bertrand, 1961.

Miller, Joseph C. *Way of Death: Merchant Capitalism and the Angolan Slave Trade, 1730–1830.* Madison: University of Wisconsin Press, 1988.

Minter, William. *Imperial Network and External Dependency: The Case of Angola.* Beverly Hills, Calif.: Sage, 1972.

Monteiro, Joachim J. *Angola and the River Congo.* 2 Vols. London: Macmillan, 1875.

Samuels, Michael Anthony. "The New Look in Angolan Education." *Africa Report* 12, no. 8 (November 1967): 63–66.

———. *Education in Angola, 1878–1914: A History of Culture Transfer and Administration.* New York: Teachers College Press, 1970.

Sharman, T. C. *Overseas Economic Surveys. Portuguese West Africa: Economic and Social Conditions in Portuguese West Africa (Angola).* London: Her Majesty's Stationery Office, 1954.

Vinhas, Manuel. *Angola Today.* Lisbon: Composto e Impresso Na NEA, 1961.

Wastberg, Olle. *Angola.* Stockholm: Bokforlaget Pan/Norstedts, 1970.

Wentzel, Volkmar. "Angola, Unknown Africa." *National Geographic* 120, no. 3 (September 1961): 347–84.

Wheeler, D. L. "The Portuguese Army in Angola." *Journal of Modern African Studies* 7 no. 3 (October 1969): 425–39.

———. "African Elements in Portugal's Armies in Africa (1961–1974)." *Armed Forces and Society* 2, no. 2 (February 1976): 233–50.

Wheeler, Douglas L., and Rene Pelissier. *Angola.* New York: Praeger, 1971.

Wilson, T. Ernest. *Angola Beloved.* Neptune, N.J.: Loizeaux Brothers, 1967.

V. STRUGGLE FOR INDEPENDENCE

Adelman, Kenneth. "Report from Angola." *Foreign Affairs* 53, no 3 (April 1975): 558–74.

All Roads to Luanda. Cairo: Permanent Secretariat of the A.A.P.S.O., 1976.

Alves, Nito. *Memoria da Longa Resistência Popular* (Memoir of the long popular resistance). Luanda: Africa Editoria, 1976.

Andrade, Mario de. *The War in Angola.* Dar es Salaam: Tanzania Publishing House, 1975.

Andrade, Mario de, and Marc Ollivier. *La Guerre en Angola* (The war in Angola). Paris: Maspero, 1971.

Angola Book Project. *With Freedom in Their Eyes.* San Francisco: People, 1976.

Angola in Arms. Dar es Salaam, Tanzania: MPLA, 1969.

Angola Solidarity Committee. *Angola.* London: Committee, 1975.

Barnett, Don. *Liberation Support Movement Interview in Angola with Spartacus Monimambu.* Oakland, Calif.: Liberation Support Movement Press, 1968.

——. *Liberation Support Movement Interview with Daniel Chipenda.* Oakland, Calif.: Liberation Support Movement Press, 1969.

——. *Liberation Support Movement.* Richmond, B.C.: LSM Information Center Press, 1971.

——. *Liberation Support Movement Interview with Sixth Region Commander Seta Likambuila.* Richmond, B.C.: LSM Information Center Press, 1971.

——. *Liberation Support Movement Interview with Daniel Chipenda.* Richmond, B.C.: LSM Information Center Press, 1972.

——. *The Revolution in Angola.* Indianapolis: Bobbs–Merrill, 1972.

——. *With the Guerrillas in Angola.* Richmond, B.C.: LSM Information Center Press, 1972.

——. *Interviews in Depth, MPLA/Angola #4.* Richmond, B.C.: Liberation Support Movement Press, 1973.

——. *Spartacus Monimambu.* Richmond, B.C.: LSM Information Center Press, 1973.

Barnett, Don, and Roy Harvey. *The Revolution in Angola: MPLA Life and Documents.* New York: Bobbs–Merrill Company, 1972.

Cann, John P. *Counterinsurgency in Africa: The Portuguese Way of War, 1961–1974.* New York: Greenwood, 1997.

Davidson, Basil. "An Inside Look at Angola's Fight for Freedom: A British Historian and Journalist Describes What He Found When He Went to See for Himself." *Africa Report* 15, no. 9 (December 1970): 16–18.

——. "Angola in the Tenth Year: A Report and an Analysis, May–July 1970." *African Affairs* 70, no. 278 (January 1971): 37–49.

——. *Walking 300 Miles with Guerrilla Through the Bush of Eastern Angola.* Pasadena, Calif.: Munger Africana Library, 1971.

——. *In the Eye of the Storm: Angola's People.* Garden City, N.Y.: Doubleday, 1972.

Davis, Jennifer. *No One Can Stop the Rain.* New York: Africa Fund, 1976.

Department of Foreign Relations of the GRAE. *Our Struggle Goes on and Will Continue Till Total Independence.* Kinshasa, Zaire: GRAE Press, 1975.

Emergency International Solidarity Conference with the People of Angola. *Emergency International Solidarity Conference with the People of Angola, Luanda, 2–4 February 1976.* Cairo: Permanent Secretariat of AAPSO, 1976.

Felgas, Hélio A. *Guerra em Angola.* Lisbon: Livraria Classica, 1961.

Fluehr-Lobban, Carolyn. "Angolan Independence: Neo-Colonialism or Socialism." *Southern Africa* 8, no. 10 (November 1975): 4–8.

Gabriel, C. *Angola in the Whirlwind of Permanent Revolution.* London: Africa in Struggle, 1976.

Gilchrist, Sidney. *Angola Awake.* Toronto: Ryerson, 1968.

Gjerstad, Ole. *The People in Power.* Oakland, Calif.: LSM Information Center Press, 1976.

Harsch, Ernest. *Angola.* New York: Pathfinder, 1976.

Harvey, Roy. *People's War in Angola.* Oakland, Calif.: Liberation Support Movement Press, 1970.

Heimer, Franz-Wilhelm. *The Decolonization Conflict in Angola.* Geneva: University Institute of International Studies Press, 1979.

Henrikson, Thomas H. "End of Empire: Portugal's Collapse in Africa." *Current History* 68, no. 405 (May 1975): 211–15, 229.

———. "Lessons from Portugal's Counter-Insurgency Operations in Africa." *Journal of the Royal United Services Institute for Defence Studies* 123, no. 6 (June 1978): 31–35.

———. "People's War in Angola, Mozambique, and Guinea-Bissau." *Journal of Modern African Studies* 14, no. 3 (September 1976): 377–39.

Howe, Russell Warren. "The Stakes in Angola." *New Leader* 52, no. 1 (January 1976): 6–8.

Jerman, William, and Caroline Reuver-Cohen, eds. *Angola: Secret Government Documents on Counter Subversion.* Rome: IDOC, 1974.

Kaunda, Kenneth. *Zambia's Stand on Angola.* Lusaka: Zambia Information Service, 1976.

Liberation Support Movement. *Interviews in Depth with MPLA: Angola, Paulo Jorge.* Richmond, B.C.: LSM Information Center Press, 1973.

———. *Making of a Middle Cadre: The Story of Rui De Pinto.* Richmond, B.C.: LSM Information Center Press, 1973.

———. *Road to Liberation: MPLA Documents on the Founding of the People's Republic of Angola.* Richmond, B.C.: LSM Information Center Press, 1976.

Marcum, John. *The Angolan Revolution: The Anatomy of an Explosion,* Vol. I. Cambridge, Mass.: M.I.T. Press, 1969.

———. "The Anguish of Angola: On Becoming Independent in the Last Quarter of the Twentieth Century." *Issue* 5, no. 4 (Winter 1975): 3–13.

Martin, Phyllis M. "The Cabinda Connection: An Historical Perspective." *African Affairs* 76, no. 302 (January 1977): 47–59.

Mason, Phillip, ed. *Angola: A Symposium Views on a Revolt.* London: Oxford University Press, 1962.

Matau, Godwin. "Angola e o Futuro." (Angola and the future) *Africa,* no. 43 (March 1975): 36–41.

McCallin, John. *Angolan Refugees in Zaire.* Geneva: International University Exchange Fund, 1974.

Mikhalev, Pavel. *Password: Anguimo.* Moscow: Novosti, 1974.

Movimento Popular de Libertação de Angola. *Angola in Arms: 4th February.* Dar es Salaam, Tanzania: People's Movement for the Liberation of Angola, 1969.

———. *Imperialist Powers Are Supporting Portuguese Colonial Repression.* Brazzaville, Congo: MPLA, 1965.

———. *Revolution in Angola.* London: Merlin, 1972.

———. *Road to Liberation.* Oakland, Calif.: LSM Information Center Press, 1976.

MPLA Central Committee Plenary. *Documents, 23–29 October 1976.* London: Mozambique, Angola, and Guinea Information Center Press, 1976.

National Union for the Total Independence of Angola. *The Armed Struggle in Angola.* Free Land of Angola: UNITA Central Committee, 1973.

Neto, Agostinho. *Messages to Companions in the Struggle.* Richmond, B.C.: LSM Information Center Press, 1972.

Okuma, Thomas. *Angola in Ferment: The Background and Prospects of Angolan Nationalism.* East Sussex, England: Beacon, 1962.

Pagano, Gaetano. *Visit to MPLA and Their Liberated Areas.* London: International University Exchange Fund, 1975.

Panikkar, K. Madhu. *Angola in Flames.* Hong Kong: Asia, 1962.

Rivers, Bernard. "Angola: Massacre and Oppression." *Africa Today* 21, no. 1 (Winter 1974): 41–45.

Samuels, Michael A., and Stephen M. Haykin. "The Anderson Plan: An American Attempt to Seduce Portugal Out of Africa." *Orbis* 23 (Fall 1979): 649–69.

Sidenko, Victor. "Angola: People against Reaction." *New Times,* no. 43 (October 1975): 14–15.

Silva, Pedro, Valdemar Moreira, and Francisco Esteves. *Angola: Comandos especiais Contra os Cubanos* (Angola: Special forces against the Cubans). Braga–Lisbon: Braga Editora, 1978.

Steenkamp, Willem. *Adeus Angola.* Cape Town: Timmins, 1976.

Teixeira, Bernardo. *The Fabric of Terror.* New York: Devin–Adair, 1965.

Uralov, K. "Angola: The Triumph of the Right Cause." *International Affairs* (Moscow) 5 (May 1976): 51–57.

Valentim, Jorge Aliceres. *Qui Libre l'Angola* (The liberation of Angola). Brussels: Michele Coppens, 1969.

Watson, Thomas H. *The Angolan Affair, 1974–76.* Maxwell Air Force Base, Ala.: Air War College Press, 1977.
Wheeler, Douglas L. "Reflections on Angola." *Africa Report* 12, no. 8 (November 1967): 60.
Wheeler, Douglas L., and Rene Pelissier. *Angola.* New York: Praeger, 1971.
Willers, David. "The Genesis of a Revolution. Angola: 1483 to Present." *South Africa International* 12, no. 1 (July 1981): 303–31.
World Council of Churches. *The Cunene Dam Scheme and the Struggle for the Liberation of Southern Africa.* Geneva: World Council of Churches, 1971.
World Peace Council. *Hands Off Angola: For Recognition of the People's Republic of Angola for Support to MPLA.* Helsinki: World Peace Council, 1976.

VI. THE ANGOLAN CIVIL WAR: 1975–2002

Aguilar, Renato, and Mario Zejan. *Angola.* Stockholm: SIDA, 1990.
Angola after Independence. London: Institute for the Study of Conflict, 1975.
Anstee, Margaret. "Angola: The Forgotten Tragedy. A Test Case for UN Peacekeeping." *International Relations* 11 (December 1993): 495–511.
——. *Orphan of the Cold War.* London: Macmillan, 1997.
Baynham, S. J. "International Politics and the Angolan Civil War." *Army Quarterly and Defence Journal* 107, no. 1 (January 1977): 25–32.
Bender, Gerald. "Angola, the Cubans and American Anxieties." *Foreign Policy* 3 (Summer 1978): 3–33.
——. "Angola: Left, Right and Wrong." *Foreign Policy* 43 (Summer 1981): 53–70.
——. "The Continuing Crisis in Angola." *Current History* 82 (March 1983): 124–25, 128, 138.
——. "Peacemaking in Southern Africa: The Luanda–Pretoria Tug-of-War." *Third World Quarterly* 11 (January 1989): 15–30.
Berridge, G. R. "Diplomacy and the Angola/Namibia Accords." *International Affairs* 65, no. 3 (Summer 1989): 463–79.
Breytenbach, Cloete. *Savimbi's Angola.* Buckinghamshire, England: Timmins, 1980.
Breytenbach, Jan. *They Live by the Sword: 32 "Buffalo" Battalion, South Africa's Foreign Legion.* Alberton, South Africa: Lemur, 1990.
Bridgland, Fred. *Jonas Savimbi: A Key to Africa.* New York: Paragon House, 1987.
——. *The War for Africa: Twelve Months That Transformed a Continent.* Gibraltar: Ashanti Press, 1990.

Brittain, Victoria. "UNITA: Outpolled but Not Overpowered." *New Statesman and Society* (March 4, 1994): 16–17, 19.

———. *Death of Dignity: Angola's Civil War.* Trenton, N.J.: Africa World, 1998.

Campbell, Horace. *The Siege of Cuito Cuanavale.* Uppsala, Sweden: Scandinavian Institute of African Studies, 1990.

———. *War and Peace in Angola.* Harare: Institute of Development Studies Press, 1995.

Catholic Institute for International Relations. *Achieving Lasting Peace in Angola: The Unfinished Agenda.* London: Catholic Institute for International Relations, 1997.

Chitunda, Jeremias K. "The Price of a Negotiated Settlement in Southern Africa, with Emphasis on Angola." *East–West Roundtable of New York* (April 3, 1984): 1–12.

Ciment, James. *Angola and Mozambique: Postcolonial Wars in Southern Africa.* New York: Facts on File, 1997.

Coetzee, David. "Angola: The Longest War." *New African,* no. 156 (September 1980): 8–17.

Conchiglia, A. *UNITA: Myth and Reality.* London: European Campaign against South African Aggression, 1990.

A Conversation with Ernesto Mulato. Washington, D.C.: American Enterprise Institute, 1979.

Crocker, Chester. "Southern Africa." *Foreign Affairs* 68, no. 4 (Fall 1989): 144–64.

———. *High Noon in Southern Africa: Making Peace in a Rough Neighborhood.* New York: Norton, 1992.

Dash, Leon. *Savimbi's 1977 Campaign against the Cubans and the MPLA.* Pasadena, Calif.: California Institute of Technology Press, 1977.

Davidson, Basil. "Angola since Independence." *Race and Class* 19, no. 2 (Autumn 1977): 133–48.

Davies, George Ola. "On a Limb: Interview with Jonas Savimbi." *Africa Events* (April 1990): 19–20.

Davis, Nathaniel. "The Angola Decision of 1975: A Personal Memoir." *Foreign Affairs* 57, no.1 (Fall 1978): 109–25.

Debay, Yves. "Angola and South West Africa: A Forgotten War (1975–89)." *Raids,* no. 44 (July 1995): 20–23, 41.

Dempster, Chris, Dave Tomkins, and Michel Parry. *Fire Power.* New York: St. Martin's, 1980.

Deutschmann, David. *Changing the History of Africa: Angola and Namibia.* Melbourne: Ocean, 1989.

Dias, Joffre P. F. *Angola: From the Estoril Peace Agreement to the Lusaka Peace Accord, 1991–1994.* Geneva: n.p., 1995.

Dixon, Glen (as told to Anthony Mockler). *Hostage.* Alberton, South Africa: Galago, 1986.

Dohning, W. *UNITA.* Angola: Kwacha UNITA, 1984.

Dreyer, Donald. *Namibia and Angola: The Search for Independence and Regional Security, 1966–1988.* Geneva: Program for Strategic and International Studies, 1988.

Ebinger, Charles K. "External Intervention in Internal War: The Politics and Diplomacy of the Angolan Civil War." *Orbis* 20, no.3 (Fall 1976): 669–701.

Fauvet, Paul. "Savimbi: Pawn or Patriot." *New African,* no. 153 (May 1980): 28–31.

Figueiredo, Xavier de. "Mavinga: Neither Honor nor Glory." *Inform Africa,* no. 12 (February 1990): 1–2.

Finkel, Vickie. "Savimbi's Sour Grapes." *Africa Report* 38, no. 1 (January–February 1993): 25–28.

Freeman, Charles W. "The Angola/Namibia Accords." *Foreign Affairs* 68, (Summer 1989): 126–41.

Gaines, Mike. "UNITA, Angola's HIND Killers." *Flight International* 129 (March 1986): 30–33.

Government of Angola. *White Paper on Acts of Aggression by the Racist South African Regime against the People's Republic of Angola, 1975–82.* Luanda: Ministry of External Relations, 1982.

Grundy, Kenneth. "The Angolan Puzzle: Varied Actors and Complex Issues." *Issue* 15 (1987): 35–41.

Guimarães, Fernando J. Andresen. "The Collapse of the New State and the Emergence of the Angolan Civil War." *Camões Center Quarterly* 1 and 2 (Winter 1993–1994): 9–16.

——. *The Origins of the Angolan Civil War: Foreign Intervention and Domestic Political Conflict.* London: Macmillan, 1998.

Gunn, Gillian. "Unfulfilled Expectations in Angola." *Current History* (May 1990): 213–17, 234.

Hamill, James. "Angola's Road from under the Rubble." *World Today* 50 (January 1994): 6–11.

Hamilton, Iain (director). *Angola after Independence: Struggle for Supremacy.* London: Conflict Studies, 1975.

Hare, Paul. *Angola's Last Best Chance for Peace: An Insider's Account of the Peace Process.* Washington, D.C.: U.S. Institute for Peace, 1998.

Hart, Keith, and Joanna Lewis, eds. *Why Angola Matters.* Cambridge: African Studies Center, 1995.

Heinbecker, Paul (chairman). *Final Report of the Monitoring Mechanism on Angola Sanctions.* New York: United Nations Security Council Committee, 2000.

Heitman, Helmoed-Römer. *War in Angola: The Final South African Phase.* Gibraltar: Ashanti, 1990.

Hermele, Kenneth. *Landrapport Angola.* Stockholm: SIDA, 1988.

Hooper, Jim. "UNITA Guerrillas Attack with Impunity." *International Defense Review 22* (June 1989): 747–49.

Hough, Michael. "The Angolan Civil War with Special Reference to the UNITA Movement." *Strategic Review (S.A.)* 7, no. 2 (November 1985): 1–11.

Human Rights Watch. *Angola: Violations of the Laws of War on Both Sides.* New York: Human Rights Watch, 1989.

———. *Angola: Arms Trade and Violations of the Laws of War since the 1992 Elections.* New York: Human Rights Watch, 1994.

———. *Angola: Between War and Peace. Arms Trade and Human Rights Abuses since the Lusaka Protocol.* New York: Human Rights Watch, 1996.

———. *Angola Unravels: The Rise and Fall of the Lusaka Peace Process.* New York: Human Rights Watch, 1999.

International Defence and Aid Fund. *Remember Kassinga.* London: IDAFSA, 1981.

James, W. Martin. "Cuban Involvement in the Angolan Civil War: Implications for a Lasting Peace." *Institute for Strategic Studies Bulletin,* no. 4 (1988): 1–15.

———. *A Political History of the Civil War in Angola, 1974–1990.* New Brunswick, N.J.: Transaction, 1992.

———. "'Peace on the Cheap': A Critical Analysis of the Angolan Electoral Process." *Small Wars and Insurgencies* 5, no. 3 (Winter 1994): 318–77.

Kapuscinski, Ryszard. *Another Day of Life: A Haunting Eyewitness Account of Civil War in Angola.* New York: Penguin, 1987.

Khan, Owen Ellison, ed. *Disengagement in Southwest Africa: The Prospects for Peace in Angola and Namibia.* New Brunswick, N.J.: Transaction, 1991.

Lazitch, Branko. *The Battle for Angola, 1974–1988: A Set-Back for Communism in Africa.* London: Better Britain Society, 1988.

Legum, Colin, and Tony Hodges. *After Angola: The War over Southern Africa.* New York: Africana Library, 1976.

Lin, Yung-Lo. "The Angola–Namibia Accords: Looking to the Future." *Issues and Studies* 26 (September 1990): 111–30.

LoBaido, Anthony. "Privatized Warfare." *New American* 18 (September 4, 1995): 21–30.

Maier, Karl. *Angola: Promises and Lies.* London: Serif, 1996.

Marcum, John A. "Lessons of Angola." *Foreign Affairs* 54, no. 3 (April 1976): 407–25.

———. *The Angolan Revolution.* Vol. 2 *Exile Politics and Guerrilla Warfare (1962–1976).* Cambridge, Mass: M.I.T. Press, 1978.

———. "Angola: Twenty-Five Years of War." *Current History* 85, no. 511 (May 1986): 193–96, 229–30.

———. "Angola: War Again." *Current History* 92, no. 574. (May 1993): 218–24.

Marcus, David Lloyd. "Letter from Angola: The Forgotten War." *Gentlemen's Quarterly* (October 1994): 165–74.

Maren, Michael. "The Right's Last Best Hope: Savimbi and Angola." *Nation* 245, no. 21 (December 1987): 744–46.

Massacre at Kassinga. Luanda: South West Africa People's Organization, 1978.

Massing, Michael. "Upside Down in Angola." *New Republic* 194 (March 1986): 16–20.

Mboukou, Alexandre. "An African Triangle: Angola/Congo/Zaire." *Africa Report* 27, no. 5 (September–October 1982): 39–44.

McColm, R. Bruce, and David Smith. "The Other Angola." *National Review,* no. 1 (January 1977): 83–86.

Mendes, Pedro Rosa. *Bay of Tigers: An Odyssey through War-Torn Angola.* San Diego, Calif.: Harcourt, 2003.

Minter, William. *Operation Timber: Pages from the Savimbi Dossier.* Trenton, N.J.: Africa World, 1988.

———. *Account from Angola: UNITA as Described by Ex-Participants and Foreign Visitors.* London: African–European Institute, 1990.

Monteiro, Anthony. "Angola's Second War of Liberation." *Freedom Ways* 16, no. 1 (1976): 47–59.

Movimento Popular de Libertação de Angola. *1st Congress.* London: Mozambique, Angola and Guinea Information Center Press, 1979.

National Union for the Total Independence of Angola. *UNITA: Identity of a Free Angola.* Jamba, Angola: Free Land of Angola, 1985.

Nesbitt, Prexy. "Angola Is Part of All of Us." *Black Scholar* 11, no. 5 (May–June 1980): 48–54.

Novak, Greg. "'Externals': A Guide to the Forces of South West Africa and Angola, 1980–1989." *Command Post Quarterly* 2 (Summer 1993): 1–56.

Oyowe, Augustine. "Renewed Aggression from the South." *Africa,* no. 68 (April 1977): 43–44.

Pelda, Kurt. "UNITA: Advancing through Angola." *Swiss Review of World Affairs* 39 (January 1990): 23–26.

Pereira, Anthony W. "Peace in the Third World? The Case of Angola." *Dissent* (Summer 1993): 291–94.

———. "Angola's 1992 Election: A Personal View." *Camões Center Quarterly 1 and 2.* (Winter 1993–1994): 1–8.

———. "The Neglected Tragedy: The Return to War in Angola, 1992–3." *Journal of Modern Africa Studies* 32, no. 1 (March 1994): 1–28.

Potgieter, Jakkie, and Richard Cornwell. "Angola—Endgame or Stalemate?" *Institute for Security Studies Occasional Paper,* no. 30 (April 1998): 1–12.

———. "Angola: At the Precipice." *Institute for Security Studies Occasional Paper,* no. 32 (July 1998): 1–5.

Pototskiy, Igor. "José Eduardo dos Santos: Friendship Tested in Struggle." *New Times* 20 (May 26, 1986): 20.

Prendergast, John. "Angola's Deadly War: Dealing with Savimbi's Hell on Earth." *United States Institute for Peace—Special Report* (October 1999): 1–20.

Roberto, Holden. "An Open Letter to the Members of the Congress of the United States of America." *F.N.L.A.* (December 17, 1981): 1–8.

Roberts, J. Milnor. "Angola: Whose Side Are We On?" *Retired Officer* (February 1986): 26–30.

Robinson, Randall. "Africa Asks of America: Are You with Us or against Us." *TransAfrica News Report* (Winter 1980–1981): 2, 7.

Rothchild, Donald. "Conflict Management in Angola." *TransAfrica Forum* 8 (Spring 1991): 77–101.

Rozès, Antoine. "Angolan Deadlock: Chronicle of a War with No Solution." *African Security Review* 10, no. 3 (2001): 1–18.

Savimbi, Jonas Malheiro. *Angola: A Resistência em Busca de Uma Nova Nação* (Angola: The resistance in search of a new nation). Lisbon: Edicão da Agência Portuguesa de Revistas, 1979.

———. "We Are Working toward One Angola." *World View* 23 (June 1980): 19.

———. *Por um Futuro Melhor* (For a better future). Lisbon: Editora Nova Novica, 1986.

———. "The War against Soviet Colonialism." *Policy Review* 35 (Winter 1986): 18–24.

Sayagues, Mercedes. "A Little Breathing Space." *Africa Report,* no. 3 (May–June 1995): 13–17.

Schmults, Robert C. "Bloodshed and Blame in Angola." *Insight* 9, no. 9 (March 1993) 16, 38–39.

Sheehan, Sean. *Angola.* Tarrytown, N.Y.: Cavendish, 1999.

Sidler, Peter. "Angola: A Country at a Dead End." *Swiss Review of World Affairs* 39 (May 1989): 6–7.

Smith, James. "FAPLA–Angola's Marxist Armed Forces." *Jane's Soviet Intelligence Review* 2 (July 1990): 306–10.

Smith, Wayne. "A Trap in Angola." *Foreign Policy* 62 (Spring 1986): 61–75.

Smith, Xan. "Inside Angola." *New York Review of Books* 30, no. 2 (February 1983): 39–45.

Spikes, Daniel. *Angola and the Politics of Intervention.* Jefferson, N.C.: McFarland, 1993.

Steenkamp, Willem. *Borderstrike!* Pretoria: Butterworths, 1983.

——. *South Africa's Border War: 1966–1989.* Gibraltar: Ashanti, 1989.

Tholin, Richard. "Angola: Confrontation or Cooperation?" *Christian Century* 98 (May 1981): 543–46.

Toussie, Sam R. *War and Survival in Southern Angola: The UNITA Assessment Mission.* Luanda: UNICEF, 1989.

Turner, John. "Angola: War in the North." *African Armed Forces Journal* (October 1994): 28–32.

——. "Angola: War in the North (Part 2)." *African Armed Forces Journal* (December–January 1995): 29–35.

Tvedten, Inge. *The War in Angola: Internal Conditions for Peace and Recovery.* Uppsala, Sweden: Scandinavian Institute for African Studies Press, 1989.

——. "U.S. Policy toward Angola since 1975." *Journal of Modern African Studies* 30, no. 1 (March 1992): 31–52.

——. "The Angolan Debacle." *Journal of Democracy* 4, no. 2 (April 1993): 108–18.

——. *Angola: Struggle for Peace and Reconstruction.* Boulder, Colo.: Westview, 1997.

União Nacional Para a Independência Total de Angola. *The People's Struggle Until Victory.* Toronto: Norman Bethune Institute, 1976.

——. *The UNITA Leadership.* Jamba, Angola: Kwacha UNITA, 1990.

United Nations. "Report on the Human Casualties and Material and Other Damage Resulting from Repeated Acts of Aggression by the Racist Regime of South Africa against the People's Republic of Angola." *United Nations* (1979): 1–64.

——. "Security Council Demands South Africa Withdraw from Angola." *UN Chronicle* 21 (February 1984): 59–78.

——. *United Nations and the Situation in Angola: May 1991–February 1995.* New York: United Nations, 1995.

Venancio, Moises. *The United Nations, Peace and Transition: Lessons from Angola.* Lisbon: Instituto de Estudos Estrategicos e Internacionais, 1994.

Venter, Al J. "The Angola War: A Classic Study of Guerrilla Warfare." *International Defense Review* 23 (June 1990): 649–52.

Vines, Alex. *One Hand Tied: Angola and the UN.* London: Catholic Institute for International Relations, 1993.

——. *Angola and Mozambique: The Aftermath of Conflict.* Washington, D.C.: Research Institute for the Study of Conflict and Terrorism, 1995.

——. *Peace Postponed, Angola since the Lusaka Protocol.* London: Catholic Institute for International Relations Press, 1998.

Vinicios, Marco, and Maria João Saldanha. *Jonas Savimbi: Um Defasio a Ditadura Comunista em Angola.* Lisbon: Edicoes Armasilde, 1977.

Virmani, K. K. *Angola and the Superpowers.* Delhi: University of Delhi Press, 1989.

Wheeler, Jack. "Fighting the Soviet Imperialists: UNITA in Angola." *Reason* 15 (April 1984): 22–30.

White, George. *The Destruction of a Nation: United States Policy toward Angola since 1945.* London: Pluto, 1997.

Williams, Christopher. *Angola to Vietnam.* New York: Distributed Art, 1992.

Windrich, Elaine. *The Cold War Guerrilla: Jonas Savimbi, the U.S. Media, and the Angolan War.* New York: Greenwood, 1992.

——. "Media Coverage of the Angolan Election." *Issue* 23 (Winter 1994), 19–23.

Wolfers, Michael. *Angola in the Frontline.* London: Zed, 1983.

Worthington, Peter. "Angola's Unknown War." *National Review* 37 (November 1985): 51–55, 77.

Wright, Robin. *Angola's Dogs of War.* New York: Patterson Foundation, 1976.

——. "The Man in the Middle: Talking with Angola's Jonas Savimbi." *New Leader* 59, no. 3 (February 1976): 6–7.

VII. GENERAL

A. Agriculture and Fisheries

Alberts, Tom. *The Fishery Sector in Angola: Development Perspectives and Swedish Support in the 1990s.* Gothenburg, Sweden: National Swedish Board of Fisheries, 1990.

——. *Fisheries and the Angolan Economy: A Review of Key Issues and Swedish Support in the 1990s.* Stockholm: DEVRO AB, 1995.

Feldbrugge, Torsten. *Economics of Emergency Relief Management in Developing Countries: With Case Studies on Food Relief in Angola and Mozambique.* New York: Peter Lang, 2001.

Fernandes, Manuel Jose. "Surface Fish of the Coastal Waters of Angola." *TAAG "Austral" Inflight Magazine,* no 21 (July–August 1997): 1–4.

Galli, Rosemary E. "The Food Crisis and the Socialist State in Lusophone Africa." *African Studies Review* 30, no. 1 (March 1987): 19–44.

MacKenzie, Debora. "African Fisheries on Brink of Collapse." *New Scientist* 175, no. 2351 (July 2002): 5.

MINADER. *Agricultural Recovery and Development Options Review.* Luanda: Ministry of Agriculture and Rural Development, 1996.

Steiner, Herbert H. *Angola's Agricultural Economy in Brief.* Washington, D.C.: Congressional Research Service, 1977.

Van Dongen, Irene S. *Sea Fisheries and Fish Ports in Angola*. Lisbon: Sociedade de Geografia, 1962.

B. Anthropology and Sociology

Carter, Hazel, et al. *Kongo Language Course—Maloongi Makikoongo: A Course in the Dialect of Zoombo, Northern Angola*. Madison: University of Wisconsin Press, 1987.

Chatelain, Heli. *Kimbundu Grammar: Grammatica Elementar Do Kimbundu Ou Lingua de Angola*. Ridgewood, N.J.: Gregg International, 1971.

Childs, Gladwyn Murray. *Umbundu Kinship and Culture: Being a Description of the Social Structure and Individual Development of the Ovimbundu of Angola, with Observations Concerning the Bearing on the Enterprise of Christian Missions of Certain Phases of Life and Culture Described*. London: Oxford University Press, 1949.

Department of Humanitarian Affairs. *Internally Displaced Persons in Angola*. Luanda: United Nations, 1995.

——. *The Identification of Social and Economic Expectations of Soldiers to Be Demobilized*. Luanda: United Nations, 1995.

——. *Study of Vulnerable Groups in Angola within the Perspective of the Peace Process*. Luanda: United Nations, 1995.

Edwards, Adrian C. *The Ovimbundu under Two Sovereignties: A Study of Social Control and Social Change among a People of Angola*. London: Oxford University Press, 1962.

Estermann, Carlos. *Ethnography of Southwestern Angola: The Non-Bantu Peoples, the Ambo Ethnic Group*. New York: Africana Library, 1979.

——. *Ethnography of South-Western Angola: The Herero People*. New York: Africana Library, 1981.

Hambly, Wilfred D. *The Ovimbundu of Angola: Frederick H. Rawson–Field Museum Ethnological Expedition to West Africa, 1929–30*. Chicago: Field Museum of Natural History, 1934.

——. *Anthropometry of the Ovimbundu, Angola*. Germantown, N.Y.: Periodicals Service, 1940.

——. *Serpent Worship in Africa—The Ovimbundu of Angola: Culture Areas of Nigeria*. Germantown, N.Y.: Periodicals Service, 1974.

Horton, A. E. *A Grammar of Luvale*. Johannesburg: Witwatersrand University Press, 1949.

Hunt, Simon, W. Bender, and S. Devereux. *The Luanda Household Budget and Nutrition Survey*. Oxford: University of Oxford Press: Food Studies Group, 1991.

Hurlich, Susan. *Cassoneka: A Socio-Economic Survey*. Luanda: Development Workshop, 1989.

——. *Formal and Informal Community Structures in the Comuna of Ngola Kiluanje*. Luanda: Development Workshop, 1990.

——. *Angola: Country Gender Analysis*. 2 Vols. Luanda: Development Workshop, 1991.

Jordan, Manuel. *Chokwe: Angola, Zambia*. New York: Rosen, 1997.

Jordan, Manuel, Gary N. Van Wyk, and Marie Louise Bastin, eds. *Chokwe! Art and Initiation among Chokwe and Related Peoples*. London: Prestel, 1998.

Kaulinge, Vilho. *Healing the Land: Kaulinge's History of Kwanyama*. Cologne: Rudiger Keoppe Verlag, 1997.

Martin, Phyllis M. *The External Trade of the Loango Coast, 1576–1870: The Effects of Changing Commercial Relations on the Vili Kingdom of Loango*. London: Oxford University Press, 1972.

McCulloch, Merran. *The Southern Lunda and Related Peoples*. London: International African Institute, 1951.

——. *The Ovimbundu of Angola*. London: International African Institute, 1952.

McKissack, Patricia. *Nzingha: Warrior Queen of Matamba, Angola, Africa, 1595 (The Royal Diaries)*. New York: Scholastic, 2000.

Mohanty, Susama. *Political Development and Ethnic Identity in Africa: A Study of Angola since 1960*. London: Stosius/Advents, 1992.

Niddrie, David L. "Changing Settlement Patterns in Angola." *Rural Africana*, no. 23 (1975): 47–48.

Njoku, Onwuka N. *Mbundu: Angola*. New York: Rosen, 1997.

Okeke, Chika. *Kongo: Angola, Congo, Zaire*. New York: Rosen, 1997.

Pearce, Richard. *The Social Dimensions of Adjustment in Angola*. Oxford: Oxford University Press, 1989.

Thomas, Elizabeth Marshall. *The Harmless People*. New York: Knopf, 1959.

United Nations Development Program. *Community Rehabilitation and National Reconciliation Program*. Luanda: United Nations, 1995.

Urquhart, Alvin W. *Patterns of Subsistence and Settlement in Southwestern Angola*. Washington, D.C.: National Academy of Sciences, 1963.

Van der Winden, Bob, ed. *A Family of the Musseque: Survival and Development in Postwar Angola*. Oxford: One World Action, 1996.

C. Arts and Literature

Antunes, Antonio Lobo. *South of Nowhere*. New York: Random House, 1983.

——. *The Return of the Caravels*. New York: Grove, 2003.

Bessa, Victor. *Poetry from Angola: Ao Som das Marimbas, Poemes Africans*. Germantown, N.Y.: Periodicals Service, 1967.

Brinkman, I. *Singing in the Bush: MPLA Songs during the War for Independence in Southeastern Angola*. Cologne: Rudiger Koppe Verlag, 2001.

Burness, Donald, ed. *Fire: Six Writers from Angola, Mozambique and Cape Verde.* Boulder, Colo.: Rienner, 1977.

Chabal, Patrick, ed. *The Postcolonial Literature of Lusophone Africa.* London: Hurst, 1996.

Chatelain, Heli. *Folk Tales of Angola.* Germantown, N.Y.: Periodical Service, 1969.

———. *Folk-Tales of Angola: Fifty Tales, with Ki-Mbundu Text, Literal English Translation, Introduction and Notes.* Germantown, N.Y.: Periodical Service, 2001.

Comrade Dr. Agostinho Neto, Namibia Mourns You. Luanda: SWAPO Information and Publicity Department, 1979.

England, Nicholas M. *Music Among the Z u'/w A-si and Related Peoples of Namibia, Botswana, and Angola.* New York: Garland Science, 1995.

Ennis, Merlin. *Umbundu Folk Tales from Angola.* Boston: Beacon, 1962.

Holness, Marga, trans. *Yaka.* Portsmouth, N.H.: Heinemann, 1996.

Jamba, Sousa. *Patriots.* London: Viking, 1990.

———. *A Lonely Devil.* London: Fourth Estate, 1993.

Khazonov, A. M. *Agostinho Neto.* Moscow: Progress, 1986.

Leakey, M. D., and L. S. B. Leakey. *Some String Figures from North East Angola.* Lisbon: Musea Do Dondo, 1949.

Neto, Agostinho. *A Renúncia Impossível* (Impossible renunciation). Luanda: Angolan Writers Union, 1982.

———. *Sacred Hope. (Sagrada Esperanca).* Luanda: Angolan Writers Union, 1986.

Pestana, Artur "Pepetela." *Yaka.* Trans. Marga Holness. Portsmouth, N.H.: Heinemann Publishers, 1996.

———. *O Retorno do Espírito da Água* (The return of the water spirit). Portsmouth, N.H.: Heinemann, 2002.

Rui, Manuel. *Yes, Comrade.* Trans. Ronald Sousa. Minneapolis: University of Minnesota Press, 1993.

Scherz, A. *Hair-Styles, Head-Dresses and Ornaments in Namibia and Southern Angola.* Johannesburg: Gamsberg Macmillan, n.d.

Visiting Arts. *Angola Arts Directory.* London: Visiting Arts Publications, 1999.

Wolfers, Michael. *Poems from Angola.* Portsmouth, N.H.: Heinemann, 1979.

———. *Mayombe.* Portsmouth, N.H.: Heinemann, 1996.

Xitu, Xuahenga. *The World of "Mestre" Tamoda.* London: Readers International, 1984.

D. Congressional Hearings and Reports

Branaman, Brenda. *Chronology of Events Relating to Angola (April 25, 1974–January 29, 1976).* Washington, D.C.: Congressional Research Service, 1976.

———. *Angola/Namibia Negotiations.* Congressional Research Service Issue Brief. Washington, D.C.: Congressional Research Service, 1989.

Copson, Raymond W., and Robert B. Shepard. *Angola and the Clark Amendment.* Congressional Research Service Issue Brief. Washington, D.C.: Congressional Research Service, 1981.

U.S. Congress. House. Committee on International Relations. *Disaster Assistance in Angola. Hearings before the Subcommittee on International Resources, Food, and Energy.* 94th Congress. 2nd Session. 1976. Report 65-115.

———. Committee on International Relations. *United States Policy on Angola. Hearings before the Committee on International Relations.* 94th Congress. 2nd Session. 1976. Report 66-572.

———. Committee on International Relations. *United States–Angolan Relations. Hearings before the Subcommittee on Africa.* 95th Congress. 1st Session. 1978. Report 29-726.

———. Committee on International Relations. *Angola: Intervention or Negotiations. Hearings before the Subcommittee on Africa.* 99th Congress. 1st Session. 1985. Report 56-508.

———. Permanent Select Committee on Intelligence. *Angola: Should the United States Support UNITA?* 99th Congress. 2nd Session. 1986. Report 61-063.

———. Committee on Foreign Affairs. *A Review of United States Policy toward Political Negotiations in Angola. Hearing before the Subcommittee on Africa.* 101st Congress. 1st Session. 1989. Report 24-781.

———. Committee on Foreign Affairs. *New Reports of Human Rights Violations in the Angolan Civil War.* Hearings before the Subcommittee on Africa. 101st Congress. 1st Session. 1989. Report 20-105.

———. Committee on Foreign Affairs. *Angola: The Aftermath of Elections. Hearing before the Subcommittee on Africa.* 102nd Congress. 2nd Session. 1992. Report 62-825.

———. Committee on Foreign Affairs. *Potential for Private Sector Activity in Angola. Hearing before the Subcommittee on Africa.* 102nd Congress. 2nd Session. 1992. Report 65-479.

———. Committee on Foreign Affairs. *The Quest for Peace in Angola. Hearing before the Subcommittee on Africa.* 103rd Congress. 1st Session. 1993. Report 80-781.

———. Committee on International Relations. *The Path toward Democracy in Angola. Hearing before the Subcommittee on Africa.* 104th Congress. 1st Session, 1995. Report 93-230.

———. Committee on International Relations. *Angola: Prospects for a Durable Peace and Economic Reconstruction.* Hearings before the Subcommittee on Africa. 2nd Session. 2002. Report 107-86.

U.S. Congress. Senate. Committee on Foreign Relations. *Angola. Hearings before the Subcommittee on African Affairs.* 94th Congress. 2nd Session. 1976. Report 67-055.

——. Committee on Foreign Relations. *Angola: Options for American Foreign Policy. Hearings before the Committee on Foreign Relations.* 99th Congress. 2nd Session. 1986. Report 39-399.

——. Committee on Foreign Relations. *Prospects for Peace and Democracy in Angola. Hearings before the Subcommittee on African Affairs.* 104th Congress. 2nd Session. 1996. Report 23-323.

Walker, Darcy A. *Cuban Military Involvement in Angola.* Washington, D.C.: Congressional Research Service, 1976.

Yu, Alan K. *The Angola Food Emergency: Extent of the Problem and Current U.S. Emergency Assistance Policy.* Congressional Research Service Report for Congress. Washington, D.C.: Congressional Research Service, 1989.

E. Disaster Assistance Programs

Brennan, T. O. *From Crisis to Catastrophe: Uprooted Angolans.* Washington, D.C.: U.S. Committee for Refugees, 1987.

Duarte, Mafalda. *Aid Policy in War-Torn Countries: Promoting Development in Conflict Situations: The Case of Angola.* Lanham, Md.: University Press of America, 2002.

European Union. *Aid Flows to Angola: An Overview.* Luanda: European Union, 2001.

——. *Angola–European Community Strategy Paper and National Indicative Programme.* Luanda: European Union, 2001.

Human Rights Watch. *Land Mines in Angola.* New York: Human Rights Watch, 1993.

——. *Still Killing: Landmines in Southern Africa.* New York: Human Rights Watch, 1997.

Interaction Member Activity Report: Angola. *A Guide to Humanitarian and Development Efforts of InterAction Member Agencies.* Washington, D.C.: American Council for Voluntary International Action, 1999.

International Committee to Ban Land Mines. *Angola: Landmine Monitor Report 2002.* Washington, D.C.: Human Rights Watch, 2002.

Jeffrey, Paul. "Making Peace a Reality in Angola." *National Catholic Reporter* 38, no. 41 (September 2002): 3–6.

Lake, Anthony. *After the Wars: Reconstruction in Afghanistan, Indochina, Central America, Southern Africa and the Horn of Africa.* New Brunswick, N.J.: Transaction, 1990.

Lanzer, Toby. *The U N Department of Humanitarian Affairs in Angola: A Model for the Co-ordination of Humanitarian Assistance.* Uppsala, Sweden: Nordic Africa Institute, 1996.

Médecins sans Frontières. *Angola: Sacrifice of a People.* New York: Doctor's without Borders, 2002.

Meldrum, Andrew. "The Maiming Machines." *Africa Report* (May–June 1995): 18–21.

Morrison, J. Stephen. *The Long Road Home: Angola's Post-War Inheritance.* Washington, D.C.: U.S. Committee for Refugees, 1991.

Robson, Paul, and Sandra Roque. *Here in the City There Is Nothing Left Over for a Lending Hand: In Search of Solidarity and Collective Action in Peri-Urban Areas in Angola.* Guelph, Ont.: Development Workshop, 2001.

Sawdon, Gary. *The Household Economies of Kuito, Bié Province.* Luanda: Save the Children, 2002.

Sawdon, Gary, John Seaman, and Anna Taylor. *Final Report on a Survey to Assess the Food Needs of the Population of Huambo, Angola.* London: Save the Children, 2000.

Sidaway, James D. "Angola: Back to Normal." *Review of African Political Economy* 28, no. 90 (December 2001): 641–42.

Simon, David. "The Bitter Harvest of War: Continuing Social and Humanitarian Dislocation in Angola." *Review of African Political Economy* 28, no. 90 (December 2001): 503–20.

Tvedten, Inge. *Report to NORAD on Selected Development Issues in Angola 1999/2000.* Bergen, Norway: Christen Michaelson Institute, 2000.

———. *Angola 2000/2001: Key Development Issues and the Role of NGOs.* Bergen, Norway: Christen Michaelson Institute, 2001.

Wright, Mark. *Food Security Assessment: Kuito 2001.* Luanda: Save the Children, 2001.

United Nations High Commissioner for Refugees. *Background Paper on Refugees and Asylum Seekers from Angola.* Geneva: Center for Documentation and Research, 1994.

F. Economy

Aguilar, Renato, and Asa Stenman. *Angola 1994: Trying to Break through the Wall.* Gothenburg: University of Gothenburg Press, 1994.

———. *Angola: Let's Try Again.* Stockholm: SIDA Planning Secretariat, 1995.

———. *Angola 1996: Hyper-Inflation, Confusion and Political Crisis.* Gothenburg: University of Gothenburg Press, 1996.

Aguilar, Renato, and Mario Zejan. *Angola: A Long and Hard Way to the Marketplace.* Gothenburg, Sweden: University of Gothenburg Press, 1991.

——. *Angola: The Last Stand of Central Planning.* Gothenburg: University of Gothenburg Press, 1992.

Andrade, Mário de, and Marc Ollivier. *The War in Angola: A Socio-Economic Study.* Dar es Salaam: Tanzania Publishing House, 1975.

Angola: Trade and Investment Guide. Washington, D.C.: Embassy of the Republic of Angola, 2001.

Benguela Railways and the Development of Southern Africa. Luanda: Editorial Vanguarda, 1987.

Bhagavan, M. R. *Angola's Political Economy, 1975–1985.* Research Report no. 75. Uppsala, Sweden: Scandinavian Institute of African Studies Press, 1986.

Carmo, Albano T. *Angola Ports Handbook and Manual.* Luanda: Actualidade Editora, 1973.

Carneiro, Dionisio D., and Marcelo de P. Abreu. *Angola: Growth and Adjustment in Scenarios of Peace.* Stockholm: SIDA, 1989.

Ernst and Young. "Investment Profile: Angola." *Ernst and Young Country Profiles* (June 1998): 1–15.

Global Investment and Business Center. *Angola: A Country Study Guide.* Washington, D.C.: International Business, 2000.

Government of Angola. *Angola: Economic Summary.* Luanda: Ministry of Finance, 1991.

Hodges, Tony. *Angola to 2000: Prospects for Recovery.* London: Economist Intelligence Unit, 1993.

——. *Angola from Afro-Stalinism to Petro-Diamond Capitalism.* Indianapolis: University of Indiana Press, 2001.

Hodges, Tony, and Walter Viegas. *Country Strategy Study.* Luanda: Norwegian People's Aid, 1998.

How to Invest in Angola. Luanda: Oficinas Graficas, 1963.

International Monetary Fund. *Angola: Recent Economic Developments.* Washington, D.C.: International Monetary Fund, 1995.

——. *Angola: Recent Economic Developments.* Washington, D.C.: International Monetary Fund, 2000.

——. *Government of Angola: Memorandum of Economic and Financial Policies.* Washington, D.C.: International Monetary Fund, 2001.

Le Billon, Philippe. *A Land Cursed by Its Wealth? Angola's War Economy (1975–1999).* Helsinki: United Nations, 1999.

——. "Angola's Political Economy of War: The Role of Oil and Diamonds 1975–2000. *African Affairs* 100 (2001): 55–80.

——. "Thriving on War: The Angolan Conflict and Private Business." *Review of African Political Economy* 28, no. 90 (December 2001): 629–35.

Malaquias, Assis. "Making War and Lots of Money: The Political Economy of Protracted Conflict in Angola." *Review of African Political Economy* 28, no. 90 (December 2001): 521–36.

McCormick, Shawn. *The Angolan Economy: Prospects for Growth in a Post-War Environment.* Washington, D.C.: Center for Strategic and International Studies, 1994.

Netto, Dionaisio Diasa Carneiro. *Angola: Growth and Adjustment Scenarios of Peace.* Stockholm: Swedish International Development Authority, 1989.

Oxfam International. *Angola's Wealth: Stories of War and Neglect.* Washington, D.C.: Oxfam International, 2001.

Roque, Fatima. *Building the Future in Angola: A Vision for Sustainable Development.* Oeiras, Portugal: Celta Editora, 1986.

———. *Building Peace in Angola: A Political and Economic Vision.* Lisbon: Edicoes Universitarias Lusofonas, 2000.

Sogge, D. *Sustainable Peace: Angola's Recovery.* Harare: Southern Africa Research and Documentation Center, 1992.

Somerville, Keith. *Angola: Politics, Economics and Society.* Boulder, Colo.: Rienner, 1986.

Special Assistance Program for Angola. Luanda: Government of the People's Republic of Angola Southern Africa Transport and Communications Commission, 1988.

União Nacional para a Independência Total de Angola. *The Angola Road to National Recovery: Defining the Principles and the Objectives.* Jamba, Angola: National Union for the Total Independence of Angola Press, 1984.

United Nations Industrial Development Organization (UNIDO). *Angola: Economic Reconstruction and Rehabilitation.* Geneva: UNIDO, 1990.

Walker, G. *Angola: The Promise of Riches.* London: Africa File, 1990.

World Bank. *Angola: An Introductory Economic Review.* Washington, D.C.: World Bank, 1991.

———. *Angola: Public Expenditures Issues and Priorities during Transition to a Market Economy.* Washington, D.C.: World Bank, 1993.

———. *Angola: Towards Economic and Social Reconstruction.* Washington, D.C.: World Bank, 1996.

G. Energy and Minerals

Anderson, Jon Lee. "Letter from Angola: Oil and Blood." *New Yorker* (August 2000): 46–59.

Campbell, Greg. *Blood Diamonds: Tracing the Deadly Path of the World's Most Precious Stones.* Boulder, Colo.: Westview, 2002.

Cilliers, Jakkie, and Christian Dietrich, eds. *Angola's War Economy: The Role of Oil and Diamonds.* Pretoria: ISS, 2000.

Frynas, Jedrzej George, and Geoffrey Wood. "Oil and War in Angola." *Review of African Political Economy* 28, no. 90 (December 2001): 587–606.

Global Witness. *A Rough Trade: The Role of Companies and Governments in the Angolan Conflict.* London: Global Witness, 1998.

———. *A Crude Awakening: The Role of the Oil and Banking Industries in Angola's Civil War and the Plunder of State Assets.* London: Global Witness, 1999.

———. *Conflict Diamonds: Possibilities for the Identification, Certification and Control of Diamonds.* London: Global Witness, 2000.

———. *All the President's Men: The Devastating Story of Oil and Banking in Angola's Privatized War.* London: Global Witness, 2002.

Helmore, Richard. "Diamond Mining in Angola." *Mining Magazine* (June 1984): 22–27.

Hodges, Tony. *Angola: Anatomy of an Oil State.* New York: Currey, 2004.

Human Rights Watch. *The Oil Diagnostic in Angola: An Update.* London: Human Rights Watch, 2001.

Johnson, Elias. "Angola." *U.S. Department of Energy: Energy Information Administration* (October 2001): 1–8.

Katsouris, Christina. "Angola: Luanda Confidential." *Energy Compass* (October 31, 2002): 1–2.

Schissel, Howard. "African Economies: What Prospects for the Oil Industry." *Africa Report* 28, no. 5 (September–October 1983): 43–48.

———. "The Lusophone Oil Boom." *Africa Report* 31, no. 1 (January–February 1986): 24–27.

Venter, Lester. "Angola: Oil, Diamonds and a Begging Bowl." *Excellence* 4, no. 3 (Spring 1988): 24–27.

Vines, Alex. "Oil, Diamonds and Death." *World Today* 58, no. 3 (March 2002): 19–20.

Walde, T. *Mineral Development in Angola.* New York: United Nations Department of Technical Cooperation for Development, 1987.

World Bank. *Angola: Issues and Options in the Energy Sector.* Washington, D.C.: World Bank, 1987.

H. Human Rights and Politics

Action for Southern Africa. *Waiting on Empty Promises: The Human Cost of International Inaction on Angolan Sanctions.* London: ACTSA, 2000.

Adelman, Kenneth Lee. "Afrocommunism: Angola, Mozambique." *Freedom at Issue,* no. 45 (March–April 1978): 12–16.

Africa Watch. *Angola: The Violations of the War by Both Sides.* New York: Africa Watch, 1989.

———. *Angola: Civilians Devastated by 15 Year War.* New York: Africa Watch, 1991.

Amnesty International. *Angola: Human Rights Guarantees in the Revised Constitution.* New York: Amnesty International, 1991.

———. *Angola: An Appeal for Prompt Action to Protect Human Rights.* New York: Amnesty International, 1992.

———. *Angola: Freedom of Expression under Threat.* New York: Amnesty International, 1999.

———. *Angola and Namibia: Human Rights Abuses in the Border Area.* New York: Amnesty International, 2000.

Angola Peace Fund. *Alvor and Beyond: Politics and Legal Issues in Angola.* Washington, D.C.: Angola Peace Fund, 1988.

———. *Angola: The Case for Reconciliation.* Washington, D.C.: Angola Peace Fund, 1989.

Bayer, T. *Angola, Presidential and Legislative Elections, September 29–30, 1992: Report of the IFES Observation Mission.* Washington, D.C.: International Foundation for Electoral Systems, 1992.

Bergerol, Jane. "Choosing the People's Representatives." *Africa,* no. 110 (October 1980): 43–44.

Carroll, Anthony J. "Lessons from Angola: An Observer Offers Advice for the Future." *News from the International Foundation for Election Systems* 5, no. 4 (October 1996): 34–35.

Chabal, Patrick. "Some Reflections on the Post-colonial State in Portuguese Speaking Africa." *Africa Insight* 23, no. 3 (1993): 129–35.

Chismar, Janet. "Jonas Savimbi: Rebel Warlord or Man of God?" *Crosswalk.com* (March 2002): 1–4.

Coetzee, David. "Neto: Giant of the Angolan Revolution." *New African,* no. 146 (October 1979): 91–93.

Eduardo Mondlane Foundation. *Democratization in Angola: Seminar Readings.* Leiden, Netherlands: African Studies Center Press, 1992.

———. *Democratization in Angola: Seminar Proceedings.* Leiden, Netherlands: African Studies Center Press, 1993.

European Parliamentarians for Southern Africa. *Angola: Election Observers, Report of an Observer Mission at the Angolan Elections, 29–30 September 1992.* Brussels: European Union Office of Information, 1992.

Falk, Pamela. "The United States, Soviet Union, Cuba, and South Africa in Angola: Negotiator's Nightmare, Diplomat's Dilemma, 1974–1980." *Pew Case Studies in International Affairs* 405 (1988): 1–22.

Falk, Pamela, and Kurt M. Campbell. "The United States, Soviet Union, Cuba, and South Africa in Angola: The Quagmire of Four Party Negotiations, 1981–88." *Pew Case Studies in International Affairs* 429 (1988): 1–36.

Felton, John. "Angola Pact Poses Policy Challenges for Bush." *Congressional Quarterly Weekly Report* 47 (February 1989): 268–71.

Henderson, Robert E., and Edward B. Stewart. *UNITA after the Cease-Fire: The Emergence of a Party.* Washington, D.C.: National Republican Institute, 1991.

Human Rights Watch. *The International Monetary Fund's Staff Monitoring Program for Angola: The Human Rights Implications.* New York: Human Rights Watch, 2000.

International Republican Institute. *Angola: Entering the 1992 Elections. An International Republican Institute Assessment.* Washington, D.C.: International Republican Institute, 1992.

Jett, Dennis C. *Why Peacekeeping Fails: A Comparative Assessment of Angola.* New York: St. Martin's, 2000.

Kaure, Alexactus T. T. *Angola: From Socialism to Liberal Reforms.* Harare, Zimbabwe: SAPES, 1999.

Kibble, Steve, and Alex Vines. "Angola: New Hopes for a Civil Society?" *Review of African Political Economy* 28, no. 90 (December 2001): 537–47.

Kone, Elizabeth M. Jamilah. "The Right of Self-determination in the Angolan Enclave of Cabinda." Paper Presented at the Sixth Annual African Studies Consortium Workshop (October 1998): 1–19.

Luke, Timothy W. "Angola and Mozambique: Institutionalizing Social Revolution in Africa." *Review of Politics* 44, no. 7 (July 1982): 413–36.

Luso–Angolan Committee for the Release of the Luanda Political Prisoners. *Aspects of the Human Rights Situation in Angola.* Washington, D.C.: Free Angola Information Service, 1994.

Maier, Karl. "Blueprint for Peace." *Africa Report* 36, no. 2 (March–April 1991): 19–22.

Malaquias, Assis. "Angola's Foreign Policy since Independence: The Search for Domestic Security." *African Security Review* 9, no. 3 (2000): 1–13.

Meldrum, Andrew. "Hungry to Vote." *Africa Report* (November–December 1992): 26–30.

Minter, William. "Angola after Savimbi." *Nation* 274, no. 16 (April 2002): 7, 24.

Munslow, Barry. "Angola: The Politics of Unsustainable Development." *Third World Quarterly* 20, no. 3 (1999): 551–68.

Novicki, Margaret A. "José Eduardo dos Santos: President, the People's Republic of Angola." *Africa Report* 31, no. 1 (January–February 1986): 4–14.

Ogunbadejo, Oye. "Angola: Ideology and Pragmatism in Foreign Policy." *International Affairs* 57 (Spring 1981): 254–69.

Pazzanita, Anthony G. "The Conflict Resolution Process in Angola." *Journal of Modern African Studies* 29, no. 1 (1991): 83–114.

Robson, Paul. "Briefing: Angola after Savimbi." *Review of African Political Economy* 29, no. 91 (March 2002): 130–32.

Saferworld. *Angola: Conflict Resolution and Peace-Building.* London: Saferworld, 1996.

Somerville, Keith. "The Failure of Democratic Reform in Angola and Zaire." *Survival,* no. 35 (1993): 51–77.

Tsongas, Paul E. "On Recognizing Angola." *Africa Report* 24, no. 3 (May–June 1979): 21–22.

Williams, Abiodun. *In Search of Peace: Negotiations and the Angolan Civil War.* Washington, D.C.: Institute for the Study of Diplomacy, Georgetown University, 1993.

Wills, Shana. "Jonas Savimbi: Washington's 'Freedom Fighter,' Africa's Terrorist." *Foreign Policy in Focus* (February 2002): 1–4.

Wolfers, Michael. "Neto's Sacred Hope for Angola." *Africa,* no. 98 (October 1979): 37–38.

Wright, George. "The Clinton Administration's Policy toward Angola: An Assessment." *Review of African Political Economy* 28, no. 90 (December 2001): 563–79.

Young, Tom. "The Politics of Development in Angola and Mozambique." *African Affairs* 87 (April 1988): 165–84.

I. Public Health and Safety

Carp, Carol, and William J. Bicknell. *Review of Health Care in Angola: Issues, Analyses and Recommendations.* Washington, D.C.: Family Health Care and Africare, 1978.

Christian Children's Fund. *Sexual Abuse and Exploitation of Children in Time of War: The Case of Angola.* Luanda: Christian Children's Fund, 1996.

Christoplos, I. *Local Service Institutions and the Humanitarian Imperative in Relief and Rehabilitation: A Case Study of the Angolan Red Cross.* Uppsala: Swedish University of Agricultural Sciences Press, 1997.

Eyber, Carola, and Alastair Ager. "Conselho: Psychological Healing in Displaced Communities in Angola." *Lancet* 360, no. 9336 (September 2002): 871–73.

Habgood, Laura. *Health and Livelihoods in Rural Angola: A Participatory Research Project.* Oxfam Working Paper. Oxford: Oxfam, 1998.

International Committee of the Red Cross. "Special Report: Angola, 1985–1986." *ICRC* (January 1986).

Rugema, Mike, and Inge Tvedten. *Survey of Expanded Educational Assistance to Refugees from Angola and Mozambique.* Nairobi: All-Africa Conference of Churches, 1991.

Ruiz, Jose Antonio, Pere P. Simarro, and Teofilo Josenando. "Control of Human African Trypanosomiasis in the Quicama Focus, Angola." *Bulletin of the World Health Organization* 80, no. 9 (2002): 738–48.

J. Religion

Baptist Missionary Society. *One Hundred Years of Christian Mission in Angola and Zaire, 1878–1978.* London: Baptist Missionary Society Press, 1978.

Grohs, Gerhard. *State and the Church in Angola, 1450–1980.* Geneva: Graduate Institute of International Studies, 1983.

Henderson, Lawrence W. *The Church in Angola: A River of Many Currents.* Cleveland, Ohio: Pilgrim, 1992.

Lewis, Thomas. *These Seventy Years.* London: Carey, 1930.

Louttit, Thomas. *Trial and Triumph in Chokweland, Central African Jubilee or Fifty Years with the Gospel in "Beloved Strip."* London: Pickering and Ingles, n.d.

Munroe, Scott. *African Manhunt: A Layman's-Eye View of the Umbundu People of Angola.* Toronto: United Church of Canada Press, 1959.

Tucker, John T. *Drums in the Darkness: The Story of the Mission of the United Church of Canada in Angola, Africa.* Toronto: United Church of Canada Press, 1927.

K. Wildlife

Breytenbach, Jan. *The Plunderers.* Johannesburg: Covos-Day, 2001.

Dean, W. J. R. *Birds of Angola.* Hertfordshire, England: British Ornithologists Union, 2000.

Greenwood, P. H. *The Haplochromine Species (Teleostei, Cichlidae) of the Cunene and Certain Other Angolan Rivers.* London: Intercept Scientific, Medical and Technical, 1984.

Walker, John Frederick. *A Certain Curve of the Horn: The Hundred Year Quest for the Giant Sable Antelope of Angola.* New York: Atlantic Monthly, 2002.

L. Women and Women's Issues

Agadjanian, Victor, and Ndola Prata. "War and Reproduction: Angola's Fertility in Comparative Perspective." *Journal of Southern African Studies* 27 (2001): 330–47.

——. "War, Peace, and Fertility in Angola." *Demography* 39, no. 2 (May 2002): 215–32.

Amado, F., and J. Van-Dúnem. "Position Paper: A Família." *Centro de Ensino e Investigação em Populção, Universidade Agostinho Neto, Luanda.* 1996.

Andrade, Henda Ducados Pintos de. *Women, Poverty, and the Informal Sector in Luanda's Peri-Urban Areas.* Luanda: Development Workshop, 1994.

Curtis, Valerie. *Water and Women's Work in Malanje, Angola.* London: London School of Hygiene and Tropical Medicine, 1988.

Dos Santos, Naiole Cohen. *Beyond Inequalities: Women in Angola.* Harare, Zimbabwe: Southern African Research and Documentation Center, 2001.

Organização da Mulher Angolana. *Organization of African Women.* London: Blackmore, 1981.
——. *Angolan Women Building the Future.* London: Zed, 1984.
Qunta, Christine, ed. *Women in Southern Africa.* London: Allison and Busby, 1987.
ToPouzis, Daphne. "Women and Children on the Frontline: Interview with Maria Eugenia Neto." *Africa Report* 33, no. 4 (July–August 1988): 37–39.
United Nations Children's Fund (UNICEF). *Situation Analysis of Women and Children in Angola.* Luanda: UNICEF, 1986.
——. *The State of Angola's Children Report.* Luanda: UNICEF, 1995.

M. Websites, Newspapers, and Journals

Africa News (www.africanews.com)
Africa Policy Information Center (www.africaaction.org)
AllAfrica (www.allafrica.com)
Angola Agency Press (www.angolapress-angop.ao)
Angola Commercial Directory (www.dcda.net)
Angola News (www.angolanews.com)
Angola Peace Monitor (www.actsa.org/Angola/apm)
Angolan Anti-Militarism Initiative for Human Rights (German) (home .snafu.de/usp/iaadh.htm)
Angolan Embassy in Portugal (www.embaixadadeangola.org)
Angolan Embassy in Washington, D.C. (209.183.193.172/index.htm)
Angolan Ministry of Industry (www.mind-angola.com/indexe)
Angolan Mission Observer (209.183.193.172/news/mission/index.html)
Angolan Republican Youth Organization (www.geocities.com/orja_angola/index)
ANGOP (official government press agency) (noticias-angop.netangola.com/index-e.asp)
British Angola Forum (195.157.131.156)
Buffalo Battalion (32nd Battalion) (www.netcentral.co.uk)
Columbia University (on Angola) (www.columbia.edu/cu/lweb/indiv/africa/cuvl/Aogen)
Frente de Libertação do Enclave de Cabinda (FLEC): Official Site of the Cabindese Government in Exile (www.cabinda.org/anglais.htm)
Frente Nacional de Libertação de Angola (FNLA) (www.fnla.org)
Foundation of José Eduardo dos Santos (www.fesa.og.ao)
Jornal de Angola (Luanda) (www.jornaldeangola.com)
Kwacha Angola (www.kwacha.org)
Kwacha UNITA Press (www.kwacha.com)

Languages of Angola (www.ethnologue.com/show_country.asp?name= Angola)

Monitoring Mechanism on Sanctions against UNITA (www.un.org/Depts/dpa/ docs/monitoringmechanism.htm)

National Bank of Angola (www.bna.ao)

National Society for Human Rights (Namibian) (www.nshr.org.na)

Peace for Angola (www.pazangola.org)

O Pensador (www.angola.org/news/pensador/index.html)

Pensador Sustainable Development (www.pensador.com)

Radio National de Angola (www.rna.ao)

Republican Party of Angola (www.geocities.com/wallstreet/bureau/6011)

Southern African Development Community (SADC) (www.mirex.gv.ao/ sadc/index)

Sports Journal (Angola) www.jornaldesportos.com

U. S.–Angola Chamber of Commerce (www.us-angola.org)

About the Author

W. Martin James is professor of political science at Henderson State University in Arkadelphia, Arkansas. He received undergraduate degrees from the University of Arkansas at Fayetteville and a Ph.D. from the Catholic University of America in Washington, D.C. Dr. James has been to Angola several times. He was an electoral observer for the 1992 Angolan elections, serving in Luanda, Huambo, and Lubango. His dissertation was on the UNITA insurgency. He is the author of many articles and books, including *A Political History of the Civil War in Angola 1974–1990,* published by Transaction Press in 1992. Dr. James lives in Benton, Arkansas, and has two sons.

About the Author